HIGH-IMPACT PRACTICES IN ONLINE EDUCATION

HIGH-IMPACT PRACTICES IN ONLINE EDUCATION

Research and Best Practices

Edited by

Kathryn E. Linder and

Chrysanthemum Mattison Hayes

Foreword by Kelvin Thompson

STERLING, VIRGINIA

Published by Stylus Publishing, LLC 22883 Quicksilver Drive
Sterling, Virginia 20166-2019

Library of Congress Cataloging-in-Publication-Data
Names: Linder, Kathryn E., editor. | Hayes, Chrysanthemum Mattison,
editor.
Title: High-impact practices in online education / edited by Kathryn E.
Linder & Chrysanthemum Mattison Hayes.
Description: First edition. |
Sterling, Virginia : Stylus Publishing, 2018. |
Includes bibliographical references and index.
Identifiers: LCCN 2017058349 (print) |
LCCN 2018013489 (ebook) |
ISBN 9781620368480 (uPDF) |
ISBN 9781620368497 (mobi, ePub) |
ISBN 9781620368466 (cloth : alk. paper) |
ISBN 9781620368473 (paperback : alk. paper) |
ISBN 9781620368480 (library networkable e-edition) |
ISBN 9781620368497 (consumer e-edition)
Subjects: LCSH: Internet in higher education. |
Education, Higher--Computer-assisted instruction. |
Web-based instruction.
Classification: LCC LB2395.7 (ebook) |
LCC LB2395.7 .H56 2018 (print) |
DDC 378.1/7344678--dc23
LC record available at https://lccn.loc.gov/2017058349

13-digit ISBN: 978-1-62036-846-6 (cloth)
13-digit ISBN: 978-1-62036-847-3 (paperback)
13-digit ISBN: 978-1-62036-848-0 (library networkable e-edition)
13-digit ISBN: 978-1-62036-849-7 (consumer e-edition)

Printed in the United States of America

All first editions printed on acid-free paper
that meets the American National Standards Institute
Z39-48 Standard.

Bulk Purchases
Quantity discounts are available for use in workshops and for
staff development.
Call 1-800-232-0223

First Edition, 2018

CONTENTS

TABLES AND FIGURES

Tables

Figures

FOREWORD

"What is the difference between a high-quality online course and a high-impact practice?" This was the question asked during a panel I moderated recently at a faculty development event. I was struck by the earnestness of the question, the intent to unsnarl the often confusing jargon of our field and the underlying desire to pursue something good for students. On reflection, though, I was reminded of my own similar, implicit question when first hearing George Kuh speak of high-impact practices (HIPs) some years ago at a live event. As someone operating from an orientation of effective online course design and faculty preparation for successful teaching, I think I had come to the event looking for new guidance related to instructional design. However, during the event, I was struck by Kuh's perspective on the broader educational experience encountered (or not encountered) by students in colleges and universities. While there were implications for course design, to be sure, in Kuh's remarks, (although no explicit mention that I can recall of "online"), there was an implicit call for disparate university departments to come together to provide a better experience, a more "impactful" experience for students that would benefit them for the rest of their lives.

In *High-Impact Practices in Online Education: Research and Best Practices*, editors Kathryn E. Linder and Chrysanthemum Mattison Hayes have provided what will likely become a foundational volume for those concerned with enriching the educational experience for all students. With an overarching emphasis on better serving the needs of traditionally underserved student populations, Linder and Hayes have assembled an impressive selection of examples of each HIP (a) implemented in an online context and (b) aligned with research and professional practice literature. The contributors are obviously knowledgeable and personally experienced. Taken as a whole the chapters are wonderfully varied, detailed, and illustrative. There is a mix of course and non-course implementations of HIPs from diverse disciplinary and institutional contexts, and when online courses are in view, multiple course design models are described (e.g., asynchronous discussion boards, synchronous video sessions, etc.). However, those looking for guidance in online experiences beyond the course will find plenty of inspiration here. Overall, the book exemplifies a high view of online practice and pedagogy and invites readers to push beyond easy answers in their own settings. As one might expect, Linder and Hayes provide framing reflection on their selection of high-impact examples. The introduction provides a helpful on-ramp to the topic and outlines the overall arc of the book. The conclusion synthesizes the various accounts of the contributors into themes summarizing the benefits, challenges, and new work to be done. It is easy to imagine follow-up volumes in which new examples, new insights, and perhaps even new HIPs are shared.

Whether you are, like me, an online education professional interested in better providing beyond-the-course HIPs to online students or whether you are currently engaged in fostering such practices in traditional settings but are curious about the "online world," I recommend this book to you with the confident hope that you will find inspiration. Read, reflect, and rally your resources. May you build on the works described by these contributors as you carry out your own visions for enriching the educational experiences of all students through implementing HIPs in online education.

Kelvin Thompson, EdD
Executive Director
University of Central Florida Center for Distributed Learning

ACKNOWLEDGMENTS

There are many people without whom this book would not have been possible. We wish to thank our editor at Stylus Publishing, Sarah Burrows, who first encouraged the creation of a volume dedicated to a holistic look at high-impact practices in the online environment. Amy Donley, who is truly a miracle worker and spent countless hours compiling, organizing, and formatting the chapters in this volume, was also a crucial team member in the completion of this book. Her skill and attention to detail are what brought clarity, consistency, and order to these pages.

In addition, we wish to thank each contributor whose experience, research, and insights make up this volume. We offer a special thank you to Deborah Smith Arthur, Kevin F. Downing, Jennifer K. Holtz, and Zapoura Newton-Calvert, to whom we reached out to for contributions much later in the process in hopes of adding some additional important perspectives. They are model colleagues who worked quickly and efficiently to produce stellar chapters on a limited timeline.

We owe a great deal of appreciation to our supervisors, Susana Rivera-Mills and Lisa Templeton, who supported our desire and allowed us the time to compile and edit this volume. We also thank our colleagues in Extended Campus and the Division of Undergraduate Studies for supporting our work on this volume and sharing in the excitement of the project.

On a more personal note, our partners, Michael Hayes and Benjamin Winter provided encouragement, patience, and perspective throughout the evolution of this process.

INTRODUCTION

Kathryn E. Linder and Chrysanthemum Mattison Hayes

In 2008, George Kuh coined the term *high-impact educational practices* (HIPs) and defined them as the following 10 components of undergraduate education: first-year seminars and experiences, common intellectual experiences, learning communities (LCs), writing-intensive courses, collaborative assignments and projects, undergraduate research, diversity and global learning, service-learning and community-based learning, internships, and capstone courses and projects (Kuh, 2008). In 2016, ePortfolios were added as the eleventh HIP. Since they were identified, HIPs have become a foundational strategy to increase student retention and completion rates in institutions of higher education and have been used as a variable to study student success (McGlynn, 2014) and engagement (Sweat, Jones, Han, & Wolfgram, 2013). HIPs have also been used to explore the needs of specific student populations such as first-year students (Tukibayeva & Gonyea, 2014) and students from traditionally underserved or underrepresented backgrounds (Sweat et al., 2013). Frequently discussed across a range of disciplines including university libraries (Murray, 2015), the presence of embedded HIPs during a student's academic career is now considered to be a fundamental metric for an institution's dedication to student success (Kilgo, Sheets, & Pascarella, 2015) and campus cultures that promote and support high-quality and effective educational practices (Laird, BrckaLorenz, Zilvinskis, & Lambert, 2014).

Although HIPs have been in the higher education lexicon for almost a decade, the literature on each practice, and how they interrelate with one another, is continuing to develop (Gagliardi, Martin, Wise, & Blaich, 2015; Landy, 2015). The current literature on HIP is often dedicated to looking at one specific practice (e.g., see Barkley, Major, & Cross, 2014; Hauhart & Grahe, 2015) and often primarily focuses on traditional undergraduate courses and programs that take place in face-to-face environments on residential campuses. Scholars are also starting to explore how HIPs relate to different types of higher education environments, such as community colleges (Price & Tovar, 2014). However, although some scholars have explored a particular HIP online (see Strait & Nordyke, 2015), no books are currently available that share comprehensive research and best practices for implementing all of the HIPs in the online environment. Moreover, no texts comprehensively explore the differences that should be taken into account for effective online implementation of HIPs.

A primary goal of *High-Impact Practices in Online Education* is to highlight the necessity of leveraging and expanding HIPs for distance-learning environments. The approaches and examples shared in this volume offer insights and recommendations on how utilizing HIPs in the online learning environment may help address key challenges that extend from several large shifts occurring in higher education. We explore just a few of them here.

The demand for high-quality college degrees is increasing. Carnevale, Smith, and Strohl (2013) estimate that by 2020, 65% of the jobs in the United States will require a postsecondary education and that skills such as decision-making, critical thinking, and communication will be the most in-demand competencies for the labor market. It is increasingly relevant and important that students are provided with the opportunities that help them build and practice these critical skills, especially in applied or real-world settings.

The demographic profile of the degree-seeking student is becoming more diverse. The 2012 Digest of Education Statistics reports that college enrollment among low-income, Black, and Hispanic students has increased over the last few decades. Simultaneously, the rate of Black and Hispanic high school graduates who attend a two- or four-year institution has nearly converged, at 67%, with the rate of White high school graduates pursuing a secondary degree (National Center for Education Statistics, 2012). Additionally, many nontraditionally aged, veteran, and returning students are enrolling to advance their job prospects. Although historical disparities in enrollment have gradually declined, significant differences across student demographic groups in terms of progression and degree attainment have persisted, signifying that work still needs to be done to satisfactorily meet the needs of the fastest growing segments of the student population. It is imperative that educators and institutions provide and expand access and support to the types of transformative educational experiences that help all students to be successful both in and beyond their academic pursuits.

Over the last 13 years, the number of students taking distance courses has steadily increased. In 2015, more than 5.8 million students representing 28% of the total higher education population reported taking at least one course online, which is an increase of 3.9% from the previous year (Allen, Seaman, Poulin, & Straut, 2015). As the landscape of higher education shifts to one where we must graduate more students from diverse backgrounds while responding to the demand for access to high-quality online and distance programs, intentional design and adoption of traditional and emerging high-impact practices becomes a critical strategy for student success.

Online students are expecting more. A recent study by Aslanian Market Research and Learning House found that students are asking for increased options for distance education via mobile devices, more career services options, and better information about whether their transfer credits can be used for different degree programs (Clinefelter & Aslanian, 2017).

In response to these changes and the growing complexity of the higher education environment, this volume presents HIPs as a constellation of opportunities that, when thought of cohesively, can provide a series of milestones that support the development of distance students throughout their entire academic journey (see Figure I.1). This premise echoes the claim of Kuh and others who consider the "cumulative effect" of the collective set of HIPs (Finley & McNair, 2013). This effect starts as students transition into college, acquire fundamental and transferable skills, gain hands-on experiences, synthesize their learning, apply their knowledge in real-world applications, and demonstrate mastery of skills that are highly valued in today's graduates.

Figure I.1. The constellation of high-impact practices.

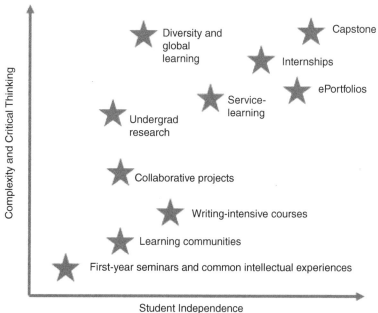

Each chapter of *High-Impact Practices in Online Education: Research and Best Practices* provides readers with concrete strategies for transitioning HIPs to the online environment that can be utilized across a range of disciplines and institution types. The authors share the value they have found in expanding HIPs to the online environment and also reference the most recent and relevant literature for each HIP. In addition to summarizing the research-based principles for what make online HIPs successful, each chapter also references the challenges that frequently arise when transitioning HIPs online, and the authors offer advice for how to overcome them. Some of the common considerations mentioned throughout the collection include: how and when to use technology effectively (rather than for novelty), leveraging HIPs in both synchronous and asynchronous courses, how to ensure high-impact and meaningful interactions, how to manage the growth and scalability of time-intensive HIPs, questions of equity and access for traditionally underserved student populations, faculty development needs related to HIPs, and considerations for new or different assessments of learning online. After reading *High-Impact Practices in Online Education*, we hope that readers will have a comprehensive overview of the current research and emerging practices for scaling HIPs to an online environment as well as a greater understanding of the value and role HIPs can play in proactively responding to the demands being placed, especially on online and distance segments of higher education.

Structure of the Volume

High-Impact Practices in Online Education is structured so that each chapter covers a specific high-impact educational practice. The chapters begin with a theoretically grounded discussion of the HIP, including a literature review of the most current research on the topic. The latter part of each chapter offers specific examples, practical suggestions for implementation, or a case study of that particular practice in online environments.

In chapter 1 "First-Year Seminars," Jennifer R. Keup of the National Resource Center for the First-Year Experience and Students in Transition, explores the potential implications and impacts of transitioning first-year experiences (FYEs) into the online environment. Rooted in a decades-long history of FYEs in the United States, Keup's analysis also draws on recent data that illustrate the growing trend of online and technology-enhanced first-year seminars in a range of institution types. Keup discusses the opportunities that online FYEs provide as well as the faculty development needs to ensure the success of transitioning these programs online. She also demonstrates the varied ways that institutions of higher education can leverage technology for successful FYE seminars and experiences, including opportunities for creative and even more frequent interaction than face-to-face FYE courses.

Chapter 2 "Common Intellectual Experience" by Jason D. Baker and Michael Pregitzer utilizes a case study from Regent University where the authors have instituted a Narrative, Engagement, Transformation (NET) model across their undergraduate curriculum to help students learn how to ask and answer "big questions." After introducing the need for common intellectual practices and highlighting the imperative to support and foster learner-to-learner, learner-to-content, and learner-to-instructor interaction and connection in the online environment, the authors provide a theoretical framework of this HIP through the NET model. Baker and Pregitzer illustrate how their flexible NET model can be used to guide online course development and delivery. The authors also share retention and engagement benefits from their own online programs and conclude with practical implementation tips for faculty, administrators, and instructional designers.

In chapter 3 "Learning Communities," Kathy E. Johnson, Amy A. Powell, and Sarah S. Baker provide an overview of the purpose and value of LCs as a HIP and consider how key elements of this HIP, such as social integration and integrated learning, become even more critical for the diverse and rapidly expanding community of distance learners. The contributors also share how, through creating the digital space and leveraging common online tools such as threaded discussions, this HIP can be readily translated to distance-learning environments. Johnson, Powell, and Baker go on to describe a "Themed Learning Community High-Impact Practice Taxonomy" that has emerged from work in the California State University System and at Indiana University–Purdue University Indianapolis, and they share preliminary evidence regarding its use and efficacy to guide faculty teams. The authors close their chapter by suggesting ways of adapting this taxonomy to ensure that LCs offered through distance education are maximally effective at supporting student success.

June Griffin, in chapter 4 "Writing-Intensive Classes," addresses the challenges of offering writing-intensive courses online and offers suggestions for mitigating the impact of the *literacy load* for both students and instructors. Specifically, she advocates the use of screencast technology to give students feedback on their writing. This chapter draws from the work of the Conference on College Composition and Communication's Committee for Effective Practices in Online Writing Instruction, the Meaningful Writing Project, and recent research on screencasting feedback to offer readers practical tips on how to focus on quality over quantity in the writing-intensive online classroom.

In chapter 5 "Collaborative Assignments and Projects," Robert John Robertson and Shannon Riggs discuss some of the common roadblocks of designing and facilitating collaborative assignments and projects in an online, asynchronous course. Collaborative work in online courses can be especially problematic because online students may seek out asynchronous online learning opportunities due to schedule demands that make synchronous class attendance and group work undesirable. In addition, many instructors are resistant to the concept for several reasons: a lack of design expertise; an aversion to the many conflicts that can arise, especially in the asynchronous environment; and a desire to meet the needs and preferences of online students. With students and instructors at least somewhat naturally predisposed against collaboration, it is crucial to articulate the benefits of collaborative work and identify and overcome the risk factors unique to the online asynchronous classes. The authors explore research which indicates that collaboration and the opportunities created by implementing this HIP in an online space are particularly valuable for students from traditionally underserved backgrounds. Throughout the chapter, Robertson and Riggs offer practical guidance for instructors looking to create collaborative assignments and projects in online courses.

Chapter 6 "Undergraduate Research in the Humanities" by Ellen Holmes Pearson and Jeffrey W. McClurken offers an in-depth exploration of a Teagle and Mellon Foundation grant-funded initiative called "Century America." This Council of Public Liberal Arts Colleges initiative involved team-taught seminars with faculty and undergraduate student researchers from campuses in 13 states and 1 Canadian province. The multicampus seminars, taught synchronously through distance-learning technology, combine the virtual and local by engaging undergraduates in conducting archival research on the histories of their campuses and communities while also collaborating across campuses to build major digital projects available to the public on the web. The authors share how this program has enabled students at public liberal arts institutions to develop research, production, and communications skills applicable to a wide variety of twenty-first-century professions and discuss broadly applicable best practices for online undergraduate research initiatives focused on the humanities.

Chapter 7 "Undergraduate Research in the Sciences" by Kevin F. Downing and Jennifer K. Holtz serves as a "sister" chapter to chapter 6 and focuses on the HIP of undergraduate research in the sciences. In this chapter, the authors offer a conceptual framework that bridges the nexus between customary undergraduate research in the sciences and online learning principles and techniques. These techniques include how undergraduate research in the sciences should be implemented, as well as instructional design considerations such as quality, student engagement, learning formats, timeframes, scaffolding, dissemination, communities of practice, mentoring, and institutional support. These guidelines serve as a roadmap for transitioning a face-to-face undergraduate research experience in the sciences into a fully distance environment.

In chapter 8 "Diversity and Global Learning," Jesse Nelson and Nelson Soto explore the interaction between two of higher education's most prominent themes: diversity and online education. Attention is given to the meaningful application of diversity and global learning within the context of online teaching and learning. Specifically, the chapter provides innovative instructional strategies addressing curriculum development, inclusive pedagogy, and assessment of student learning. Additionally, it addresses the role of faculty in creating diverse and inclusive experiences. The chapter concludes by considering some of the most salient emerging issues associated with diversity and online education.

Jean Strait and Katherine Nordyke, authors of chapter 9 "eService-Learning," outline the practices and structures for a range of eService-learning models that are complementary to distance education. This instructor-focused chapter is full of insight, practical strategies, and thought-provoking ideas about how to incorporate service-learning into online courses. Strait and Nordyke highlight the "how-tos" and various models currently in practice across the United States. In particular, the authors report on a model for eService-learning created by a national team, sharing their research studies and providing models for readers interested in incorporating eService-learning into their own online classrooms or programs.

In chapter "10 Internships," Pamela D. Pike explores several approaches and functions of online or remote internships. Although the outward-facing structure of online internships may vary based on factors such as whether students attend their internship in person or remotely, the best practices for internships around preparation, communication, and reflection for integrated learning remain central and vital. This chapter also emphasizes and illustrates the value of providing distance internships within the context of teacher education programs. Teaching internships provide students with opportunities to interact with others, practice concepts presented in class, and make greater meaning of the material than would otherwise be possible in either a typical class or face-to-face setting. Best practices from research and interviews with experts in this emerging online field are discussed, and practical tips for implementation are provided throughout the chapter.

Chapter 11 "Capstone Courses and Projects," by Zapoura Newton-Calvert and Deborah Smith Arthur, describes the development and instruction as well as mentoring and facilitation practices needed for effective capstone projects in undergraduate degrees and certificates in distance-education programs. The authors describe Portland State University's capstone program and the critical role that institutional support plays in its longevity and success. Newton-Calvert and Arthur share best practices in the areas of social presence and teaching presence as well as experience-based examples of the challenges for both students and instructors in online capstone courses and strategies to address them. In considering capstone courses through an equity lens, this chapter explores the ways in which this HIP offers a powerful mechanism to encourage students to synthesize, communicate, and demonstrate high-level learning. The value and benefits of this type of experience may be amplified for nontraditional and underrepresented students.

Representing the most recent HIP, chapter 12 "ePortfolios," by Jennifer Sparrow and Judit Török, illustrates how ePortfolios act as a nexus for other HIPs. The authors describe three categories of ePortfolios that may be used to that end. As a space outside of the learning management system in which students in online programs curate and reflect on a collection of artifacts documenting their educational journeys, ePortfolios connect learners with cocurricular activities such as experiential learning, project-based learning, and career exploration. Throughout the chapter, Sparrow and Török explore the benefits of ePortfolios, including increased levels of student engagement, a holistic view of students' progress toward degree completion, and the opportunity for authentic assessment of learning.

Although not a HIP in itself, use of library resources is fundamental to the success of many HIPs. In chapter 13 "High-Impact Practices and Library and Information Resources", Stefanie Buck provides an overview of the kinds of information resources and pedagogical support services libraries provide to faculty and instructors in support of HIPs in the distance-education environment. Buck reviews the current literature on HIPs and libraries and offers examples of successful library integration into activities and programs that support these practices. In addition, Buck discusses how improving student information literacy skills can increase the success of HIPs in the online learning environment.

To conclude this volume, in "Future Directions for High-Impact Practices Online," the editors discuss the common themes across the volume's chapters around opportunities and challenges for successful implementation of HIPs in the online environment and present a practical guide of several best practice principles. We also explore what it means to transition HIPs across modalities as well as review the principles relevant to all HIPs, regardless of delivery mode. As technology use in all classrooms increases, we argue that faculty development models that focus on modality first and best practices second may need to be flipped, and that significant opportunities are available to learn from the advances and creative approaches that emerge consequentially from transitioning HIPs online. Finally, we conclude by offering some ideas of HIPs that may need to be added to the list with the advent of adaptive and personalized learning and the rising use of learning analytics across the university landscape.

Conclusion

High-Impact Practices in Online Education: Research and Best Practices offers the first comprehensive guide to how HIPs are being implemented in online environments and how HIPs can be adjusted to meet the needs of online learners. As a collection, *High-Impact Practices in Online Education* is a multidisciplinary response to the phenomenon of online HIPs that can, ultimately, assist faculty and administrators in better implementing HIPs in distance-education courses and programs.

References

Allen, E., Seaman, J., Poulin, R., & Straut, T. T. (2015). *Online report card tracking online education in the United States*. Retrieved from http://onlinelearningsurvey.com/reports/onlinereportcard.pdf

Barkley, E. F., Major, C. H., & Cross, K. P. (2014). *Collaborative learning techniques: A handbook for college faculty*. San Francisco, CA: Jossey-Bass.

Carnevale, A. P., Smith, N., & Strohl, J. (2013). *Recovery: Job growth and education requirements through 2020*. Retrieved from https://cew.georgetown.edu/wp-content/uploads/2014/11/Recovery2020.FR_.Web_.pdf

Clinefelter, D. L., & Aslanian, C.B. (2017). *Online college students 2017: Comprehensive data on demands and preferences*. Louisville, KY: The Learning House.

Finley, A. P., & McNair, T. (2013). *Assessing underserved students' engagement in high-impact practices*. Washington DC: Association of American Colleges & Universities.

Gagliardi, J. S., Martin, R. R., Wise, K., & Blaich, C. (2015). The system effect: Scaling high-impact practices across campuses. *New Directions for Higher Education, 2015*(169), 15–26.

Hauhart, R. C., & Grahe, J. E. (2015). *Designing and teaching undergraduate capstone courses*. San Francisco, CA: Jossey-Bass.

Kilgo, C. A., Sheets, J. K. E., & Pascarella, E. T. (2015). The link between high-impact practices and student learning: Some longitudinal evidence. *Higher Education, 69*(4), 509–525.

Kuh, G. D. (2008). *High-impact education practices: What are they, who has access to them, and why they matter*. Washington DC: Association of American Colleges & Universities.

Laird, T. N., BrckaLorenz, A., Zilvinskis, J., & Lambert, A. (2014, Nov. 19–22). *Exploring the effects of a HIP culture on campus: Measuring the relationship between the importance faculty place on high-impact practices and student participation in those practices.* Roundtable paper presented at the Association for the Study of Higher Education Conference, Washington DC. Retrieved from http://nsse .indiana.edu/pdf/presentations/2014/ASHE14-HIPCulturePaperFINAL.pdf

Landy, K. (2015). Structure, connectivity, and authenticity: The how and why of high-impact practices. *About Campus, 19*(6), 29–32.

McGlynn, A. P. (2014). Report shares high-impact practices for student success. *Hispanic Outlook.* Retrieved from https://www.wdhstore.com/hispanic/data/pdf/ march24-ccsse.pdf

Murray, A. (2015). Academic libraries and high-impact practices for student retention: Library deans' perspectives. *Portal: Libraries and the Academy, 15*(3), 471–487.

National Center for Education Statistics. (2012). *Digest of education statistics 2012.* Retrieved from https://nces.ed.gov/pubsearch/pubsinfo.asp?pubid=2014015

Price, D. V., & Tovar, E. (2014). Student engagement and institutional graduation rates: Identifying high-impact educational practices for community colleges. *Community College Journal of Research and Practice, 38*(9), 766–782.

Strait, J. R., & Nordyke, K. (Eds.). (2015). *eService-learning: Creating experiential learning and civic engagement through online and hybrid courses.* Sterling, VA: Stylus.

Sweat, J., Jones, G., Han, S., & Wolfgram, S. M. (2013). How does high impact practice predict student engagement? A comparison of white and minority students. *International Journal for the Scholarship of Teaching and Learning, 7*(2), 17.

Tukibayeva, M., & Gonyea, R. M. (2014). High-impact practices and the first-year student. *New Directions for Institutional Research, 2013*(160), 19–35.

FIRST-YEAR SEMINARS

Jennifer R. Keup

F ar from a recent innovation in higher education, first-year seminars (FYS) can be traced back to the nineteenth century. Their persistence as an efficient and effective intervention for students transitioning to college has been, in large part, due to their flexibility as a pedagogical and student support tool. In the modern era of higher education, this flexibility among FYS must adapt and shift once again to incorporate technology, online components, and models for online education to accommodate traditional students who prefer or require this type of delivery method, as well as to allow for the growing population of online learners to access this high-impact practice (HIP) in their transition to college. This chapter will explore the history, current practices, and future directions of FYS with particular emphasis on the application of this HIP in an online and distance-learning environment.

Background on First-Year Seminars

The transition to the first year of college holds great potential for incredible success or profound disappointment for the millions of students who start their undergraduate journeys at colleges and universities across the United States. Although all students entering higher education will have a first-year experience (FYE) regardless of institutional effort or intervention, a high-quality FYE is composed of "an intentional combination of academic and cocurricular efforts within and across postsecondary institutions" (Koch & Gardner, 2006, p. 2). Further, hallmarks of institutional excellence in the first year of college have been well documented and codified (Barefoot et al., 2005; Greenfield, Keup, & Gardner, 2013; Upcraft, Gardner, Barefoot, & Associates, 2005; Young & Keup, in press). Specific criteria include

(a) "evidence of an intentional, comprehensive approach to the first year that is appropriate to the institution's type"; (b) "evidence of assessment of the various initiatives that constitute this approach"; (c) "evidence of a broad impact on significant numbers of first-year students, including, but not limited to, special student subpopulations"; (d) "strong administrative support for first-year initiatives, evidence of institutionalization, and durability over time"; and (e) "involvement of a wide range of faculty, student affairs professionals, academic administrators, and other constituent groups" (Barefoot et al., 2005, pp. 24–25). These characteristics are in service to a range of positive undergraduate experiences and outcomes, including: "a strong emphasis on critical inquiry, frequent writing, information literacy, collaborative learning, and other skills that develop students' intellectual and practical competencies" (Kuh, 2008, p. 9); a sense of institutional connection, involvement, and belonging; and, ultimately, learning, persistence, and success (Greenfield et al., 2013; Hunter & Linder, 2005; Upcraft et al., 2005).

One of the most common components of an FYE is the FYS. An *FYS* is defined as

> a course intended to enhance the academic and/or social integration of first-year students by introducing them (a) to a variety of specific topics, which may vary by seminar type, (b) to essential skills for college success, and (c) to selected processes, the most common of which is the creation of a peer support group. (Barefoot, 1992, p. 49)

Born out of campus orientation initiatives, early evidence of FYS can be identified in higher education history as of the late nineteenth and early twentieth centuries (Drake, 1966; Dwyer, 1989). The expedient growth in orientation programs and the rapid professionalization of student support and services from the 1920s through the 1960s make it difficult to document the specific rates of FYS use and growth, but "by 1966, 92% of US colleges and universities offered some sort of formalized experience aimed at assisting with first-year student transitions" (Kronovet, 1969, p. 5).

In the 1970s, the FYS began to distinguish itself from orientation programming, which was a watershed moment in the FYE movement in U.S. higher education. As seminars became more pervasive, assessment and research activities on both institutional and national levels began to document their structural and instructional characteristics as well as their outcomes. The most significant of these empirical efforts was the National Survey of First-Year Seminars administered by the National Resource Center for the First-Year Experience and Students in Transition, which was administered triennially from 1988 to 2012. Data from this survey helped create a lexicon for these courses to advance scholarly, practical, and policy-based discussions about FYS. For example, these data helped identify a typology of seminars that includes six categories: extended orientation, academic seminars with uniform content across sections, academic seminars with variable content across sections, preprofessional/discipline-linked courses, basic study skills, and FYS that represent a combination of two or more other types (Barefoot, 1992; Young & Hopp, 2014).[1] The most recent administration of the National Survey of First-Year Seminars indicated that approximately 90% of two- and four-year institutions across the country offer FYS and they with the most common type of seminars being extended orientation (40%) followed closely by academic seminars (both of uniform and variable content; 38%) (Young & Hopp, 2014). Further, national data show that institutions are generally pleased with the student learning outcomes of FYS and the value for their resource investment in these courses, and they have even begun to use academic/transition seminars as an intervention for sophomores, transfer students, juniors, and seniors (Barefoot, Griffin, & Koch, 2012).

Given the momentum and pervasiveness of FYS, it is perhaps not surprising that the Association of American Colleges & Universities identified them as 1 of 10 HIPs that facilitate twenty-first-century learning outcomes such as "knowledge of human cultures and the physical and natural world, intellectual and practical skills, personal and social responsibility, [and] integrative and applied learning" (Brownell & Swaner, 2010; Kuh, 2008, p. 4). The impact of HIPs, including FYE and FYS, on these outcomes is contingent on their inclusion of eight key elements: (a) high expectations; (b) significant investment of time and effort; (c) substantive interaction with faculty and peers; (d) experiences with diversity; (e) frequent, timely, and constructive feedback; (f) reflection and integrative learning practices; (g) real-world application; and (h) demonstration of learning and competence (Keup & Young, 2018; Kuh & O'Donnell, 2013). When these elements are present in FYS, they have the capacity to enhance engagement, learning, development, and retention among all students, with particular gains noted for historically underrepresented and at-risk student populations (Brownell & Swaner, 2010; Finley & McNair, 2013; Keup & Young, 2018; Kuh, 2008). Because FYS are often the first HIP to which college students are exposed as well as a hub for other HIPs (e.g., learning communities, intensive writing, service-learning, diversity/global learning, collaborative assignments and projects, and undergraduate research), they have the potential for substantial educational and equity implications for higher education (Keup & Young, 2018; Young & Hopp, 2014).

First-Year Seminars in an Online Learning Space

Given the incredible pace of technological advancement over the past several decades, our newest cohorts of students have been exposed to online and computer technologies since birth. As digital natives, "today's first-year students use the Internet and technology in ways that were unknown to previous generations of students" (Junco, 2005, p. 223) and are often learned habits and acquired competencies for the faculty and administrators at their colleges and universities. National trends on entering first-year students collected by the Cooperative Institutional Research Program's annual survey indicate that using a personal computer and using the Internet for research or homework are nearly universal experiences for these students. Among students entering college in 2015, 83% reported that they at least "occasionally" used online instructional websites to learn something on their own, and 56% used them as assigned by a class in their last year of high school (Eagan et al., 2016). These same data show that social media use has grown in the past decade, such that 78% of students entering four-year colleges and universities in 2015 reported spending at least one hour per week engaged in online social networks, 13% spent more than 10 hours per week in these online spaces, and approximately 5% spent more than 20 hours per week engaged in social media activities (Eagan et al., 2016). Although evidence still indicates a persistent digital divide with respect to technological access and use for low-income, rural, African American, and Latino/a students, it is clear that online technologies are a pervasive force in the lives of a vast majority of first-year college students (Junco, 2005).

Thus, it is perhaps not surprising that the use of learning technologies and online learning has increased substantially in higher education over the past several decades. Recent national survey results show that 6.1 million students, just over 31% of those enrolled in higher education, took at least one course online, which is a substantial increase from the 1.6 million students who reported similar course-taking habits in 2002 and a rate that far outpaced the growth in overall student body for the same time period (Allen & Seaman, 2011). This momentum toward distance learning is motivated, in part, by institutional necessity to accommodate new populations of students who are unable to attend traditional classrooms or prefer online learning environments as well as to address limitations of classroom space on campus (Allen & Seaman, 2011; Junco, 2005; Mixson-Brookshire & Goldfine, 2011; Poirier & Feldman, 2005). These same sources also acknowledge that online education represents a more student-centered effort to allow for a diversity of learning styles, address students' interest in new technologies and engagement with social media, and recognize the importance of lifelong learning and the demand for retraining in a modern economy.

Online courses provide several advantages, including accessibility, flexibility, the ability to accommodate self-paced learning, a more comfortable environment for students who are fearful of public speaking, customization of learning, just-in-time scenarios, and continuous assessment (Allen & Seaman, 2011; Junco, 2005; Kerka, 1996; Poirier & Feldman, 2005). Further, online learning tends to incorporate more writing assignments and may even allow for more interaction between faculty and students than in traditional classrooms. Both practices are hallmarks of high-quality, engaging, and student-centered pedagogies (e.g., Chickering & Gamson, 1987; Goodman, Baxter Magolda, Seifert, & King, 2011; Kuh & O'Donnell, 2013; Swing, 2002), despite the elimination of in-person contact between faculty and students (Poirier & Feldman, 2005). However, online courses also have limitations, including difficulty understanding and expressing tone in an online space, reliance on computer technologies that may be dated or unreliable, difficulty assessing student learning, and the need for students to have advanced time management, communication, and self-responsibility skills (Allen & Seaman, 2011; Kerka, 1996; Poirier & Feldman, 2005; Yukselturk & Bulut, 2007). Despite these limitations, research studies that examined student evaluations of the course, satisfaction, sense of community, and academic performance did not yield statistically or practically significant differences between online/hybrid courses and traditional, in-person instruction (Allen & Seaman, 2011; Bishop & Verleger, 2013; Graham, 2001; Hiltz, 1993; Institute for Higher Education Policy, 1999; Lawson, 2000; Poirier & Feldman, 2004; Russell, 1999; Waschull, 2001; Wegner, Holloway, & Garton, 1999).

Prevalence and Effectiveness of Online First-Year Seminars

Despite the widespread use of technology among first-year students and the abundance of studies and reports on the prevalence and effectiveness of online and distance learning in higher education generally, there is a lack of scholarly and practical literature accounts the pervasiveness, experience, and outcomes of this educational medium for students in FYS. The majority of articles about online education and FYS are program case studies or research with a single-institutional sample, which are informative but difficult to generalize. The only source of national data specific to this topic comes from the National Survey of First-Year Seminars administered triennially by the National Resource Center for The First-Year Experience and Students in Transition. A question piloted on the 2003 survey asked institutions to report the percentage of sections of their most prominent FYS type that incorporated an online component as well as whether campuses offered at least one FYS section in an online-only format. Data collected in 2006, 2009, and 2012 to 2013 are reported in Figure 1.1.[2]

Figure 1.1. Percentage of first-year seminar sections with online components.

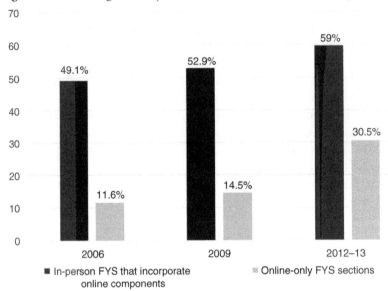

These data show that institutions have consistently reported greater use of online components in in-person FYS than online-only sections. These data also show that, consistent with national data on all higher education courses, institutional use of both online components and online-only sections for FYS has grown substantially from 2006 to 2013. However, the rate of growth for online-only sections of the FYS has outpaced the percentage point increase for sections that incorporate online components by a rate of almost two-to-one. Further, analyses of the data collected in 2012–2013 show that both online-only FYS and those that incorporate online components are more common at public institutions and two-year campuses. These data also show that academic FYS with variable content are far less likely to incorporate online components or be offered in an online-only format than other types of FYS (Young & Hopp, 2014).

A closer examination of the data collected via the most recent administration of this instrument provides more information about the proportion of online-only sections of FYS that were offered on campuses responding to the survey. Although 31% of institutions responding to the 2012–2013 National Survey of First-Year Seminars indicated that they offered at least one section in an online-only format, more than half of those institutions also shared that less than 10% of all their FYS sections were offered in this format (Figure 1.2). In addition, 85% of institutional respondents reported that less than 30% of FYS sections at their campus were delivered in an online-only

Figure 1.2. Percentage of online-only first-year seminar sections offered on campus.

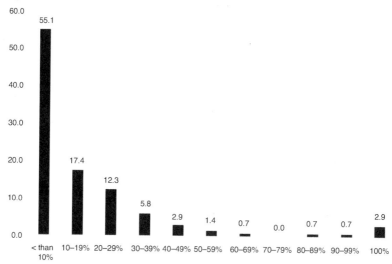

format, as shown in Figure 1.2 (Young & Hopp, 2014). Conversely, only 3% of institutions responding to the questionnaire reported that all of their FYS sections were offered online. Thus, it appears that although the proportion of institutions that offer some online-only FYS is expanding nationwide, the prominence and reach of this type of instructional delivery for FYS is still rather limited and likely considered more of a boutique or specialty offering.

These statistics may be an early measure of innovation and institutionalization of online-only FYS (shown by the percentage of institutions offering these sections) or may represent the intractable nature of traditional classroom delivery methods (illustrated by the limited reach of online-only FYS on each campus). It remains to be seen whether online learning seminars are an emerging trend or will struggle at the margins of the FYE curriculum, but it is worthy of additional institutional assessment and national research.

Online First-Year Seminar Pedagogy and Instruction

Analyses of data gathered across various administrations of these national surveys (Padgett & Keup, 2011; Tobolowsky, 2005; Tobolowsky & Associates, 2008; Young & Hopp, 2014) and select institution-specific studies of FYS (Costa, 2008; Foote & Mixson-Brookshire, 2013, 2014; Mixson-Brookshire & Goldfine, 2011) allow for a glimpse into the reasons for student participation in FYS delivered online and the types of educational technologies incorporated therein. Similar to the reasons for enrollment in online learning overall, students who participate in FYS in this format do so because of the flexibility that the course provides, the ability to work ahead and otherwise manage the pace of the course, and the highly organized and detailed nature of the course modules (Foote & Mixson-Brookshire, 2013). First-year students also reported a clear understanding of the skills that are necessary for success in an online seminar, most notably time management, communication, self-motivation, and a clear understanding of the professor's expectations, although they did not always report a high level of confidence in their personal abilities on these success metrics (Mixson-Brookshire & Goldfine, 2011).

This same body of research also indicates the methods by which online courses are able to address these needs and concerns among students in online and hybrid FYS. These sources suggest that the most common use of information technology (IT) in an FYS is transactional in nature, such as using course management systems; administering placement tests, quizzes, exams, and other learning assessments; posting course information, assignments, readings, and the syllabus; and engaging with document-sharing and information-exchange platforms. Communication strategies between instructor and students, as well as among students in the course, are other ways that IT often is engaged in FYS, including e-mail, social media channels, and discussion boards. Delivery of content, particularly asynchronously, is frequently cited as yet another means of engaging online technologies in the FYS (e.g., PowerPoint, online lectures, videos, podcasts, reviewing websites of campus resources).

True interactive engagement with the course content and the classroom community, which are foundational to the success of an FYS and hallmarks of HIPs (e.g., Brownell & Swaner, 2010; Garner, 2012; Greenfield et al., 2013; Hunter & Linder, 2005; Keup & Petschauer, 2011; Kuh, 2008; Kuh & O'Donnell, 2013), is the area that is most lacking in the literature on online FYS. Although this area needs future research, the few engaging pedagogies identified in the literature for online and hybrid FYS (Costa, 2008; Foote & Mixson-Brookshire, 2013, 2014; Garner, 2012; Junco, 2005; Mixson-Brookshire & Goldfine, 2011; Tobolowsky, 2005; Tobolowsky & Associates, 2008) include:

- interactive modules to introduce and orient online first-year students to web-based platforms, etiquette for online learning spaces, and expectations for distance learning;
- development of the online academic community through virtual collaborative exercises, group projects, wikis, and peer review of writing;
- course presentations, discussion boards, and communication of content;

- problem-based learning, active experimentation, game-based exercises, case studies, and hands-on application assignments; and
- reflection exercises such as blogs, online journals, reflective observations, and self-assessments.

In a best-case scenario (and as is suggested by the order presented previously), these tactics are intentionally introduced within the course at the optimal time for student developmental and content readiness and arranged into a "dynamic digital scaffolding" (Wilcox, Sarma, & Lippell, 2016) that allows for effective integration of distance learning pedagogies and strategies. Further, these common online teaching and learning strategies are easily connected to the (a) eight tenets of HIPs, and (b) primary outcome areas of high-quality FYE programs (i.e., skill development, community and connection, and persistence and success), both of which are noted earlier in this chapter and require more scholarly examination and practical development in an online learning space.

As with most FYS, course instructors and their ability to use the educational environment for engagement and learning are the key resource for first-year student and FYS success in an online setting. Foote and Mixson-Brookshire (2013) identify three key elements of course structure that led to positive results in an online FYS: (a) thoughtful consideration of the introduction, timing, and layering of course content; (b) clear communication of expectations for communication (e.g., "netiquette," what is appropriate for synchronous versus asynchronous interaction), performance (e.g., assignments, assessments of learning), and course learning outcomes; and (c) development of an online community via course expectations, use of interactive technologies, and commitment to engaging pedagogies. Garner (2012) validated and expanded on these points about integrating technology into FYS in both face-to-face and online environments:

> The challenge for faculty remains one of balancing several key elements: (a) remaining abreast of current technologies, (b) assessing the degree to which emerging technologies can be applied in the classroom, and (c) creating ways to integrate technology . . . in a manner that enhances the learning experience for all participating students. (p. 104)

The use of technology in an FYS must remain connected to the course mission and student learning outcomes and never become about the medium or tool itself (Garner, 2012). It can be tempting to add online content for the sake of increasing student engagement, but this can often represent the "tail wagging the dog" and lead to drift from the student learning outcomes for the seminar, which is captured by Costa (2008) in her reflection that "it is a mistake . . . to add technology at the expense of it being instructionally sound" (p. 7).

Unfortunately, many faculty remain suspicious of online instruction, and "nearly two-thirds . . . believe that the learning outcomes for an online course are inferior or somewhat inferior to those for comparable face-to-face courses" (Allen, Seaman, Lederman, & Jaschik, 2012, p. 2; see also Foote & Mixson-Brookshire, 2014). This skepticism among professors is a function of concern about academic rigor in an online environment as well as comfort with teaching practices via distance technologies (Garner, 2012; Junco, 2005). The 2013–2014 HERI Faculty Survey indicates that relatively few faculty members are teaching in a distance-learning environment for FYS and overall. Instead, faculty seem to be making greater advancements with incorporating "various forms of technology into their courses" (Eagan et al., 2014, p. 5), perhaps as a larger effort toward engaging pedagogy and student-centered teaching practices.

Some of the trepidation of faculty may reflect a concern that online learning will replace teachers in the classroom. Yet the outcome of that conversation is most often a resounding "no": "the role of teachers is essential and irreplaceable—rather . . . the value of in-person education can be enhanced by blending in online experiences" (Wilcox, Sarma, & Lippell, 2016, p. iii). Yet the critical component of much online learning success is faculty training and development to equip instructors with tools to effectively engage with students and facilitate learning in these online spaces. According to data collected by Allen and Seaman (2011), more than 90% of institutions provide at least some training for their faculty teaching online courses. When compared to faculty training opportunities for blended and face-to-face courses, professors and instructors of online courses received at least as much if not more training support than their peers teaching in hybrid and more traditional environments (Allen & Seaman, 2011). Although faculty development for FYS instruction is widely acknowledged as a place to provide support for innovative pedagogies (Cuseo, 2009), it is unclear whether the 70% of institutions offering training for FYS instructors incorporate online instruction tools and techniques into their faculty development modules (Young & Hopp, 2014). Thus, it appears that there is vast, untapped potential for FYS programs to be a space to support faculty development in online instruction and to provide skills that could be generalized to the other courses that they teach.

Conclusions and Future Directions

An overwhelming increase has taken place in students' interest in and comfort with IT, demand for online learning opportunities in the undergraduate experience, and incorporation of online educational technologies in the undergraduate curriculum. Yet this medium appears to be vastly underutilized in the delivery of FYS and underrepresented in the scholarly and practical literature on these courses. There are challenges to using online delivery methods for FYS while maintaining the tenets of HIPs and quality undergraduate education (e.g., lack of in-person contact with faculty and fellow students, challenges with feedback and learning assessments, and limited experiences with diversity). However, online learning is a means of addressing issues of access and demands for scalability for FYS, which represent one of the most widely used HIPs across colleges and universities of all types. With thoughtful course design and in-depth faculty training and development initiatives as the cornerstones of online seminar delivery, higher education is likely to see gains in metrics of success and positive impact on student learning outcomes and utilization of online learning technologies.

As educators and higher education scholars look to the future, there are many exciting directions to advance research and practice related to online FYS development and delivery. This chapter highlights the need for ongoing evaluation of the prevalence and reach of online FYS on campus rather than just counting the number of institutions offering these courses. It also points to the need for additional examination of FYS in online learning spaces and their ability to uphold the tenets of HIPs and outcomes of high-quality FYS. Additionally, a dearth of large-scale (i.e., multi-institutional or national) studies have identified the pedagogical practices used in online FYS, determined their effectiveness, and examined faculty development initiatives focused on these online instructional strategies. Finally, FYS represent only one program in an integrated, comprehensive FYE, and additional work is needed to fill the gap in the scholarly and practical literature based on other FYE practices (e.g., orientation, advising, tutoring, mentoring) delivered via online and distance-learning methods. These advancements would be invaluable to administrators and faculty who would like to implement or refine online learning overall and especially for first-year students in online learning seminars.

Key Takeaways

- Institutions should strive to move beyond transactional uses of IT in FYS and instead use IT and distance-learning technologies to facilitate interactive engagement in online FYS that is both dynamic and scaffolded for optimal learning.
- Course instructors and their ability to use the educational environment for engagement and learning are key resources for successful first-year students and seminars in an online setting.

- First-year seminar programs offer the potential to support faculty development in online instruction and provide skills that are transferable to other courses.
- Equipping faculty with tools to effectively engage with students and facilitate learning in an online environment is a critical component to much of the success with online learning.
- Ongoing evaluation is needed to determine the prevalence and reach of online FYS.

Notes

1. A combined approach to the seminar is often referred to as a *hybrid* in the FYE literature but does not indicate the medium of delivery as inclusive of both face-to-face and distance education. However, given that this term has a unique meaning in the online education body of scholarship, the term *hybrid* in reference to the type of FYS will be avoided in this chapter.

2. The 2012–2013 survey is the most recent administration of the National Survey of First-Year Seminars. The next administration of the instrument is scheduled for spring of 2017.

References

Allen, E., & Seaman, J. (2011). *Going the distance: Online education in the United States, 2011.* Babson Park, MA: Babson Survey Research Group and Quahog Research Group, LLC.

Allen, E., Seaman, J. Lederman, D., & Jaschik, S. (2012). *Conflicted: Faculty and online education, 2012.* Babson Park, MA: Babson Survey Research Group and Quahog Research Group, LLC.

Barefoot, B. O. (1992). *Helping first-year college students climb the academic ladder: Report of a national survey of freshman seminar programming in American higher education* (Unpublished doctoral dissertation). College of William and Mary, Williamsburg, VA.

Barefoot, B. O., Gardner, J. N., Cutright, M., Morris, L. V., Schroeder, C. C., Schwartz, S. W., Siegel, M. J., & Swing, R. L. (2005). *Achieving and sustaining institutional excellence for the first year of college.* San Francisco, CA: Jossey-Bass.

Barefoot, B. O., Griffin, B. Q., & Koch, A. K. (2012). *Enhancing student success and retention throughout undergraduate education: A national survey.* Brevard, NC: The John N. Gardner Institute for Excellence in Undergraduate Education.

Bishop, J. L., & Verleger, M. A. (2013). *The flipped classroom: A survey of the research.* Research paper presented at the 120th American Society for Engineering Education (ASEE) Annual Conference & Exposition, Atlanta, GA.

Brownell, J. E., & Swaner, L. E. (2010). *Five high-impact practices: Research on learning outcomes, completion, and quality.* Washington DC: Association of American Colleges & Universities.

Chickering, A. W., & Gamson, Z. G. (1987). Seven principles for good practice. *AAHE Bulletin, 39*(7), 8–10.

Costa, K. (2008). Teaching the first-year seminar online: Lessons learned. *E-Source for College Transitions, 5*(6), 7–8, 12.

Cuseo, J. (2009). The first-year seminar: A vehicle for promoting the instructional development of college faculty. *E-Source for College Transitions, 7*(2), 4–5, 8.

Drake, R. (1966). *Review of the literature for freshman orientation practices in the United States.* Fort Collins, CO: Colorado State University.

Dwyer, J. O. (1989). A historical look at the freshman year experience. In M. L. Upcraft & J. N. Gardner (Eds.), *The freshman year experience* (pp. 25–39). San Francisco, CA: Jossey-Bass.

Eagan, K., Stolzenberg, E. B., Lozano, J. B., Aragon, M. C., Suchard, M. R., & Hurtado, S. (2014). *Undergraduate teaching faculty: The 2013–2014 HERI Faculty Survey.* Los Angeles, CA: Higher Education Research Institute, UCLA.

Eagan, K., Stolzenberg, E. B., Ramirez, J. J., Aragon, M. C., Suchard, M. R., & Rios-Aguilar, C. (2016). *The American freshman: Fifty-year trends, 1966–2015.* Los Angeles, CA: Higher Education Research Institute, UCLA.

Finley, A., & McNair, T. (2013). *Assessing underserved students' engagement in high-impact practices.* Washington DC: Association of American Colleges & Universities.

Foote, S. M., & Mixson-Brookshire, D. (2013). Finding balance: Creating hybrid first-year seminars. *E-Source for College Transitions, 10*(2), 8–10.

Foote, S. M., & Mixson-Brookshire, D. (2014). Enhancing learning with technology: Applying the findings from a study of students in online, blended, and face-to-face first-year seminar classes. *Currents in Teaching and Learning, 6*(2), 35–41.

Garner, B. (2012). *The first-year seminar: Designing, implementing, and assessing courses to support student learning and success: Vol. III. Teaching in the first-year seminar.* Columbia, SC: University of South Carolina, National Resource Center for the First-Year Experience and Students in Transition.

Goodman, K. M., Baxter Magolda, M., Seifert, T. A., & King, P. M. (2011). Good practices for student learning: Mixed-method evidence from the Wabash National Study. *About Campus, 16*(1), 2–9.

Graham, T. A. (2001). Teaching child development via the Internet: Opportunities and pitfalls. *Teaching of Psychology, 28*(1), 67–71.

Greenfield, G. M., Keup, J. R., & Gardner, J. N. (2013). *Developing and sustaining successful first-year programs: A guide for practitioners.* San Francisco, CA: Jossey-Bass.

Hiltz, S. R. (1993). Correlates of learning in a virtual classroom. *International Journal of Man-Machine Studies, 28*, 61–71.

Hunter, M. S., & Linder, C. W. (2005). First-year seminars. In M. L. Upcraft, J. N. Gardner, B. O. Barefoot, & Associates (Eds.), *Challenging and supporting the first-year student: A handbook for improving the first year of college* (pp. 275–291). San Francisco, CA: Jossey-Bass.

Institute for Higher Education Policy. (1999). *What's the difference? A review of contemporary research on the effectiveness of distance learning in higher education.* Washington DC: Institute for Higher Education Policy.

Junco, R. (2005). Technology and today's first-year student. In M. L. Upcraft, J. N. Gardner, B. O. Barefoot, & Associates (Eds.), *Challenging and supporting the first-year student: A handbook for improving the first year of college* (pp. 221–238). San Francisco, CA: Jossey-Bass.

Kerka, S. (1996). *Distance learning, the Internet, and the World Wide Web.* Washington DC: Office of Educational Research and Improvement (ERIC Document Reproduction Service No. ED395214).

Keup, J. R., & Petschauer, J. W. (2011). *The first-year seminar: Designing, implementing, and assessing courses to support student learning and success: Vol. 1. Designing and Administering the Course.* Columbia, SC: University of South Carolina, National Resource Center for The First-Year Experience and Students in Transition.

Keup, J. R., & Young, D. G. (2018). Investigating first-year seminars as a high-impact practice. In R. S. Feldman (Ed.), *The first year of college: Research, theory, and practice on improving the student experience and increasing retention* (pp. 93–125). Cambridge, UK: Cambridge University Press.

Koch, A. K., & Gardner, J. N. (2006). The history of the first-year experience in the United States: Lessons from the past, practices in the present, and implications for the future. In A. Hamana & K. Tatsuo (Eds.), *The first-year experience and transition from high school to college: An international study of content and pedagogy.* Tokyo, Japan: Maruzen Publishing.

Kronovet, E. (1969). Current practices in freshman orientation. *Improving College & University Teaching, 17*(3), 204–205.

Kuh, G. D. (2008). *High-impact educational practices: What they are, who has access to them, and why they matter.* Washington DC: Association of American Colleges & Universities.

Kuh, G. D., & O'Donnell, K. (2013). *Ensuring quality & taking high-impact practices to scale.* Washington DC: Association of American Colleges & Universities.

Lawson, T. J. (2000). Teaching a social psychology course on the web. *Teaching of Psychology, 27*(4), 285–289.

Mixson-Brookshire, D., & Goldfine, R. (2011). Moving the first-year seminar online. *E-Source for College Transitions, 9*(1), 11–13.

Padgett, R. D., & Keup, J. R. (2011). *2009 National Survey of First-Year Seminars: Ongoing efforts to support students in transition* (Research Report No. 2). Columbia, SC: University of South Carolina, National Resource Center for the First-Year Experience and Students in Transition.

Poirier, C. R., & Feldman, R. S. (2004). Teaching in cyberspace: Online vs traditional instruction using a waiting-list experimental design. *Teaching of Psychology, 31*(1), 59–62.

Poirier, C. R., & Feldman, R. S. (2005). Going online: Promoting student success via distance learning. In R. S. Feldman (Ed.), *Improving the first year of college: Research and Practice* (pp. 161–175). Mahwah, NJ: Lawrence Erlbaum Associates.

Russell, T. L. (1999). *The no significant difference phenomenon.* Raleigh, NC: North Carolina State University, Office of Instructional Technologies.

Swing, R. L. (2002). *Series of essays on the First-Year Initiative Benchmarking Study.* Brevard, NC: Policy Center on the First-Year of College.

Tobolowsky, B. F. (2005). *The 2003 national survey on first-year seminars: Continuing innovations in the collegiate curriculum* (Monograph No. 41). Columbia, SC: University of South Carolina, National Resource Center for the First-Year Experience and Students in Transition.

Tobolowsky, B. T., & Associates (2008). *2006 National Survey of First-Year Seminars: Continuing innovations in the collegiate curriculum* (Monograph No. 51). Columbia, SC: University of South Carolina, National Resource Center for the First-Year Experience and Students in Transition.

Upcraft, M. L., Gardner, J. N., Barefoot, B. O., & Associates. (2005). *Challenging and supporting the first-year student.* San Francisco, CA: Jossey-Bass.

Waschull, S. B. (2001). The online delivery of psychology courses: Attrition, performance, and evaluation. *Teaching of Psychology, 28*(2), 143–147.

Wegner, S. B., Holloway, K. C., & Garton, E. M. (1999). The effects of Internet-based instruction on student learning. *Journal of Asynchronous Learning Networks (JALN), 3*(2), 98–106.

Wilcox, K. E., Sarma, S., & Lippell, P. H. (2016). *Online education: A catalyst for higher education reforms.* Boston, MA: Massachusetts Institute of Technology, Online Education Policy Initiative.

Young, D. G., & Hopp, J. M. (2014). *2012-2013 National Survey of First-Year Seminars: Exploring high-impact practices in the first college year* (Research Report No. 4). Columbia, SC: University of South Carolina, National Resource Center for the First-Year Experience and Students in Transition.

Young, D. G., & Keup, J. R. (in press). *CAS cross-functional framework: First-year experience.* Washington DC: Council for the Advancement of Standards in Higher Education.

Yukselturk, E., & Bulut, S. (2007). Predictors for student success in an online course. *Educational Technology and Society, 10*(2), 71–83.

2

COMMON INTELLECTUAL EXPERIENCE

Jason D. Baker and Michael Pregitzer

The rise of online learning over the past two decades has had a profound impact on higher education. Most chief academic officers report that online learning is critical to their long-term strategy and that online courses are as educationally effective as face-to-face courses (Allen, Seaman, Poulin, & Straut, 2016). Students have also embraced online learning, with more than one quarter of all university students enrolled in at least one online course (National Center for Education Statistics, 2016). Students regularly report convenience and flexibility as primary motivators for choosing online learning over traditional campus-based instruction (e.g., Cole, Shelley, & Swartz, 2014; Jaggars, 2014).

As institutions have diversified their learning modalities, educators have questioned whether undergraduates should be required to complete a common core curriculum. Lewis (2007) summarized this attitude: "The contention is that students just don't have that much in common—nothing is 'relevant' to all of them—and we should not 'privilege' one way of looking at the world over another" (para. 2). Similarly, Staley and Trinkle (2011) assess the present state of the core curriculum as, "in many ways a vestige of the nineteenth-century common curriculum" (p. 19) that has largely been overshadowed by the elective system. They note that students are active participants in this shift when they assume the general education core is less valuable than their career-preparation and skills-building courses.

The Common Intellectual Experience in the Online Environment

In his presentation of high-impact educational practices, Kuh (2008) framed the common intellectual experience:

The older idea of a "core" curriculum has evolved into a variety of modern forms such as a set of required common courses or a vertically organized general education program that includes advanced integrative studies and/or required participation in a learning community. . . . These programs often combine broad themes—e.g., technology and society, global interdependence—with a variety of curricular and co-curricular options for students. (p. 9)

Traditionally, the approach toward implementing a common intellectual experience for undergraduates has been focused on campus-based curricular and cocurricular activities, such as summer sessions, orientations, first-year seminars (sometimes spanning multiple semesters), and common reading programs (Greenfield, Keup, & Gardner, 2013). Interestingly enough, however, Kuh's (2008) introduction of common intellectual experiences offers an example that is campus-independent.

Bringing a common intellectual experience into an online learning environment frequently driven by convenience, flexibility, and choice produces an inherent tension between the potential benefits of recognizing the student-centered characteristics of many online instructional models (e.g., immediate enrollment, self-paced learning, asynchronous discussions) and the significant limitations resulting from fragmented learning. How do we acknowledge and harness the practical understanding of the student at the center of his or her own learning experience while emphasizing that the student is not the center of the universe? How do we bring disparate students together, particularly in an environment in which they are physically separated, to learn within community rather than as a collection of discrete individuals?

In his chart connecting liberal education learning outcomes with high-impact practices (HIPs), Kuh (2008) parenthetically refers to "exploring 'big questions' in history, cultures, science, and society" (p. 6). This use of "big questions" is integral to our approach because it serves as the means by which narrative, engagement, and transformation are promoted in the online classroom. Regent University's College of Arts & Sciences has chosen to use narrative as the organizing framework for the learning experience and to use big questions to provide a common intellectual guide for the students throughout their academic journey. Although students may have enrolled in our undergraduate degree program with the goal of earning a degree, we believe that their journey is far grander than merely completing a credential. The educational experience has at its heart students' own personal transformation as well as the opportunity for them to go into the world and be agents of transformation to promote human flourishing. To this end, we advocate a Narrative, Engagement, Transformation (NET) approach that applies a common intellectual experience to the online environment. Such a framework can be used to guide online course development and delivery to promote online learning engagement and retention. While narrative, engagement, and transformation are most fully experienced in our general education core curriculum, the NET approach also contributes to a design and pedagogical philosophy that can cut across content areas.

NET Model

The mission of Regent University's College of Arts & Sciences is to "graduate exceptional students deeply committed to Christ's calling to cherish character, challenge culture, and serve the world" (Regent University, n.d.). By leveraging a NET model, consistent with Kuh's Common Intellectual Experience, the college is seeking to foster in students the moral and intellectual character necessary to engage the culture with a Christian understanding of the good, the true, and the beautiful. Equipped with this knowledge, wisdom, and understanding, students are encouraged to humbly and wisely serve others by building businesses, helping the poor, feeding the hungry, governing citizens, educating children, managing homes, and performing other acts of service to humanity.

Narrative

Within their first online course, students are given a vision of this overarching narrative concept and introduced to the core curriculum that is built around three enduring questions of humanity: Who is God? What is a human being? What is good, true, and beautiful? Within individual courses, content is regularly framed within this narrative context. Students should be led on a journey—not an endless or a wandering journey—but one that has a specific destination: the good, the true, and the beautiful. As evident by the questions, this journey reflects our institutional identity as a Christian university, but Kuh's (2008) concept of framing the common intellectual experience around "big questions" applies to our context and can similarly benefit other institutions.

In the first week of a first-term online course, GENE 100: The Making of the Christian Mind, the chair of the general education department addresses the students in a brief video and provides this narrative context:

> In sum, societies have had some definition about what the good life is. They've had a definition or vision for what a flourishing human being or what a flourishing society looks like. . . . In our general education here at Regent University, we want to train you with the necessary skills—reading,

writing, scientific reason, critical thinking, analytical skills—to thoughtfully examine these enduring questions. We want to help you to answer these enduring questions. . . . We do not believe here at Regent that general education are simply throw-away classes, boxes to be ticked off, obstacles to overcome so that you can get to your "real classes." No. We believe that general education is at the center of what we want for you: human flourishing. . . . GENE 100 is designed to be a starting point in this quest. (McMullen, n.d.)

The role of narrative and the use of these enduring questions provide both a comprehensive organizing paradigm for the common intellectual experience as reflected in our general education core curriculum and are also explicitly revisited within individual online courses. Syllabi, instructor video presentations, and discussion questions regularly hearken back to these questions to help the student contextualize their learning within this larger journey toward human flourishing.

Engagement

Another component of Kuh's (2008) model for the common intellectual experience is engagement. A frequent cause of student dissatisfaction in online courses is lack of interaction (Cole et al., 2014; Croxton, 2014; Parahoo, Santally, Rajabalee, & Harvey, 2016). Historically, interaction within distance and online learning has been categorized into three distinct types: learner–content, learner–instructor, and learner–learner (Moore, 1989). Learner–content interaction is essentially the engagement between the student and the course content or instructional material, learner–instructor represents the communication between the student and the professor, and learner–learner is the interaction that occurs among the students themselves. When students express concerns about lack of interaction, they are generally referring to learner–instructor and learner–learner interaction (Croxton, 2014), meaning that they had limited opportunities to engage with their professor or classmates (Parahoo et al., 2016). A course limited to learner–content interaction resembles a correspondence course rather than an engaging online course. This may explain why the U.S. Department of Education differentiates between correspondence courses and distance education in part based on "regular and substantive interaction" (Poulin, 2012, n.p.) between students and faculty.

Accordingly, in addition to narrative, engagement is essential to our common intellectual experience and takes many forms. Students engage with the content. By design the content is presented in weekly units (typically eight weeks for a three-credit online course), each of which includes a variety of content presentations (e.g., videos, audio, reading). Much of the content is presented in shorter chunks or modules rather than the lengthy hour-long lectures that mark much of traditional higher education. This shift in format reflects findings within cognitive science that attention lapses are frequent within the long-form lecture style (Risko, Anderson, Sarwal, Engelhardt, & Kingstone, 2012). This is not to say that lengthy material cannot be presented, but that it is more effective to present it in smaller chunks with opportunities for engagement or active learning than to assume that students maintain a consistent high level of focus for 60 to 90 minutes at a time (Schacter & Szpunar, 2015).

In addition to chunking content to increase attentiveness, engagement is enhanced by supplementing content presentation with opportunities for reflective discussion and assessment such as discussion board prompts, online quizzes and self-assessment, collaborative group work, and long-form written assignments. In several courses in Regent's general education curriculum, reflective journals are also included to permit students to engage more personally with the material, as well as to allow for more personal interaction between the instructor and student. The design goal is to increase opportunities for high-frequency, quick feedback, low-stress engagement opportunities and assessments rather than having long stretches of impersonal content presentation followed by high-stakes assignments.

A more recent addition to our online engagement aspect of the NET model has been our Regent Live initiative. Regent Live is a university-wide initiative to ensure that all online students are given the opportunity for meaningful live engagement with their course faculty. During the first week of every course, faculty invite online students to a live synchronous engagement event, such as an online videoconference (e.g., Blackboard Collaborate, Google Hangouts, Skype), that is scheduled for sometime within the first two weeks of the course. A similar invitation is extended during the third week of the courses for an activity to be scheduled in week three or four. These live online events serve as opportunities for personal and academic engagement between the faculty and students and reduce the possibility that students will experience online learning as a mere correspondence course. Additionally, it serves as yet another opportunity for the professor to contextualize the course content within the broader narrative or big questions perspective. To respond to the student desire for convenience and flexibility, these live engagement opportunities are optional (faculty are responsible for the invitation and event but not for student attendance), and most events are recorded and archived for subsequent viewing by students unable to attend.

These engagement opportunities reflect an application of media richness theory to the online learning environment. Media richness theory is based on the premise that communication has a fundamental purpose of reducing uncertainty and ambiguity, particularly when tasks are to be accomplished (Daft & Lengel, 1986). Furthermore, media richness theory assumes that various media differ in their suitability for various tasks, such as writing being better suited for unequivocal instructions and verbal communication working better when there is ambiguity involved in the task. By incorporating multiple communication media in the learning experience, such as video presentations from faculty, readings from relevant sources, written online class discussions around key questions, and live audio/video meetings among students and faculty, students can engage with course content and people using media best suited to the tasks associated with their learning experiences.

Transformation

Transformation marks the final aspect of the NET framework. As evident by the human flourishing questions, we believe that the online learning environment is not limited to information transfer or even knowledge acquisition, but that it can include wisdom that transforms learners and enables students to serve and transform the world around them to promote human flourishing. This reflects a perspective on education that looks beyond students merely mastering content but incorporates their whole person. It encompasses engagement with themselves through reflection, engagement with other students through discussion, and engagement with faculty using various social communication tools, including discussion boards, chats, and video conferencing.

This journey of transformation is particularly reflected in the student activities and assignments in GENE 402 The Making of a Christian Leader, the capstone course in the students' common learning experience completed in their junior or senior year (for more on capstone courses as a HIP, see chapter 11, this volume). In this course, students are challenged to consider all that they have learned to date and reflect on ways in which they can lead to make their world better. Here are the learning outcomes for the course:

1. Identity and reflect on the Biblical foundations and transformative nature of Godly character and leadership.
2. Formulate views on leadership through the study and evaluation of exceptional historical figures.
3. Examine and evaluate critical cultural issues and the application of Biblical leadership principles to provide transformative, creative solutions.
4. Explore the foundational Biblical principles of character-based service and leadership and apply those principles to leadership learning experiences.

Various assignments support these outcomes. In one assignment, students are required to watch a segment of the film *Defiance* (Zwick & Jan Brugge, 2008) and discuss the qualities that were required to lead a resistance movement against the Nazis in World War II. Another assignment requires students to critically evaluate the moral failings that led to the Watergate, Enron, and Madoff scandals. Students are also required to evaluate the leadership skills employed by Coach Herman Boone as portrayed in the film, *Remember the Titans* (Bruckheimer, Oman, & Yakin, 2000), as he endeavored to overcome racism at a southern high school in the 1970s. As a final project, students are required to interview a leader related to their major field of study, evaluate that leader's effectiveness, and reflect on the ways in which that individual has been a successful change agent in his or her sphere of influence. Overall, the course—through books, articles, and videos—offers students insights into personal transformation so that they may become transformational leaders for the betterment of humankind.

It should be noted that although this common intellectual experience is built around narrative, engagement, and transformation, the specifics will vary by course and instructor. Some general courses such as theology, philosophy, or psychology are more conducive to overt reflection and consideration of the overarching big questions than, say, courses in mathematics or statistics. Even in those courses, however, faculty are expected to contextualize the course content within this larger framework. Without such activities, the common intellectual experience gets reduced to merely a uniform collection of courses rather than a narrative, engaging, and transformational learning experience. Similarly, the students should recognize that they are investing in a transformational quest and not merely consuming online course content. Without a commitment to such personal investment and engagement, students will never experience the type of transformation that we strive to promote.

Programmatic Perspective

To implement a common intellectual experience, we have found it essential that the general education core curriculum be designed as an integrated whole rather than a collection of discrete courses. This is not to say that one cannot simply design individual online education courses, but the development of a common intellectual experience described previously demands integration among the courses to ensure that the program is more than the sum of the discrete courses. This works only if courses fit into a program (with overarching goals, guiding program learning outcomes, etc.) rather than exist as a collection of courses taken to meet distribution requirements. Although many academic degrees are initially designed with an overall program in mind, individual courses are then created by faculty who may know little about the content in other courses within the program. To promote this programmatic perspective, and thus to protect the integrity of the common intellectual experience, we have implemented three separate but complementary online design initiatives: master courses, course review, and program review.

Master Courses

The first component of this programmatic perspective is our master course model. Many of our early online course development efforts paralleled our traditional course development in that they were faculty-centric. Faculty would be assigned to specific courses and would then design and develop the courses, including course content, sequencing, text selection, and learning outcomes, in the manner they deemed best. This reflected historic teaching practices with which faculty were familiar, but it produced courses that were potentially idiosyncratic and inconsistent student experiences and outcomes. Two different sections of the same course could have different professors as well as different texts, different content, different assignments, and entirely different student experiences. It is difficult to maintain a common intellectual experience across multiple courses when such a model inhibits a common experience across multiple sections of the same course. Thus, we developed a master course model in which lead faculty, under the supervision of department and program chairs, collaborate with instructional designers from the Center for Teaching and Learning in the development of a master online course shell.

These master courses contain all of the course content, including syllabi, readings, instructional videos, discussion prompts, assignment descriptions, and any other content necessary to teach the course. The master course serves as the authoritative version that is then copied into each online course shell prior to the start of the term. Every section of a given online course is thus fundamentally identical in all major aspects. Individual faculty can then focus primarily on the student engagement experience rather than designing each section from scratch. This focused engagement includes critical pedagogical practices of substantive discussion board interaction, detailed feedback on written assignments and projects, and encouraging and informative weekly announcements. Faculty have the freedom to supplement their particular course section by sharing additional content, but they cannot remove or replace the materials found in the master courses. This serves as a form of quality control and contributes to a coherent common intellectual experience. Finally, faculty who are involved in the development of these master courses are required to complete a training course that outlines the best

Figure 2.1. Life cycle of a master course.

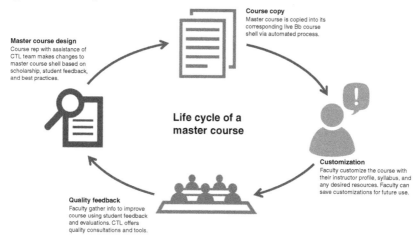

Note. Courtesy of Regent University Center for Teaching and Learning for Teaching and Learning.

practices required to maintain consistency in course structure and design (see Figure 2.1).

Course Review

The second component of this programmatic perspective is the course review process. On completion of the master course design, and periodically thereafter, every online course is reviewed by a professor or administrator who was involved in the development of the overall program. He or she reviews the course for academic quality, depth of content, effective interaction opportunities, connection to the program goals and outcomes, use of technology and media, and overall student learning experience. Each course is then scored on a spreadsheet, which is returned to the lead instructor for review and modification. Additionally, when new instructors are hired, they receive an online "visit" in their courses to ensure that their engagement with the course content and students is consistent with institutional expectations. These peer review activities, which examine both courses and instructors, serve as yet another form of quality control to promote a coherent and quality online learning experience.

Program Review

Third, in conjunction with our regional accreditation process, all degrees undergo a program review process by the faculty and under the leadership of the program or department chair every six years, with an interim report due in the third year. Each degree program is examined to consider faculty activity and support, institutional and programmatic benchmark comparisons, curriculum mapping, syllabi review, assessment review, student performance, enrollment trends, and future plans. This program review is also evaluated by the university director of assessment and compliance to ensure that this level of quality control also considers the institutional perspective and not merely the programmatic one.

These activities have served as essential components of ensuring a high-quality online learning experience during a time of rapid institutional growth. Due to the demand for online learning, the university has grown more than 50% in the past two years, with online students accounting for approximately 70% of the enrollment. In the midst of rapid growth, we have been able to maintain a high level of quality, as evidenced by strong retention and graduation rates within the online population as well as student reports of high levels of satisfaction with their courses and faculty. Retention levels in our online courses exceed our national peer set, with part-time students showing particularly high retention rates compared with our peers. Our most recent undergraduate retention analysis, including online learners, showed that retention of full-time students was 12 percentage points higher than the four-year private university average, whereas our part-time retention was 32 percentage points higher than the comparative average. We believe that the design of our online undergraduate program is integral to these positive performance metrics.

Recommendations

When considering the design and development of online learning programs, it is tempting to devise them with one eye on their traditional counterparts. Such a comparison is built on the assumption (whether explicit or tacit) that the traditional classroom experience is the standard by which all education should be measured. Because on-campus classroom instruction remains the dominant form within higher education, it is reasonable to use it as a standard of comparison. However, when online instructional design is approached from this perspective, the result is more likely to be an online learning experience that is but a mere shadow of its campus counterpart.

Because of the nature of the online classroom, it is also tempting to focus online learning research and practice on issues of technology rather than pedagogy. Distance education existed long before the Internet and is not dependent on any particular technology or media. Online learning is the current and most popular model, but even that has significant diversity therein.

Asynchronous online learning, in which courses are largely designed as discussion-heavy online seminars, has been perhaps the most common type of online learning, but this model does not represent the totality of online instructional models. Synchronous online learning with real-time streaming classes; mobile online courses delivered on smartphones or tablets; blended or hybrid learning, which combines online and on-campus instruction; and even massive open online courses represent a variety of instructional models for online learning. New wearable technologies, artificial intelligence, and machine learning algorithms offer the promise of even more technologically sophisticated and personalized online learning experiences than are possible right now. The technology will continue to change, and it is likely that online teaching methods will adapt accordingly.

Kuh's (2008) model of common intellectual experience is so beneficial to online program development because it is not rooted in the physicality of the campus classroom or the vicissitudes of any particular technology, but rather is based on a more fundamental academic principle. By focusing both the faculty and students on the "why" of the educational experience, this model provides an environment in which to make sense of the "what" and the "how" of teaching and learning. Offering online students a common intellectual experience—in our case rooted in narrative, engagement, and transformation, and presented through the lens of enduring questions of humanity—changes the students' online learning experience entirely. No longer is the online class focused on mere information transfer or technological glitz; rather, students are led on a journey of discovery in community with their faculty and peers.

Effective online education thus would be strengthened through the use of common intellectual experiences. Although this can be accomplished simply by having students complete a core group of classes, we would argue that an overarching programmatic approach would produce better outcomes. By deliberately structuring the online program as a unified whole, rather than a collection of independent courses, and guiding students through their program with the use of an overarching narrative filled with rich and frequent engagement opportunities, students are more likely to have a transformational rather than transactional learning experience. Furthermore, such an environment should contribute to increased student learning and satisfaction outcomes.

Key Takeaways

- Applying a common intellectual experience to the online environment is useful in guiding online course development and delivery to promote online learning engagement and retention.

- The implementation of a common intellectual experience serves to protect the integration of courses within a cohesive and coherent program.
- Students will be more likely to have a transformational experience through deliberate structuring of the online program as a unified whole and the use of an overarching narrative with frequent engagement opportunities.

References

Allen, I. E., Seaman, J., Poulin, R., & Straut, T. T. (2016). Online report card: Tracking online education in the United States. Retrieved from http://onlinelearningsurvey.com/reports/onlinereportcard.pdf

Bruckheimer, J. (Producer), Oman, C. (Producer) & Yakin, B. (Director). (2000). *Remember the titans* [Motion Picture]. United States: Walt Disney Pictures.

Cole, M. T., Shelley, D. J., & Swartz, L. B. (2014). Online instruction, e-learning, and student satisfaction: A three year study. *The International Review of Research in Open and Distance Learning, 14*(6). Retrieved from http://www.irrodl.org/index.php/irrodl/article/view/1748/3123

Croxton, R. A. (2014). The role of interactivity in student satisfaction and persistence in online learning. *MERLOT Journal of Online Learning and Teaching, 10*(2), 314–325.

Daft, R. L., & Lengel, R. H. (1986). Organizational information requirements, media richness and structural design. *Management Science, 32*(5), 554–571.

Greenfield, G. M., Keup, J. R., & Gardner, J. N. (2013). *Developing and sustaining successful first-year programs.* San Francisco, CA: Jossey-Bass.

Jaggars, S. S. (2014). Choosing between online and face-to-face courses: Community college student voices. *American Journal of Distance Education, 28*(1), 27–38.

Kuh, G. D. (2008). *High-impact education practices: What are they, who has access to them, and why they matter.* Washington DC: Association of American Colleges & Universities.

Lewis, H. R. (2007, September 7). A core curriculum for tomorrow's citizens. *The Chronicle of Higher Education.* Retrieved from http://www.chronicle.com/article/A-Core-Curriculum-for/26454

McMullen, J. (n.d.). *The enduring questions* [course video]. Retrieved from http://regent.blackboard.com

Moore, M.G. (1989). Three types of interaction. *The American Journal of Distance Education, 3*(2), 1–6.

National Center for Education Statistics. (2016). *Fast facts: Distance learning.* Retrieved from https://nces.ed.gov/fastfacts/display.asp?id=80

Parahoo, S. K., Santally, M. I., Rajabalee, Y., & Harvey, H. L. (2016). Designing a predictive model of student satisfaction in online learning. *Journal of Marketing for Higher Education, 26*(1), 1–19.

Poulin, R. (2012). *Is your distance education course actually a correspondence course?* Retrieved from https://wcetfrontiers.org/2012/04/20/correspondence-definition/

Regent University. (n.d.). *Faculty essentials: Resources for current and prospective faculty at Regent.* Retrieved from https://www.regent.edu/acad/undergrad/faculty/

Risko, E. F., Anderson, N., Sarwal, A., Engelhardt, M., & Kingstone, A. (2012). Everyday attention: Variation in mind wandering and memory in a lecture. *Applied Cognitive Psychology, 26,* 234–242.

Schacter, D. L., & Szpunar, K. K. (2015). Enhancing attention and memory during video-recorded lectures. *Scholarship of Teaching and Learning in Psychology, 1*(1), 60–71.

Staley, D. J., & Trinkle, D. A. (2011). The changing landscape of higher education. *EDUCAUSE Review, 46*(1), 16–32.

Zwick, E., & Jan Brugge, P. J. (Producers), & Zwick, E. (Director). (2008). *Defiance [Motion picture].* United States: Bedford Falls Productions.

3

LEARNING COMMUNITIES

Kathy E. Johnson, Amy A. Powell, and Sarah S. Baker

Since the dramatic rise of online education in the 1990s, a chief concern among educators has been how best to foster student interaction, collaboration, and coconstruction of knowledge among learners who might be scattered across geographical regions or who have never actually met (Beldarrain, 2006; Palloff & Pratt, 2007). There is a critical semantic distinction between fostering a community of learners through educational strategies supported by technologies (Moller, 1998; Moller, Harvey, Downs, & Godshalk, 2000) and the design of a learning community (LC)—the intentional linking of college courses and assignments as a means of fostering curricular coherence and deep, integrated learning (Lardner & Malnarich, 2008; Smith, MacGregor, Matthews, & Gabelnick, 2004). Although LCs may vary in terms of their structure, they typically include a common set of learning goals and opportunities for collaborative dialogue and construction of learning; they also foster among students and faculty a sense of shared purpose, responsibility for learning, a feeling of belonging, and a sense of trust and connection to others (Yuan & Kim, 2014).

In this chapter, we provide an overview of the purpose and value of LCs as a high-impact practice (HIP) and consider mechanisms for adapting them to online education. We also consider how outcomes and process assessment can be used as strategies to foster maximal benefits to students engaging in an LC. In particular, we share an evolving "Themed Learning Communities High-Impact Practice Taxonomy" that has emerged from our work at Indiana University–Purdue University Indianapolis (IUPUI), and we consider ways of adapting this taxonomy to ensure that LCs offered through online education are maximally effective at supporting student success.

Learning Communities in Postsecondary Education

LCs are curricular approaches, frequently structured as a common cohort of students, that intentionally link or cluster two or more courses, often around an interdisciplinary theme or issue (Smith & MacGregor, 2009; Smith et al., 2004). These linked courses promote connections between and across disciplines and beyond the classroom (Schmidt & Graziano, 2016). Brownell and Swaner (2010) identify LCs in their simplest form as a collection of courses students complete together in a small group. LCs demand a skillful balancing at the structural, pedagogical and cross-disciplinary levels (Lardner & Malnarich, 2008). When implemented well, LCs help to enhance student learning while strengthening the quality of academic communities in a cost-effective manner (Gaff & Ratcliff, 1997; Smith et al., 2004).

LCs can be implemented in a variety of ways, even taking the form of a single interdisciplinary course. More commonly, students coenroll in a block of courses, which could include a residential component (Soven, Lehr, Naynaha, & Olson, 2013). Linkages are at the heart of LCs. Some link two traditional courses together, whereas others link a first-year experience (first-year seminar) or freshman interest group with an interdisciplinary or a gateway course (for more on first-year seminars as a HIP, see chapter 1, this volume). LCs might focus on a "big question" or be designed around a theme, such as IUPUI's *Molecules to Medicines* or *Philanthropy: It's Not Just for Millionaires*. Additionally, LCs can be conducted face-to-face, as a hybrid model, or online. Although a variety of models exist, Shapiro and Levine (1999) argue that LCs typically share core characteristics, including the organization of faculty and students into small groups that are supportive and encourage integration across the curriculum while providing opportunities to socialize students to the expectations of college. A comprehensive review of the history of LCs is presented by Smith and colleagues (2004).

Although scholars have identified a range of pedagogies and practices promoting student learning, research based on the National Survey of Student Engagement has identified a constellation of approaches as HIPs. Their impact is grounded in a record of evidence that convincingly establishes their effectiveness at engaging students in their learning, thus yielding an overall positive impact on student retention and academic success (Felten et al., 2016; Kuh, 2008). LCs are HIPs because they promote deep, active, and collaborative learning, and they are associated with higher levels of academic challenge and student–faculty interactions (Kuh & O'Donnell, 2013; Swaner & Brownell, 2008).

LCs are well positioned to be combined with other HIPs, which is compelling given that it has been demonstrated that engagement in multiple HIPs is particularly beneficial for students from underserved groups (Finley & McNair, 2013). They naturally promote interactions with faculty and peers, and they enable students to make connections across their courses. Service-learning projects provide natural opportunities for students to apply their learning from multiple courses, and they can readily be incorporated into LCs and applied at a distance (Strait & Nordyke, 2015; Waldner, McGorry, & Widener, 2012; see also chapter 9, this volume). Finally, LCs can take full advantage of ePortfolios as a powerful mechanism that supports students' deep learning and reflection across learning contexts (Harring & Luo, 2016; see also chapter 12, this volume).

Learning Communities at a Distance

We know of no empirical studies that have systematically compared student or faculty outcomes associated with LCs delivered through online versus face-to-face environments. However, other literature points to the possibilities of transitioning LCs to online environments with positive outcomes. For example, because many positive outcomes of LCs are associated with the connections that are their hallmark, learning technologies that support effective collaboration are likely key to replicating these benefits at a distance. Many studies have demonstrated that through intentional design, course structure, and facilitation, a sense of community can be created in the online environment (Garrison, Cleveland-Innes, & Fung, 2010; Palloff & Pratt, 2007; Ramli, 2010; Shea & Bidjerano, 2009; Shea, Li, & Pickett, 2006; Shea, Li, Swan, & Pickett, 2005). Presence created through threaded discussions, making space for both content-based and social interactions; the use of a variety of learning activities and active learning strategies; and the engagement of students in collaborative and structured group work to grapple with content are all approaches that build community. Through these learner-centered approaches, students feel a higher sense of belonging as indicated by high levels of student interactions about both content and noncontent matters; a shift from instructor-focused questions to peer interactions that encourage, support, and critically evaluate each other's work; and coconstruction of meaning through discussion and shared resources (Palloff & Pratt, 2007).

A survey of attendees at the Annual Conference on Learning Communities and Collaboration found that core LC principles, such as clustering two classes around an interdisciplinary theme, were considered by attendees to be readily applicable to online environments

(DiRamio & Wolverton, 2006). The use of engaging online pedagogies to build community in a single online course can serve as the foundation for extending the online LC to a group of linked online courses. The following strategies for establishing a sense of community (DiRamio & Wolverton, 2006; Lenning, Hill, & Saunders, 2013; Murdock & Williams, 2011; Palloff & Pratt, 2007; Ramli, 2010; Yuan & Kim, 2014) are particularly translatable for creating and sustaining LCs online:

- Creating a welcome page in each course, establishing the purpose and goals of the LC
- Including a shared space for students to engage in discussions, exchange ideas, share experiences, socialize, and reflect on their learning in the LC
- Designing a shared space for all instructors to engage with students in discussion
- Utilizing coordinated syllabi for each LC course to clearly indicate activities and assignments that cross course boundaries as part of the LC
- Establishing guidelines for communication and interactions early on, especially in regard to questions and discussions that cross course boundaries
- Engaging in continuous efforts by the instructional team to plan, coordinate activities, and reflect on the LC before, during, and after implementation
- Incorporating a variety of instructional approaches in each of the LC courses
- Facilitating collaborative learning or small-group work in each of the LC courses

Supporting faculty development in online teaching and learning pedagogies is paramount to the successful design and implementation of online and hybrid courses. Effective applications of these principles have the potential to positively impact students engaged in online programs, including post-traditional learners who may be juggling work and family responsibilities while pursuing a postsecondary degree.

When shifting LCs to the online environment, there are several decisions about key factors that help ensure that benefits reaped in the face-to-face context are not lost, as depicted in Figure 3.1. The first consideration is the structure of the LC: Will all courses in the cluster be fully online, or will there be a mix of online and hybrid courses? The location of the student and faculty population, local or distant, will influence both the LC structure and the development of cocurricular and experiential learning activities.

Figure 3.1. Factors to consider in deploying learning communities at a distance.

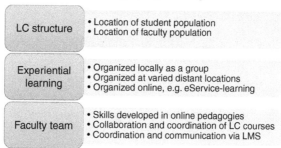

Once the structure of the LC is established, logistics for experiential, cocurricular, and community engaged learning should be considered. A student population close enough to campus to meet will offer opportunities for face-to-face engagement in experiential learning with the faculty team, whereas a distant population opens doors to distributed experiences in each student's locale. An important factor to consider in the online environment is the use of pedagogies aimed at building community and choosing faculty who are comfortable engaging students in the online environment. Also, in the online environment, the faculty team will need to consider how members will track and communicate regarding student needs based on patterns of engagement and participation, ideally capitalizing on the learning management system (LMS) and its embedded technologies.

Just as there are multiple models for creating LCs in the face-to-face environment, a range of options exists for creating online LCs (see Figure 3.2). Decisions about which model is best will depend on the population

Figure 3.2. Models of learning communities at a distance.

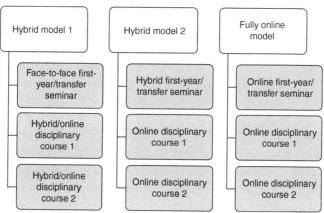

served by the course. When students are living either on campus or locally, a hybrid model may work well because students are available to collaborate on campus. For institutions that serve students across the nation and even internationally, a fully online model will allow access to more students taking the courses from a distance.

Hybrid model 1 addresses the situation where students are available to meet face-to-face for some portion of the LC. The first-year seminar course is typically taken in the first semester of college and may take the form of a transfer seminar for transfer students, because the purpose of the seminar course is to acclimate students to the university and act as a unifying space for reflective and integrative learning. If there is one course offered face-to-face, then it should be this one. Because experiential learning activities are a key component of LCs, a face-to-face seminar course will give students opportunities to engage in community-based learning experiences as a cohort.

Hybrid model 2 is a viable option when students are living close enough to the institution to participate in a small number of face-to-face sessions. Face-to-face sessions will help students begin to make connections, build a climate of trust, and develop a sense of community (Chen & Chiou, 2014; Kaleta, Skibba, & Joosten, 2007). Although a significant portion of the seminar meetings will occur online, intermittent face-to-face sessions will provide opportunities for students to come together for community-based learning experiences. These face-to-face experiences are also an opportunity for the entire faculty team to come together with students to discuss the theme through the perspective of multiple disciplinary lenses and to help students integrate their learning through dialogue and critical reflection.

The fully online model works for institutions with online programs and is the best option for participants who do not live sufficiently close to campus for any face-to-face meetings. Because a key component of LCs is out-of-class or community-engaged learning, the instructional team will need to be creative in identifying distributed opportunities for students to engage in activities in their home community rather than as a single cohort or explore online opportunities for engagement, for example, eService-learning (Guthrie & McCracken, 2010; Strait & Nordyke, 2015; Waldner et al., 2012). The faculty team may choose to create some synchronous meetings at critical moments in the term to engage in dialogue aimed at promoting integrative learning and critical reflection.

Equity of access to LCs, as well as other HIPs, may depend on determining how best to support their implementation at a distance because first-generation students, posttraditional learners, and students from other underserved groups may be constrained in terms of the amount of time they are able to spend on college campuses. Faculty would do well to envision how the most critical components of LCs could be applied to the fully online environment. Publishing the results of such explorations would provide a significant contribution to a literature that is still quite nascent.

Assessment of Outcomes and Processes: Keys to Improvement

Assessment and evaluation are key to the successful implementation of any LC. These activities provide a framework for faculty to engineer desired outcomes through intentional design, and they provide data that can facilitate iterative improvements over time. A challenge in the literature related to LCs has been that the preponderance of evidence for positive outcomes has been derived through readily accessed data, such as retention rates and student grades, with relatively fewer studies of actual learning (what students understand and know how to do as a result of their engagement) or how faculty teams improve in their ability to work together effectively (Lardner & Malnarich, 2009). New instruments for measuring integrative learning, such as the Association of American Colleges & Universities Valid Assessment of Learning in Undergraduate Education (VALUE) rubric on integrative learning (Rhodes & Finley, 2013) or the collaborative assessment protocol developed through the National Assessment Project (Boix-Mansilla, 2009; Lardner & Malnarich, 2008), provide tools for directly measuring the impact of LCs on students and faculty and may be readily adapted to the online environment. Assessment helps to verify that learning has occurred while also providing insights regarding how the process of learning might be improved. In the online environment, tremendous potential exists to capitalize on "learning analytics," or data captured through an LMS on how, when, and in what ways students engage with course content, faculty, and each other (Prineas & Cini, 2011).

Using Taxonomies to Guide Process Evaluation and Improve Practice

An important mechanism for scaling LCs across face-to-face and online contexts is process evaluation, or assessment aimed at determining how a program is being implemented. Process evaluation is key to understanding a program's fidelity to an established model or determining whether there is equity of access to the program among underserved groups (Finley & McNair, 2013). It also can help to address the problem of weaker outcomes connected to HIPs that are rapidly taken to scale. Programs deemed to be highly effective based on small pilot projects often benefit from the self-selection of outstanding faculty who are highly motivated to engage in a pilot. Benefits can drop off precipitously when programs scale up unless careful attention is paid to how they are implemented and investments are made toward ongoing faculty development as well as appropriate levels of compensation. Process evaluation can help to safeguard against the weakening of positive outcomes as implementation is extended across schools, campuses, and learning modalities.

Taxonomies can provide a helpful framework for process evaluation, as well as scaling LCs and other HIPs across contexts, including online education. The California State University (CSU) system has invested considerable resources in ensuring that students have access to HIPs during the undergraduate experience and that effective practices are scaled across campuses. Taxonomies of HIPs were developed by and for faculty and campus leaders as a means of establishing common definitions and guiding effective practice across campuses (O'Donnell, 2014). The taxonomies help to categorize, describe, and guide replication of the elements of HIPs that are most effective in promoting student learning and academic success. At IUPUI, we saw tremendous potential value in these taxonomies and have since engaged communities of practice and various advisory councils in adapting them to our campus context. Like the CSU system, the IUPUI campus is highly decentralized, with 17 schools conferring degrees from Indiana University. Two of those schools also confer Purdue University degrees. IUPUI has since developed and implemented taxonomies focused on service-learning (Hatcher, Bringle, & Hahn, 2016), internships, study abroad, and LCs, among others.

Our goals associated with this work have been to support institutional assessment and research on HIPs and to develop resources to support faculty development efforts aimed at improving the quality of the student experience in HIPs. Perhaps most importantly, they can be used together with institutional research data to determine which of our students are engaging in quality HIPs and which are not. If online education is going to become an increasingly normative means of delivering curricula at IUPUI, then we must adapt these taxonomies to online and hybrid learning environments to ensure equity of access to the most impactful elements of the undergraduate experience.

A Case Study: IUPUI's Themed Learning Community Taxonomy

At IUPUI, we recently developed a taxonomy to guide process evaluation of the Themed LC (TLC) program, and this taxonomy is being modified to support the piloting of a hybrid TLC in the near future. The IUPUI TLC Advisory Board (2016) developed the "Themed Learning Communities High-Impact Practice Taxonomy" based on the CSU framework. The taxonomy serves as a guide for implementing a TLC in a high-impact manner. The document identifies the five attributes that define a TLC at IUPUI (see Table 3.1). In a more extensive document, each of the five attributes is described at

TABLE 3.1

Themed Learning Communities High-Impact Practice Taxonomy-Based Recommendations for Online Education

Key Attribute	Recommendation for Implementation in Online Environment
1. Interdisciplinary theme shapes each TLC community course's design	• Instructors create a welcome page in their course sites describing how their courses will explore the theme, fundamental question, and learning outcome for the TLC throughout the semester • Instructors share a meaningful experience from their life connected to the theme with students • In each course, readings, activities, and discussions are connected to the theme, with students reflecting on and sharing their experiences that connect to the theme
2. Integration of course content in each TLC course is intentional; course design encourages integrative thinking in students	• Each instructor creates a course outline or schedule that clearly identifies assignments and activities that are integrated with the other courses in the TLC • Instructors intentionally use agreed-on language for connecting concepts across courses in discussions, assignments, and activities • Instructors cocreate a rubric(s) for integrative assignments, with criteria connected to each course, completed as a team for grading • Through discussion and activities, students are asked to identify and examine connections they have made between courses; instructors use an integrative learning rubric for scoring as a team • Through an ePortfolio, students are asked to create a collection of artifacts from the TLC courses, including critical reflections that make connections between the courses and life experiences; students engage in peer reviews and share their ePortfolios

(*Continues*)

Table 3.1 (*Continued*)

Key Attribute	Recommendation for Implementation in Online Environment
3. Out-of-class activities enhance academic content integrative thinking and interdisciplinary theme	• In hybrid environments, face-to-face sessions are designed as community-engaged, service-learning, or other campus cocurricular events; students engage in critical reflections to process the experiences and make connections between courses and to the theme • In online environments, instructors set parameters for local community-engaged learning experiences, and students propose a local activity to engage in; course design provides students opportunities to share their experiences and critically reflect; all instructors are present and engaged in online discussions regarding these experiences
4. Active learning strategies are central to each TLC course	• Instructors model online presence and establish guidelines for engagement and purpose consistently across each course • Instructors act as facilitators, encouraging self-directed learning, meaning-making, and the social construction of knowledge • Critical reflection occurs throughout each course • Students engage in collaborative and group learning • Instructors implement a variety of learning activities and active learning strategies throughout each course
5. Faculty collaboration fosters integrative approach, exploration of theme, out-of-class experiences, and student development	• Course instructors meet multiple times before and during the semester to plan individual course design reflecting the theme, points of integrative learning, and out-of-class activities • Course instructors discuss and come to consensus on acceptable levels of student engagement in the LMS, and communicate throughout the semester any concerns regarding students' level of engagement with their course and the TLC • Course instructors establish an online meeting space for students to engage with the faculty as a team; faculty model substantive cross-disciplinary engagement and discussion • In hybrid environments, the full faculty team is present to engage with students face-to-face during out-of-class activities

Note. See full IUPUI Themed Learning Communities Taxonomy at https://rise.iupui.edu/taxonomies/

incremental levels, demonstrating implementation of the eight key elements of HIPs (Kuh & O'Donnell, 2013). The purpose of the taxonomy is to provide planning guidance to teams, provide input to the program office on faculty development needs, and serve as a tool for guiding program fidelity.

Key strengths of the taxonomy include giving the instructional team a common language to use when planning and clearly indicating which elements are important to guide and prioritize the work. It clearly describes what makes a TLC a different experience for faculty and students than the same courses experienced separately. The taxonomy also is an important recruitment tool to communicate with faculty about what to expect when teaching in this context. The taxonomy is a tool that will allow for further scaling of the TLC program at IUPUI while maintaining program fidelity during growth.

We believe that the TLC taxonomy may readily be modified to accommodate faculty who are developing LCs in an online environment through strategies depicted in Table 3.1. Although the five attributes of a TLC remain the same, the descriptors for implementation change to account for the unique structural and pedagogical elements of the online environment. For example, the interdisciplinary theme will shape the design of each online or hybrid course, incorporated through the use of the online course site for readings, activities, discussions, and the sharing of experiences. Our strategy for populating courses in the LC is to take advantage of existing clusters of online foundational courses that cultivate degrees to provide targeted support for faculty development in online pedagogies (Murdock & Williams, 2011). A comprehensive needs assessment and a preliminary assessment plan will be completed before the hybrid TLC is designed to identify the student population(s) to be targeted in relation to specific online degree(s) or meta-majors.

Conclusion

When LCs are implemented well, they have the potential to significantly benefit students' integrative learning, social integration, and overall success, and these benefits are magnified, particularly for underrepresented students, when LCs are coupled with other HIPs. For example, ePortfolios may readily be incorporated into the design for LCs and may be particularly beneficial for helping students to reflect on and apply their learning at a distance (for more on ePortfolios as a HIP, see chapter 12, this volume). Although the elements of LCs most critical to reaping these benefits seem readily adaptable to online education formats, the literature on LCs (as a pedagogical structure) and online education has remained quite separate, and no empirical comparisons of student outcomes have been conducted across face-to-face and online LCs. Online education provides heightened access to postsecondary credentials for many learners, and the creation of online LCs could be a particularly effective strategy for promoting successful transfer (and aligning curricula) across two- and four-year institutions.

Key Takeaways

- Well-implemented LCs have the potential to significantly benefit students' integrative learning, social integration, and overall success.
- Location of student and faculty populations will influence both the LC structure and the development of cocurricular and experiential learning activities.
- Process evaluation and assessment are important mechanisms for scaling LCs across face-to-face and online contexts.
- Taxonomies can provide a helpful framework for process evaluation and the scaling of LCs in online education.

References

Beldarrain, Y. (2006). Distance education trends: Integrating new technologies to foster student interaction and collaboration. *Distance Education, 27*(2), 139–153.

Boix-Mansilla, V. (2009). Productive shifts: Faculty growth through collaborative assessment of student interdisciplinary work. *Journal of Learning Communities Research, 3*(3), 21–26.

Brownell, J. E., & Swaner, L. E. (2010). *Five high-impact practices: Research on learning outcomes, completion and quality.* Washington DC: Association of American Colleges & Universities.

Chen, B. H., & Chiou, H. (2014). Learning style, sense of community and learning effectiveness in hybrid learning environment. *Interactive Learning Environments, 22*(4), 485–496.

DiRamio, D., & Wolverton, M. (2006). Integrating learning communities and distance education: Possibility or pipedream? *Innovative Higher Education, 31*(2), 99–113.

Felten, P., Gardner, J. N., Schroeder, C. C., Lambert, L. M., Barefoot, B. O., & Hrabowski, F. A. (2016). *The undergraduate experience: Focusing institutions on what matters most.* San Francisco, CA: Jossey-Bass.

Finley, A., & McNair, T. (2013). *Assessing underserved students' engagement in high-impact practices.* Washington DC: Association of American Colleges & Universities.

Gaff, I. G., & Ratcliff, J. L. (1997). *Handbook of the undergraduate curriculum.* San Francisco, CA: Jossey-Bass.

Garrison, D. R., Cleveland-Innes, M., & Fung, T. S. (2010). Exploring causal relationships among teaching, cognitive and social presence: Student perceptions of
the community of inquiry framework. *The Internet and Higher Education, 13,*
31–36.

Guthrie, K. L., & McCracken, H. (2010). Making a difference online: Facilitating
service-learning through distance education. *The Internet and Higher Education,
13*(3), 153–157.

Harring, K., & Luo, T. (2016). ePortfolios: Supporting reflection and deep learning
in high impact practices. *Peer Review, 18*(3), 9–12.

Hatcher, J. A., Bringle, R. G., & Hahn, T. W. (2016). *Research on student civic
outcomes in service learning: Conceptual frameworks and methods.* Sterling, VA:
Stylus.

IUPUI TLC Advisory Board. (2016). Themed learning communities high-impact
practice taxonomy. Retrieved from http://rise.iupui.edu/taxonomies.

Kaleta, R., Skibba, K., & Joosten, T. (2007). Discovering, designing, and delivering hybrid courses. In A. G. Picciano & C. D. Dziuban (Eds.), *Blended learning
research perspectives* (pp. 111–144). Needham, MA: Sloan-C.

Kuh, G. D. (2008). *High-impact educational practices: What they are, who has access
to them, and why they matter.* Washington DC: Association of American Colleges
& Universities.

Kuh, G. D., & O'Donnell, K. (2013). *Ensuring quality & taking high-impact practices to scale.* Washington DC: Association of American Colleges & Universities.

Lardner, E., & Malnarich, G. (2008). A new era in learning-community work: Why
the pedagogy of intentional integration matters. *Change, 40,* 30–37.

Lardner, E., & Malnarich, G. (2009). Assessing integrative learning: Insights from
Washington Center's National Project on Assessing Learning in Learning Communities. *Journal of Learning Communities Research, 3*(3), 1–20.

Lenning, O. T., Hill, D. M., & Saunders, K. P. (2013). *Powerful learning communities: A guide to developing student, faculty, and professional learning communities to
improve student success and organizational effectiveness.* Sterling, VA: Stylus.

Moller, L. (1998). Designing communities of learners for asynchronous distance
education. *Educational Technology Research & Development, 46*(4), 115–122.

Moller, L., Harvey, D., Downs, M., & Godshalk, V. (2000). Identifying factors that
effect learning community development and performance in distance education.
Quarterly Review of Distance Education, 1(4), 293–305.

Murdock, J., & Williams, A. M. (2011). Creating an online learning community: Is
it possible? *Innovative Higher Education, 36,* 305–315.

O'Donnell, K. (October 19–21, 2014). *What's at stake: Learning outcomes assessment
as the expression of educational quality, priorities, and values.* Paper presented at the
2014 Assessment Institute, Indianapolis, IN.

Palloff, R. M., & Pratt, K. (2007). *Building online learning communities: Effective
strategies for the virtual classroom* (2nd ed.). San Francisco, CA: Jossey-Bass.

Prineas, M., & Cini, M. (2011, October). *Assessing learning in online education: The
role of technology in improving student outcomes* (NILOA Occasional Paper no.
12). Urbana, IL: National Institute for Learning Outcomes Assessment.

Ramli, R. (2010). Technology enhanced learning: Fostering cooperative learning through the integration of online communication as part of teaching and learning experience. *World Academy of Science, Engineering and Technology, 69*, 611–614.

Rhodes, T., & Finley, A. (2013). *Using the VALUE rubrics for improvement of learning and authentic assessment*. Washington DC: Association of American Colleges & Universities.

Schmidt, L. C., & Graziano, J. (2016). *Building synergy for high-impact educational initiatives: First year seminars and learning communities*. Columbia, SC: National Resource Center for the First Year Experience & Students in Transition.

Shapiro, N. S., & Levine, J. H. (1999). *Creating learning communities: A practical guide to winning support, organizing for change, and implementing programs*. San Francisco, CA: Jossey-Bass.

Shea, P., & Bidjerano, T. (2009). Community of inquiry as a theoretical framework to foster "epistemic engagement" and "cognitive presence" in online education. *Computers and Education, 52*(3), 543–553.

Shea, P., Li, C., Swan, K., & Pickett, A. (2005). Developing learning community in online asynchronous college courses: The role of teaching presence. *Journal of Asynchronous Learning Networks, 9*(4), 59–82.

Shea, P., Li, C. S., & Pickett, A. (2006). A study of teaching presence and student sense of learning community in fully online and web-enhanced college courses. *Internet and Higher Education, 9*(3), 175–190.

Smith, B. L., & MacGregor, J. (2009). Learning communities and the quest for quality. *Quality Assurance in Education, 17*(2), 118–139.

Smith, B. L., MacGregor, J., Matthews, R., & Gabelnick, F. (2004). *Learning communities: Reforming undergraduate education*. San Francisco, CA: Jossey-Bass.

Soven, M., Lehr, D., Naynaha, S., & Olson, W. (2013). *Linked courses for general education and integrative learning: A guide for faculty and administrators*. Sterling, VA: Stylus.

Strait, J. R., & Nordyke, K. J. (2015). *eService-learning: Creating experiential learning and civic engagement through online and hybrid courses*. Sterling, VA: Stylus.

Swaner, L. E., & Brownell, J. E. (2008). *Outcomes of high impact practices for underserved students: A review of the literature*. Washington DC: Association of American Colleges & Universities.

Waldner, L. S., McGorry, S. Y., & Widener, M. C. (2012). E-service-learning: The evolution of service-learning to engage a growing online student population. *Journal of Higher Education Outreach and Engagement, 16*(2), 123–150.

Yuan, J., & Kim, C. (2014). Guidelines for facilitating the development of learning communities in online courses. *Journal of Computer Assisted Learning, 30*, 220–232.

4

WRITING-INTENSIVE CLASSES

June Griffin

Educators have long turned to writing assignments and exams as a means to gain insight into what their students understand about the subjects they teach. Recognizing the cognitive processes involved in writing (e.g., goal setting, planning, selecting, applying, analyzing, synthesizing, evaluating, etc.), teachers have used writing assignments as catalysts to learning. In his original monograph on high-impact practices (HIPs), Kuh (2008) makes the case for including writing-intensive classes in his list by pointing to a study by Light (2004), which indicated that more pages written for a class equated to more time spent on it, increased perceptions of challenge, and increased engagement in the course. Although the field of composition and rhetoric has been studying the connection between writing and learning for more than 80 years, recent research has complicated the simplistic advice to assign more writing to ensure better learning outcomes. Perhaps not so surprisingly, quality counts more than quantity in writing assignments, and, in online classes in particular, more writing does not necessarily lead to better learning. This chapter summarizes research into what does and does not make writing-intensive courses "high impact" and suggests ways to integrate writing into online courses that will most enhance student learning and engagement.

What Makes Writing a High-Impact Practice?

Perhaps the most compelling study of the relationship between student writing and gains in learning and personal development comes from collaboration between the Council of Writing Program Administrators and the National Survey of Student Engagement (NSSE). A team of researchers appended a set of questions about writing (derived from best practices in writing as identified by writing specialists[1]) to the NSSE survey administered in 2010 and 2011 to more than 70,000 first-year students and seniors on 80 U.S. campuses (Anderson, Anson, Gonyea, & Paine, 2015, 2016). Using confirmatory factor analysis, the team identified the following latent constructs for effective writing assignments: (a) clear writing expectations, (b) meaning-making writing tasks, and (c) interactive writing practices. They then correlated how often students participated in these constructs with their responses to the indicators of learning and development long established by NSSE's main survey. The researchers also assessed the relationship of the constructs to students' responses to questions about the number of writing assignments of varying lengths they completed. They found that although other forms of engagement (e.g., amount of assigned reading, group work, high institutional expectations, involvement in other HIPs, and the amount of writing students did) accounted for a considerable amount of the variation in student responses to the NSSE indicators of learning and indicators of development, controlling for these other variables still yielded gains in two of the three deep learning scales and all three of the perceived gains scales. As Anderson and colleagues (2016) explain, "In every case, the net effects of our three constructs exceeded the net effect of the amount of writing, which explained less than 1% of the variance. In sum, . . . the quality of assignments and what students do to produce them appear to contribute to these aspects of student development more strongly than quantity alone" (para. 18).

The recommendation to focus more on the quality of assignments than the quantity of pages that students write may be even more critical in online classes than in face-to-face ones. Online classes are often text-intensive even when instructors use audio and video in their presentation of material. In 2012, Griffin and Minter compared the "literacy loads" (the reading and writing word counts) for students and instructors in four first-year writing classes and found that both students and instructors wrote and read a great deal more in online classes than they did in face-to-face classes. Further, they found that for each student added in online courses, the reading load increased exponentially for everyone in the class. They hypothesize that literacy load may give us insight into high rates of D and F grades and withdrawals in online courses and caution that a high literacy load is likely to have a disproportionate impact on English-language learners. Griffin and Minter (2012) encourage instructors to take literacy load into account when making decisions about coursework and course tools, and they encourage administrators to consider it when making decisions about class caps in writing-intensive courses online. The takeaway should be clear: Although being "writing intensive" can make a course high impact, simply assigning more writing does not lead to better student learning or engagement. In online classes in particular, more writing can quickly become too much, especially if online classes lean heavily on text-based delivery modes.

Anyone who has tried to adopt HIPs has realized that, to get the most out of them, one must understand what it is about them that make them effective. In their 2013 monograph, *Ensuring Quality & Taking High-Impact Practices to Scale*, Kuh and O'Donnell try to meet this need by identifying the following quality dimensions which help ensure that HIPs meet their objectives:

- Performance expectations set at appropriately high levels
- Significant investment of time and effort by students over an extended period of time
- Interactions with faculty and peers about substantive matters
- Experiences with diversity
- Frequent, timely, and constructive feedback
- Periodic, structured opportunities to reflect and integrate learning
- Opportunities to discover relevance of learning through real-world applications
- Public demonstration of competence (p. 8)

This list is helpful, but some items more than others speak to the qualities that make writing-intensive courses effective. Looking for a more succinct articulation of the principles for all HIPs, Landy (2015) condensed Kuh and O'Donnell's (2013) eight principles to a trim list of three in her article, "Structure, Connectivity, and Authenticity: The How and Why of High-Impact Practices." Landy (2015) argues that to make an institution's use of HIPs effective, it should ensure that the HIPs are thoughtful in the way they are structured, connect to learning outcomes and/or curricular objectives, and avoid feeling inauthentic or contrived. Landy's (2015) principles are easy to interpret in terms of writing assignments; in fact, they overlap with two of the three constructs identified by Anderson and colleagues (2016) in the study discussed at the beginning of this chapter. In their article on HIP writing assignments, they identified three high-impact writing practices positively associated with several established constructs in the NSSE survey relating to students' learning and practical and personal development.

Putting these two lists side by side (see Table 4.1) highlights the general principles in terms that are easy to remember while highlighting an opportunity that writing-intensive courses offer that can make a critical difference in fulfilling the promise of HIP. The third item, Connectivity/Interactive Writing Processes, might seem to pose the greatest challenge for instructors

TABLE 4.1

Two Views for What Makes Writing a High-Impact Practice

Landy (2015)	Anderson, Anson, Gonyea, and Paine (2015)
Structure	"Clear Writing Expectations occur when instructors provide students with an accurate understanding of what they are asking the students to demonstrate in an assignment and the criteria by which the instructors will evaluate the students' submissions" (p. 207).
Authenticity	"Meaning-Making Writing Tasks . . . occur when students engage in some form of integrative, critical, or original thinking" (p. 207).
Connectivity	"Interactive Writing Processes occur when student writers communicate orally or in writing with one or more persons at some point between receiving an assignment and submitting the final draft" (pp. 206–207).

who teach online, but in truth all three require instructors to think about their assignments from their students' perspectives and to think creatively about the affordances of online classes. In what follows, I address the three constructs (Anderson et al., 2016), summarize research on writing instruction that corroborates their effectiveness, and suggest different ways that faculty might operationalize the constructs in their online classes.

Structure/Clear Writing Expectations

Although this construct may strike readers as obvious and easy to implement, it has caused a surprising degree of consternation for faculty and students alike. Often the assignments that faculty believe are clearly written are opaque to students because they are steeped in disciplinary conventions students find "COIK" (i.e., "clear only if known"). In face-to-face classes, these concerns are often recognized and addressed in class discussions when students ask questions as an assignment is introduced. Online, instructors can make a space for conversation about assignments by creating a discussion thread devoted to it. These discussion threads can be beneficial, but their benefit is still limited to addressing the questions students have. When possible, it is best to determine and address COIK instructions before giving the assignment to students by providing faculty members the means to share and discuss their assignments with faculty members in other disciplines through programs run by a campus teaching and learning center, Writing Across the Curriculum (WAC) or Writing in the Disciplines (WID) program, or Writing Center. Some faculty express concerns about being too explicit about their expectations in their assignments, saying they do not want to "spoon feed" their students and limit the learning potential of the assignment. In light of Anderson and colleagues' (2015) findings, it seems the latter worry is unfounded. Their regression analysis of responses to the prompts related to clear writing expectations[2] indicated that students who reported their instructors had done these things in all or most of their assignments "also reported that they themselves engaged more often in Deep Approaches to Learning, and reported greater perceived gains from their experience at their institution" (Anderson et al., 2015, pp. 228–229) than students whose teachers had not. Instructors can go a step further when providing sample student work by annotating it with comments explaining key features that students should emulate. Annotated examples are especially helpful in online classes because they both anticipate questions students are likely to have but might be reluctant to ask, and they call attention to aspects of assignments that students might have overlooked.

Providing a discussion thread for questions about assignments and giving students annotated samples go a long way toward meeting the need to provide structure/clear writing expectations in online courses. However, before they can provide clear instructions to students, faculty need to be clear on the purposes of their assignments. WAC programs and WID initiatives have long offered teachers and administrators concrete suggestions for integrating writing into courses in any discipline and developing effective writing assignments. As recently as 2014, the International Network of Writing Across the Curriculum Programs and the Committee for College Composition and Communication endorsed the "Statement of WAC Principles and Practices" recommendations for establishing effective WAC programs and identifying four principles and practices for WAC pedagogy drawn from scholarship in rhetoric and composition. These principles can inform instructors' understanding of the nature of writing and the potential purposes of writing assignments in any discipline.

> Writing as rhetorical: Texts are dynamic and respond to the goals of the writer(s), goals of the reader(s), and the wider rhetorical context, which may include culture, language, genre conventions, and other texts . . .
>
> Writing as a process: For high-stakes writing (writing that will be graded), the writing process is long and complex, with the writer revising in response to developing ideas, reader feedback, and a deeper understanding of the rhetorical situation . . .

> Writing as a mode of learning: [often referred to as "Writing to Learn"]
> Writing has long been recognized as enhancing the learning process. Writ-
> ing makes thinking visible, allowing learners to reflect on their ideas. Fur-
> ther, writing facilitates connections between new information and learned
> information, and among areas of knowledge across multiple domains . . .
>
> Learning to Write: Effective writers are those who have learned to
> write across a variety of rhetorical situations, for a variety of audiences, and
> for a variety of purposes. Learning-to-write assignments are often higher-
> stakes assignments that require the writer to write with attention to the
> conventions of a rhetorical context (i.e. within the genre and discourse
> conventions of a specific community) and to move through a multi-draft
> writing process . . . (p. 5)

These principles are grounded in research and practice in the field of
composition and rhetoric and offer faculty members ways of thinking about
their assignments that highlight both the complexity of the act of writing and
the different purposes writing might serve in their classes.

To create clear writing assignments that are well structured and connect
to learning objectives, faculty must begin with their objectives. The four previous principles offer faculty prompts to think about the purposes of their
writing assignments that then lead to types of assignments and activities—
or ways to structure them—based on the instructor's purpose. For example, if an instructor of an online psychology class decides the purpose of a
particular assignment is to use writing to help students learn material, then
he or she would want to keep it informal and low stakes so students can
focus on understanding the material rather than perfecting their prose. The
assignment might ask students to post to a personal blog or discussion board
prompts in response to questions such as,

> Suppose you had a theory that laboratory rats fed a steady diet of beer and
> hot dogs could learn to find their way through a maze faster than rats fed
> a steady diet of squash, spinach, and broccoli. How would you design a
> scientific experiment to test this hypothesis? In your discussion, use the
> terms *experimental group, control group, independent variable,* and *dependent
> variable.* (Bean, 2011, p. 128)

Alternatively, if the instructor wants students to enter into the discourse
of the discipline and adopt its habits of mind and modes of expression, then
it is best to create a learning-to-write assignment asking for a traditional
academic genre common in that discipline. For example, an instructor in an
online Economics course might offer the following assignment: "To what
extent do the attached economic data support the hypothesis 'Social service
spending is inversely related to economic growth?' First create a scattergram
as a visual test of the hypothesis. Then create a verbal argument analyzing

whether the data support the hypothesis" (Bean, 2011, p. 109). Providing a prompt that has a focused question and an annotated sample essay (addressing a different question), and indicating where students can find useful resources and direct their questions, help to ensure that the writing online instructors assign will be impactful.

Authenticity/Meaning-Making Writing Tasks

Sadly, it appears that much of the writing assigned to undergraduates does not promote higher order thinking or deep engagement in learning. In a study of more than 21,000 writing assignments in 100 courses across the disciplines at 100 different institutions, Melzer (2009) found that nearly a quarter were short answer, and the majority—about two-thirds—had students address a teacher-as-examiner. Assignments such as these fall far short of the goal of enriching students' engagement and deepening their understanding of demanding course material and instead focus students' attention on delivering correct answers most often in simplistic prose.

In contrast, meaning-making writing tasks "require students to engage in some form of integrative, critical, or original thinking" (Anderson et al., 2015, p. 207). What counts as meaning-making tasks are evident from the prompts researchers connected to that construct in NSSE:

- Narrate or describe one of your own experiences;
- Summarize something you read, such as articles, books, or online publications;
- Analyze or evaluate something you read, researched, or observed;
- Describe your methods or findings related to data you collected in lab or fieldwork, a survey project;
- Argue a position using evidence and reasoning;
- Explain in writing the meaning of numerical or statistical data;
- Write in the style and format of a specific field (engineering, history, psychology, etc.); include drawings, tables, photos, screenshots, or other visual content in your written assignment;
- Create the project with multimedia (web page, poster, slide presentation such as PowerPoint, etc.). (Anderson et al., 2015, p. 208)

Asking students to complete these kinds of writing tasks rather than reporting back information provided through lecture or course reading yields clear results. Anderson and colleagues (2015) found that, "for both first-year and senior students, the strongest relationship with all three Deep Approaches to Learning was observed for the frequency with which students reported being given Meaning-Making Writing Tasks" (p. 222).

Landy's (2015) category, *Authenticity*, is, by comparison, a bit vague and defined in terms of what it is not: "forced," "inauthentic," or "fabricated." Still, it evokes something that many have intuited is critical for promoting student engagement in learning. Perhaps the best study of what we might call authenticity in writing assignments is "The Meaningful Writing Project," a multi-institution study led by Eodice, Geller, and Lerner (2017). The team surveyed 707 seniors at 3 different types of institutions, asking questions about the qualities of meaningful writing experiences in and out of classrooms. They conducted follow-up interviews with 27 seniors, surveyed 160 faculty who were repeatedly cited as offering meaningful assignments, and followed up with 60 one-on-one interviews with some of these faculty. The researchers report the following broad trends in the writing projects that students found meaningful:

- they "were something they had never done before but that they felt would be connected to the writing they would do as professionals";
- they "were connected to students' lives and interests beyond school, as well as writing projects that helped them learn or explore course content more deeply"—more than one in three students described personal connection as a reason why their project was meaningful;
- they "frequently had requirements but also offered students considerable choice in topic or approach." (Eodice et al., n.d.)

It is worth noting where the students surveyed wrote their most meaningful writing projects: 52% wrote them in their major, 17% in an elective course, 29% in a general education course, and 52% in a required course. Although neither the project's website nor the book, *The Meaningful Writing Project: Learning, Teaching, and Writing in Higher Education* (Eodice et al., 2017), include any findings concerning online versus face-to-face classes, some student responses described assignments from online classes. One notable response to the question, "What was the project you described as meaningful?," highlights the significance of assignments that connect to students lives:

> A ten page assignment that required presenting three different scenarios to solve a problem . . . the problem was meaningful to me because I used a real-life work situation to base my paper on. The writing project gave me the chance to explore three different scenarios to solve this work situation and led to a better working environment for me. (pp. 15–16)

Although there is no way to ensure that students will choose topics connected to their lives or to what they will do as professionals, giving students opportunities to do so in both formal (learning to write) and informal (writing to learn) assignments will increase the likelihood that students feel engaged in the course and recognize the value of the assignment to their learning in their online classes.

Connectivity/Interactive Writing Processes

Perhaps the best way to understand "interactive writing processes" is as activities in which students write and faculty respond to their writing. However, reading and responding to writing assignments is time-consuming. Although rubrics can help faculty members manage the workload that comes with writing assignments and can offer students important information about faculty members' expectations, they are not necessarily the best choice for giving students feedback on drafts. To understand why, it is helpful to consider the difference between feedback and assessment. Although both assist writing development, they serve different purposes:

- Assessment gives writers information about how well their text meets the expectations set for the assignment.
- Feedback tells writers how readers understand and respond to their writing.

Rubrics are designed for assessment; they can help faculty assess student work quickly and with greater equity. When distributed with an assignment sheet, students can use a final grading rubric for self-assessment of drafts, or faculty can modify the rubrics into checklists to make them even more useful to students for this purpose. However, when students are engaged in working on their writing, they benefit most from hearing how other readers respond to their texts. If the goal of assigning writing is to engage students in their work and assist them in developing their ideas, then they need more than assessment; they need feedback on in-process writing from real readers who care about what the writer has to say, who will ask questions, and, even when they disagree or raise a concern, will signal their support for the writer.

Qualities of Effective Feedback and Peer Review

In an early study of student achievement, Hattie (1999) synthesized more than 500 meta-analyses (more than 180,000 studies in all) to better understand the effect of more than 100 influences on student learning. He found that feedback had twice the effect of typical schooling (a benchmark arrived at through the study's meta-analyses) and was in fact one of the most significant influences studied, falling in the top 10 strongest influences on achievement, along with direct instruction, reciprocal teaching, and students' prior cognitive ability; it was even more powerful than socioeconomic influences. Extending that study, Hattie and Timperly (2007) created a model for feedback focusing on the task and processes students use to complete the task (and avoiding feedback that comments on the student him- or herself). Their model was simplified and summarized by Wiggins (2012)[3] and then adapted by McLeod, Hart-Davidson, and Grabill (n.d.) for guiding instructor and peer feedback on writing.[4] For these scholars, effective feedback on writing is the following:

- Formative: It focuses on improving student performance or understanding (in contrast to summative, which evaluates how students performed).
- Timely: It happens at times conducive to learning or changing (i.e., it is more effective to give feedback when students have an opportunity to revise than when they have completed an assignment and will not work on it further).
- Descriptive: It names what the student has done.
- Goal-referenced: It refers back to the assignment.
- Goal-directed: It offers students suggestions for what they might do next.

Faculty are not the only people who can give effective feedback. Peers can give effective feedback, too, particularly when they are taught and/or prompted to give feedback that meets these criteria and does not merely make judgements (e.g., "I like it" or "awkward"). McLeod and colleagues (n.d.) offer the following specific suggestions for crafting prompts for peer review:

- "Consider the cognitive load of a review" and have students review short texts or portions of a text for specific goals.
- "Start with the learning goals and work backwards." Use checklists, ratings, and scales to have peer reviewers focus on a text's alignment with an assignment's criteria or to indicate their reaction to particular aspects of a text. Use open-ended questions to invite peer reviewers to elaborate on answers or offer suggestions.
- "Prompt reviewers with specific, detailed questions," such as, "Which of the following requirements do you see in this draft?" and "Give the writer at least two comments. As you write comments, be sure to describe what you see happening, evaluate its effectiveness using these criteria, and suggest changes the writer might make."

Peer review makes it possible to offer students more feedback on their work and also gain further insights by thinking through their peers' writing.

In online classes, it is even more important to make sure prompts for peer review focus students' attention on the aspects of the assignment that are most critical to the learning goals they are meant to foster because peer review adds to the courses' already heavy literacy load. There should be a balance in how much feedback is provided by peers and how much by instructors. Even instructor feedback can add to the literacy load of a course and is, of course, time-consuming for instructors.

Screencast Feedback

One solution to these concerns comes from an updated form of an old practice of creating audio recordings of feedback. From its earliest implementation, practitioners have praised this approach to feedback for reducing the "distance" between students and faculty by turning commenting into something more like a conversation, assisting faculty in focusing on the most significant macro issues rather than less significant surface issues, and giving faculty a means to model the kinds of thinking they want their students to develop (Mrkich & Sommers, 2016). Since about 2010, faculty have been using screencasts—video-capture technology that allows faculty to record their voice along with their movements on a screen—for this purpose. Often instructors will quickly preread an essay, highlight sections they want to discuss with a student, and then record a short (3- to 10-minute) screencast in which they directly address the student and talk with him or her about the assignment. Screencasting makes it possible to talk with students about their writing, point to specific things on the page, scroll to other sections of their texts or presentations, or even bring up other documents, such as an assignment sheet or one of the texts a student has cited. Recent research on screencast comments has compared written feedback with screencast feedback and found a number of benefits to screencasting.

Anson, Dannels, Laboy, and Carneiro (2016) and Anson (in press) have conducted a series of studies comparing screencast and written feedback to assess both differences in the content of the feedback and in student perceptions of it. First, they compared transcripts of screencast comments with written marginal and end comments in eight classes, five face-to-face sections of first-year writing and three online sections of different courses (Introduction to Psychological Research, Women and Gender Studies, and Women and Health). Teachers' written responses averaged 109 words per paper, whereas teacher's spoken words in screencasts averaged 745 words per paper. Composition and rhetoric scholars have long advised teachers to avoid giving too much feedback so as not to overwhelm students or making it appear as if the instructor has taken over the students' writing. However, this study showed that the more words did not address more things, but rather instructors offered more elaboration on the aspects of the paper they addressed and made more personal connections with students.

In the second part of the study, researchers administered a survey to all 141 students in the original study to gather demographic information and impressions of both modes of feedback and then conducted structured interviews with 17 of them. Anson and colleagues (2016) summarize their findings:

> Students consistently reported that screencast technology played a role in (a) facilitating personal connections between teacher and student, (b) creating transparency about the teacher's evaluative process and identity, (c) revealing the teacher's feelings, (d) providing visual affirmation, and (e) establishing the conversational tone for the evaluative process. (p. 392)

The researchers understand the significance of these findings in light of the concept of *face*, a term used in social science research that refers to the self-image a speaker desires in his or her interactions with others. The term is most familiar to English speakers through the idiom, "to save face," and roughly equates to one's sense of dignity or prestige. In their study, Anson and colleagues (2016) point to earlier research suggesting that a central component of students' perceptions of and reactions to feedback depends on the ways it enables or restricts their ability to mitigate face threats. The clear advantage that screencasting feedback offers faculty to balance elaborate, detailed feedback with rapport-building makes it an especially useful practice in online courses, where a lack of physical presence eliminates important opportunities for students to pick up on their instructor's identity cues or face-mitigating interactions that can help them interpret the feedback they receive on their assignments. The findings by Anson and colleagues (2016) about the positive responses students give to this form of feedback are echoed by other research, summarized well in Sommers's (2013) useful research bibliography on the topic. They also highlight the advantage in time saving, saying, "nearly all anecdotal and empirical articles [reported] audio response can save time for the commenter" (p. 3).

As faculty consider the design of their online classes and the roles writing may play in them, they would do well to remember that the quantity of pages that students write has less impact on student learning and engagement than the following three constructs identified by Anderson and colleagues (2015; 2016): clear writing expectations, meaning-making writing tasks, and interactive writing processes. Faculty can mitigate the literacy load that typically occurs (for students and faculty alike) in feedback-rich classes by using structured peer review and screencast technology to provide rich, rapport-building responses to students.

Key Takeaways

- Focus on the quality of writing assignments in an online class rather than quantity.
- It is more effective to ask students to complete meaning-making writing tasks than report back information provided through lecture or course reading.
- Faculty can mitigate literacy loads that typically occur (for students and faculty) in feedback-rich classes by using structured peer review and screencast technology to provide rapport-building responses to students.

Notes

1. The questions were shaped from discussions at the 2007 annual meeting of the Council of Writing Program Administrators, expanded through discussions on the organization's electronic mailing list, WPA-L, and later condensed to 27 questions that then were refined through extensive focus group testing.

2. The questions associated with Clear Writing Expectations included the following: "Provided clear instructions describing what he or she wanted you to do"; "Explained in advance what he or she wanted you to learn"; "Explained in advance the criteria he or she would use to grade your assignment"; "Provided a sample of a completed assignment written by the instructor or a student" (p. 208).

3. Wiggins (2012) identified seven components of effective feedback: goal-referenced, tangible and transparent, actionable, user-friendly (specific and personalized), timely, ongoing, and consistent.

4. McLeod, Hart-Davidson, and Grabill (n.d.) developed a digital environment for instructors to use to scaffold and guide peer feedback. Their tool, Eli Review, is a commercial product. Visit elireview.com for more information about their approach to feedback and their tool.

References

Ad Hoc Committee, International Network of Writing Across the Curriculum Programs. (2014). Statement of WAC principles and practices. Retrieved from http://wac.colostate.edu/principles/statement.pdf

Anderson, P., Anson, C. M., Gonyea, R. M., & Paine, C. (2015). The contributions of writing to learning and intellectual development: Results from a large-scale national study. *Research in the Teaching of English, 50*, 199–235.

Anderson, P., Anson, C. M., Gonyea, R. M., & Paine, C. (2016). How to create high-impact writing assignments that enhance learning and development and reinvigorate WAC/WID programs: What almost 72,000 undergraduates taught us. *Across the Disciplines, 13*(4). Retrieved from http://wac.colostate.edu/atd/hip/andersonetal2016.cfm

Anson, C. M. (in press). "She really took the time": Students' opinions of screen capture response to their writing in online courses. In C. Weaver and P. Jackson (Eds.), *Writing in online courses: How the online environment shapes writing practices*. Gorham, ME: Myers Education Press.

Anson, C. M., Dannels, D. P., Laboy, J. I., & Carneiro, L. (2016). Students' perceptions of oral screencast responses to their writing exploring digitally mediated identities. *Journal of Business and Technical Communication, 30*(3), 378–411.

Bean, J. C. (2011). *Engaging ideas: The professor's guide to integrating writing, critical thinking, and active learning in the classroom.* New York, NY: John Wiley & Sons.

Eodice, M., Geller, A., & Lerner, N. (n.d.). *The Meaningful Writing Project.* Retrieved from http://meaningfulwritingproject.net/

Eodice, M., Geller, A., & Lerner, N. (2017). *The meaningful writing project: Learning, teaching, and writing in higher education.* Logan, UT: Utah State University Press.

Griffin, J., & Minter, D. (2012, March 21–24). Expert views from student voices regarding fully online and hybrid OWI. A presentation from the 2012 Conference on College Composition and Communication, St. Louis, MO.

Hattie, J., & Timperley, H. (2007). The power of feedback. *Review of Educational Research, 77*(1), 81–112.

Hattie, J. A. (1999). *Influences on student learning.* Inaugural professorial address, University of Auckland, New Zealand. Retrieved from http://www.arts.auckland.ac.nz/staff/index.cfm?P=8650

Kuh, G. (2008). *High-impact educational practices: What they are, who has access to them, and why they matter.* Washington DC: Association of American Colleges & Universities.

Kuh, G., & O'Donnell, K. (2013). *Ensuring quality & taking high-impact practices to scale.* Washington DC: Association of American Colleges & Universities.

Landy, K. (2015). Structure, connectivity, and authenticity: The how and why of high-impact practices. *About Campus, 19*(6), 29–32.

Light, R. (2004). *Making the most of college: Students speak their minds* (2nd ed.). Cambridge, MA: Harvard University Press.

McLeod, M., Hart-Davidson, B., & Grabill, J. (n.d.). Feedback and revision: The key components of powerful writing pedagogy. Retrieved from http://elireview.com/content/td/feedback/

Melzer, D. (2009). Writing assignments across the curriculum: A national study of college writing. *College Composition and Communication, 61*(2), 240–261.

Mrkich, S., & Sommers, J. (2016, July). Audio response to student writing. WPA-CompPile Research Bibliographies, No. 26. *WPA-CompPile Research Bibliographies*. Retrieved from http://comppile.org/wpa/bibliographies/Bib26/Audio_Response.pdf

Sommers, J. (2013). Response 2.0: Commentary on student writing for the new millennium. *Journal of College Literacy and Learning, 39*, 21–37.

Wiggins, G. (2012). Seven keys to effective feedback. *Educational Leadership, 70*(1), 10–16.

5

COLLABORATIVE ASSIGNMENTS AND PROJECTS

Robert John Robertson and Shannon Riggs

The Association of American Colleges & Universities (AAC&U) has identified the use of collaborative assignments and projects as a high-impact educational practice because these activities combine "learning to work and solve problems in the company of others, and sharpening one's own understanding by listening seriously to the insights of others, especially those with different backgrounds and life experiences" (Kuh, 2008, p. 9). Given the nature of collaborative assignments and projects in combining these patterns of thinking and behaviors, they can be understood to support AAC&U's Essential Learning Outcomes, developed as part of the Liberal Education and America's Promise (LEAP) initiative, in the categories of intellectual and practical skills; personal and social responsibility; integrative and applied learning; and, depending on the subject of the assignment or project, perhaps also knowledge of human cultures and the physical and natural world.

In addition, group assignments and projects require increased time on task; require that students interact with peers and faculty about substantive matters over extended periods of time; provide opportunities to give, receive, and consider more feedback than independent assignments and projects; and provide skill-building opportunities valued in many places of employment where collaboration is necessary to conduct business successfully. Nathan and Sawyer (2015) have also identified several ways in which collaboration improves learning: communicating and listening to explanations, making implicit knowledge explicit, revealing knowledge gaps in comparison with other group members, and reflecting on one's own arguments and the arguments of others in the process of collaboration.

Designed well, collaborative projects and assignments can also provide more authentic learning experiences than traditional assessments, such as exams. Authentic learning experiences provide opportunities for skill-building as well as several other benefits, including greater relevance for current or future work environments, opportunities to approach problems from a multidisciplinary standpoint, and encouraging students to achieve higher order learning outcomes (Windham, 2007). Given the rise of globalization, asynchronous collaboration is increasingly common in professional workplaces; therefore, asynchronous collaboration in coursework, regardless of the topic, is by its nature an authentic learning experience. Students participating in online, asynchronous collaboration within their major disciplines and/or modeling professional collaborations benefit from even greater degrees of authenticity.

In addition to providing the benefits outlined previously, collaboration may be especially valuable for those students for whom the AAC&U and LEAP initiative identify as historically underserved (Kuh, 2008). Interestingly, these historically underserved students comprise many of the same student populations that online providers of higher education are trying to serve by bringing higher education to where they are, rather than requiring that they relocate to a physical campus and overcome obstacles such as disabilities, family responsibilities, and economic pressures, which make leaving employment to pursue full-time studies challenging. Given this overlap between the student populations that online providers are trying to serve and the student populations identified as benefiting from high-impact practices (HIPs), promoting collaborative activities online is becoming more essential.

Asynchronous Online Environments

Today's online learning environments are constructed using many different technologies, multimedia components, and design features, and they are facilitated from a range of pedagogical perspectives. However, they fall into two basic design categories: those that require synchronous participation and those that do not. Synchronous online courses are those that require regularly scheduled virtual class meetings, where all students and the instructor must be online and communicating in real time, usually in a Web conference environment. Asynchronous online courses allow students and the instructor to participate per their own schedules, usually according to weekly deadlines.

Asynchronous course designs better meet the schedule flexibility needed by most adult online learners. In asynchronous course designs, class members are not required to log in to the course management system or other virtual meeting location at a designated time. Rather, students may log in to participate in asynchronous class discussions and other learning activities at any time of the day or night. Instructors facilitate and respond to student work on their own timetables as well. Importantly, asynchronous course designs do require modifications of many learning activities to accommodate asynchronous participation and to ensure that students meet the same learning outcomes. For some instructors new to online education, the simple act of adjusting lecture delivery for an asynchronous environment seems like a difficult challenge; learning to manage small groups of geographically dispersed people engaged in collaborative learning, in comparison, can seem like an insurmountable obstacle.

Despite the challenge, including collaborative learning in online asynchronous courses may be desirable simply because, among other HIPs, collaborative learning can be made available to a wide array of online students across disciplines. Although providing collaborative learning opportunities online is challenging, with sufficient design consideration and guidance, it can be done.

What Is Collaborative Learning?

Before venturing into how to implement collaborative learning in an online, asynchronous course, it is necessary to define what we mean by *collaborative*, as a vast array of learning experiences are described using this word. AAC&U (Kuh, 2008) defines *collaborative learning* as, "learning to work and solve problems in the company of others, and sharpening one's own understanding by listening seriously to the insights of others, especially those with different backgrounds and life experiences" (p. 10). Stahl, Koschmann, and Suthers (2014) provide a helpful distinction between collaboration and cooperation. In cooperative learning, "learning is done by individuals, who then contribute their individual results and present the collection of individual results as their group product" (p. 481). With collaborative learning, however, "individuals are involved as members of the group, but the activities that they engage in are not individual-learning activities, but group interactions like negotiation and sharing . . . with a shared task that is constructed and maintained by and for the group" (p. 481). Although cooperative learning can be beneficial and is certainly easier to manage in an online, asynchronous course, collaborative learning provides perhaps even greater educational benefit.

Because collaborative learning requires negotiation, argumentation, and continually making implicit knowledge explicit, it demands a greater cognitive load. Nathan and Sawyer (2015) suggest that more simplified cooperative learning tasks, where instructors reduce the need for negotiation and argumentation, especially, will result in students "process[ing] the information passively and shallowly, with little learning occurring" (p. 31). On the contrary, when true collaboration is required, students must argue and reason with each other, are encouraged by the demands of the task to work together to make sense of challenging content, and must make generalizations that can be transferred to other situations they encounter in the future.

Several scholars have explored what it means to create successful teams within a range of learning environments. Miyake and Kirschner (2015) present a model of team-learning beliefs and behaviors that can be used to inform the design of collaborative learning experiences for online, asynchronous classes. This model suggests that a collection of beliefs (interdependence, social cohesion, task cohesion, group potency, and psychological safety) lead to team behaviors (construction, constructive conflict, and coconstruction), which then lead to mutually shared cognition and team effectiveness. For asynchronous online collaborative activities, this model would suggest the need to incorporate a team-building activity early in the process, as well as the creation of a plan for constructively working through conflict before it arises. Hurst and Thomas (2004) also identify several key practices in successful online teaming: "agreement on how teams will work together, how accountability is assigned, how progress is monitored, and how social interaction is incorporated" (p. 456). These practices might include specifying individual roles, as well as acceptable and nonacceptable modes of communication, including how to ensure inclusion of members who are not available for a planned synchronous communication within the group. Table 5.1 outlines examples of several pre- and postcollaborative project activities that can help students identify, analyze, and synthesize skills, communication practices, and behaviors that contribute to positive group work learning experiences.

Nathan and Sawyer (2015) caution that good collaboration does not happen naturally. Rather, learners "need modeling, guidance, or direct instruction and scripts to develop and apply collaboration skills, such as turn-taking, active listening, critical evaluation, and respecting others' opinions" (Nathan & Sawyer, 2015, p. 34). All instructors, regardless of modality, would be wise to offer such guidance. Instructors of online asynchronous courses, however, would also need to provide direct instruction about online asynchronous collaboration prior to launching a primary group project.

Challenges to Collaborative Activities in Online Asynchronous Environments

Given the context and connections outlined earlier and the value of collaborative learning, what are some of the challenges in implementing this

TABLE 5.1

Scaffolding Examples for Collaborative Learning to Assist With Team Learning Beliefs, Values, and Skills

Collaborative Project Scaffolding	How It Works	Intended Collaboration Effects
Two Truths and a Lie Activity	In small-group discussion, each member shares three personal "facts," two of which are true and one of which is a lie. Group members post their guesses about which facts are actually lies. After a fixed interval, members self-disclose which fact was a lie.	Builds social connections, demonstrates accountability, models the use of interim milestones in longer projects, and begins to establish psychological safety
Valuing Constructive Conflict	Teams share examples of conflicts in past experiences with group work, perhaps from childhood, professional, or college experiences. Teams discuss when conflicts have yielded positive outcomes and then compare and contrast constructive and destructive conflict.	Builds group potency, establishes boundaries for acceptable communication, creates group value of diversity, identifies benefits of constructive conflict, and creates a shared and nuanced vocabulary about conflict
Reflecting on Strengths and Challenges of Group Work	Before the project begins, group members brainstorm a collaborative document expressing strengths and challenges of group work, noting specific strengths and challenges for online, asynchronous group work. Teams generate a list of strengths and concerns and then collectively prioritize them based on degree of severity.	Builds task cohesion, increases psychological safety, establishes the value of proactively avoiding problems, builds awareness of role responsibility, and establishes group values about which behaviors are most undesirable for the team
Preventing and Addressing Team Problems	Building on the prioritized list of concerns, teams discuss strategies for preventing problems and dealing with them if they do arise. Teams produce a strategy document that helps teams agree on a plan for preventing concerning situations and responding to concerns as they arise.	Reduces apprehension, builds team and task cohesion, increases psychological safety, creates a shared understanding of team dynamics, and builds team interdependence
Advice for Future Groups	At the conclusion of the group project, teams can create a letter or video message for students in future terms providing advice for approaching collaborative work productively. These artifacts can be used in future terms to orient students to collaborative work.	Provides authentic student-to-student feedback on collaborative work, introduces nuances specific to the context of the class itself, and normalizes collaborative work as a valuable educational practice

HIP online? What obstacles do instructors and students face in collaborating online? In this section, the challenges are classified into several categories. We will review each in detail, outlining how these challenges might manifest in the asynchronous, online setting. Later in the chapter, we will discuss strategies for overcoming these challenges.

Schedule Incompatibility

Scheduling collaborative work can be challenging regardless of the course modality. In an on-campus environment, however, the synchronous schedule can help students find a common time for collaboration and allows for impromptu meetings and timely instructor intervention. In an online, asynchronous environment, the variety of schedules and time zones that drive students to choose online courses can make finding a common pattern of work, by default, difficult. One strategy to assist student coordination efforts is to allow students to self-select into groups based on typical availability, such as those who are typically available during early morning hours on weekdays, long stretches of time on weekends, or late evenings. For institutions that attract students worldwide, it can be helpful to clarify the home institution time zone.

In addition, procrastination, while challenging for all collaborative projects, can easily snowball in the online environment and have a substantial impact on a group's work schedule. Furthermore, in an online environment, unresponsive students can more easily avoid both group members and the instructor. This situation can have serious consequences on a group's ability to do the work, the group's schedule, and the overall morale of the group. To discourage procrastination, it can be helpful to build in regular milestones with incremental deliverables. Missed milestones early on can be addressed with interventions, such as instructor counseling of group members or group work improvement plans. Also helpful in discouraging procrastination is requiring a representative of each group to periodically report progress to the full class. Status reports can help groups that are encountering difficulties learn how other groups are managing similar concerns.

Online Communication Gaps and Misunderstanding

All collaboration relies heavily on clear communication; however, the asynchronous online medium exacerbates the possibility of communication gaps and misunderstanding. Aggressive or inflexible collaborators can be a challenge in any group effort; however, the intermediation of a screen and a heavy reliance on text without intonation or facial expression can, regardless of whether the strength of feeling was intentional, lead to perceived aggression or inflexibility. Additionally, given the scheduling lag times and delays between responses, misunderstandings can have more time to fester, which can diminish trust among collaborators.

Cultural influences are also important to consider. Online courses have an increased likelihood of involving students from a variety of countries, cultural contexts, and backgrounds across a wider range of demographics than on-campus courses. Although this can be a great strength, it also creates a greater likelihood that language will be used and understood differently and that humor and other cultural referents will not be understood, making group members feel alienated, confused, or offended.

Technical Difficulties

A range of tools are available to support online collaboration: e-mail, discussion boards, screen recorders, virtual poster boards, and Web-conferencing platforms. These tools can help ease communication and enrich group collaboration. Unfortunately, this plurality of choice in infrastructure can also lead to related challenges for students as they seek to get tools and technologies to work and to figure out how to use them effectively. One technical challenge is compatibility. Differing versions of computers, browsers, operating systems, and tools can provide challenges for even the most technically literate students.

Other technical challenges may arise if group members assume that all members have the same access to broadband, a personal computer, a mobile device, a webcam, a microphone, or a quiet space at a particular time. Even when the instructor bears formal accessibility requirements in mind when picking tools to use, group members picking their own tool may not initially think of this, and other students who need accommodation may feel uncomfortable asking for it.

Finally, all new technologies share the technical challenge of requiring a learning curve to master use. Whether the tool is assigned by the instructor or chosen by other group members, constantly having to learn how to use new tools can create a cognitive overhead that may be off-putting for learners or diminish their enthusiasm.

Challenges in Assessing Collaborative Work

One of the challenges with collaborative work in any modality is the question of whether to assess students individually or as a group. For online students, the risk of depending on other students for a grade can be amplified because online students often balance work; demanding schedules; and other commitments, such as military service or caring for their family or relatives.

Given these constraints, as well as sacrifices they and others make to support their studies, online students may be concerned about making any part of their grade reliant on others.

Additionally, in collaborative work in any modality, equity in grading can be problematic. There are various approaches to grading collaborative work, such as grading individually, having peer-assigned balancing points, or assigning a single grade for each group member. All such approaches can be perceived as inequitable in some form: individual grading diminishes the collaborative nature of the work and may reward those who can best exploit their peers, balancing points changes the group dynamic and may possibly reward acting politically rather than collaboratively, and a uniform group grade might allow a student to coast along and benefit from the work of others. The perception of the fairness or unfairness of such situations may be amplified given asynchronous online environments, but, as importantly, it may also diminish the options that the group or the instructor has to assess and address those perceptions.

Authenticity of Collaboration

A challenge exists to make collaborative assignments feel authentic for students, and in an online environment, the relative paucity of the surrounding social context and the varying degree of life experience of the student cohort can add to this challenge in several important ways. First, collaborative work in any course can be perceived as contrived and artificial. On-campus instructors may have an advantage here, however, because they have the option to build up to the relevancy of a collaborative activity by peppering prior lectures with connections to working practice or asides about the wider purpose of that activity; the often focused and highly condensed online parallels rarely afford the luxury of such asides. Second, without the immediate support of a synchronous course's time frame, students' engagement with each other is one more step to be arranged, and collaborating with relative strangers can make the activity feel strained. Third, much of the commentary about students needing to learn to collaborate assumes the traditional transition from high school to college. However, for mature students, especially those who have been in the workforce or military, learning to collaborate may not be new, and the academic activity may feel forced and unnecessary.

Strategies to Overcome Challenges

Although many challenges are inherent in creating collaborative learning experiences in online asynchronous courses, there are compelling reasons to make the effort. Online educators can apply a number of strategies and approaches to overcome these challenges to implement collaborative learning successfully.

Reflecting About How Collaboration Aligns With Your Pedagogy and Course Design

Overcoming the challenges outlined previously begins with thinking through your epistemological beliefs, as well as the pedagogy reflected in the design and teaching of your course. Considering how you believe students learn can help you clarify first for yourself, and then for your students, why you expect your students to collaborate, what the purpose and benefit of collaboration is for them, which learning outcomes the collaboration addresses, and how best to evaluate the activity. Reflecting on your chosen pedagogy can help you design a collaborative project that aligns with your beliefs and therefore comes across more consistently and coherently to your students, thus minimizing confusion and maximizing motivation.

For example, if you are using a social constructivist pedagogy, you view knowledge not as something passed from the instructor to the students, but rather as something students construct through social interactions that help them build on prior learning, reflection and metacognition, and active learning (Anderson & Dron, 2011). Your collaborative learning assignments, therefore, might include the following: the opportunity for students to recall related prior knowledge, ample time and means to collaborate with debate and deliberation as opposed to simply cooperating to assemble a final product, and active learning that provides the opportunity to interact meaningfully with content as well as a requirement for reflection and metacognition, such as a journal or cover letter for the assignment.

However, if you are using a connectivist pedagogy, you believe that learning is about connecting learners with resources and other people in a manner that allows them to work on applied, real-world problems (Anderson & Dron, 2011). In this case, your collaborative learning assignments might include the following: guidance in helping students find relevant and reputable resources; available experts and/or suggestions for finding such experts; sufficient time for students to make exploratory connections before finding those that will be fruitful for the given assignment; and regularly updated, real-world problems that do not have ready-made, already-realized solutions.

Finally, if you are using an open pedagogy, you believe that knowledge and information should be freely available, people bear a certain responsibility to innovate and contribute to this collective knowledge, and communication is necessary for creating, sharing, and ensuring quality (Hegarty, 2015). Collaborative learning assignments using this pedagogy might include the following: a project that calls for creation or innovation; means for students to communicate and collaborate from a distance; a process that includes opportunity for substantial, formative feedback and/or peer review; and a final product that is shared publicly.

Other pedagogies are certainly possible; these are offered simply as illustrations. That said, once your pedagogy is clear in your own mind, you will be able to make better decisions about the design of your collaborative assignment. You will also be able to address student concerns about the challenges inherent in online, asynchronous collaborative work more persuasively.

Make Communication in Collaborative Assignments Transparent

Establishing clear expectations for student communication is a key piece of setting up a successful online group. How will the group communicate and collaborate? What pieces of that need to be visible to the instructor and how do the tools and practices chosen support these expectations? In addition, instructors will also find it helpful to address several other components. First, in the same way that an instructor can set the tone of a discussion board in a course through their initial posts or response, they have the opportunity to set the tone of the collaborative activity. Hurst and Thomas (2004) outline one approach in which teams explicitly develop a charter for how they will interact and structure social interaction into their team communication process. Such a charter might include provisions for the frequency of team communication, expectations for response times between meetings, preferred communication methods, how to communicate emergencies such as illness, building time allowances for contingencies, and how to proceed with decision making in the absence of unanimity (i.e., majority rules or consultation with the instructor). Of importance, and also related to tone, is ensuring that collaborators feel safe in their groups. Although student conduct codes might exist and offer a process to address problems, reminding students about these policies in the context of the collaborative work and striving to create an active sense of obligation to each other can help establish a baseline of conduct and create a needed safe space (Miyake & Kirschner, 2015).

In addition, group conflict will likely occur. The critical factor in the success of the activity is not that there be an absence of all conflict, but that conflict is anticipated, valued for its ability to strengthen the process and product, and negotiated successfully and civilly. Another key element is the need to build in the expectation that collaboration—from scheduling to working with technology—will not run smoothly and that anticipating, evaluating, and responding to challenges are essential parts of the activity rather than unintended and undesirable problems to be avoided (Hurst & Thomas, 2004).

Finally, although online asynchronous courses by definition do not require synchronous participation for the entire class, this does not preclude smaller groups of students negotiating synchronous meetings, in person or virtually, as part of the collaborative process. Although this option might not be possible in all institutions or programs, it may be available in some cases.

Make Grading Criteria and Processes Explicit

As with other assessments, students' collaboration works more smoothly when they understand what is being evaluated. In collaborative work, this may be each student's mastery of a topic or skill, the process of collaboration, the final product, the metacognitive reflection on the process, or a combination of these factors. If a combination, how they are weighted relative to each other is an important piece of information to make clear. Assessment plans and rubrics will—and should—vary depending on discipline, course topic, level, and learning outcomes being assessed. Clarifying the collaborative assignment's purpose in relation to the learning outcomes being assessed can be helpful. For example, an instructor using a collaborative report writing assignment might emphasize the content of the report, with the collaboration involved intended to enrich the content. Alternatively, an instructor of a technical writing course might equally weight the product and process because professional technical writers need to develop skills to work with a variety of stakeholders to produce useful documentation. The instructor must be intentional in creating the assessment plan and must communicate the plan and rationale behind it clearly. Forthright directions and explanations of why particular activities are evaluated the way they are can avoid unnecessary problems in the collaborative activity and can help students negotiate conflict in constructive ways.

Instructors should also clarify when they might interfere in the group process, which circumstances might lead them to remove people from groups, and how they will deal with unequal workloads or unresolvable conflict. These grading strategies will be helpful in any collaborative work. For online asynchronous courses, however, instructors must also take into account how to make all of these components transparent to students and themselves as evaluators to avoid piecing together evidence at the end of a term to make a fair determination. Rubrics, peer evaluation forms, written check-ins, and communication and decision logs can help document criteria, expectations, participation, and performance, and ease grading concerns in the asynchronous learning environment.

Emphasize Authenticity

As previously discussed, authenticity can be especially difficult to achieve with diverse groups of online students who may be naturally averse to the idea of collaborating—indeed, this may be one reason that they have intentionally sought out an asynchronous learning environment. Finding ways to emphasize the authenticity of collaboration can increase student motivation by making the value of the activity more apparent. For example, the collaborative project might call for students to emulate the writing, editing, and negotiation of project specifications or reports called for in many careers, or it may ask that students use tools they will be required to engage with in future professional situations.

In addition to creating authentic assessments that students can perceive as skill-building for future professional practice, authentic assessments might also aim to create artifacts that have life and an audience beyond the course. Whether creating a shared summary of the course, a time line of events, or a project shared in some other public form, the context of the collaborative work can seem more authentic when it moves beyond the disposable assignment to something more meaningful (Wiley, 2013).

In the context of online learning, the geographically dispersed and diverse nature of students can be a real advantage. Learners located in many different places with many different backgrounds required to participate in collaborative learning experiences afford students the opportunity to learn more from each other more than they might in a homogenous group.

Concluding Thoughts

Collaborative activities in an asynchronous online environment have their challenges; however, they also have enormous potential to support and develop all students. Instructors who find that collaborative learning suits their pedagogy and can be supported in their course designs would do well to remember that collaboration does not happen naturally and needs to be defined, taught, and modeled for students (Nathan & Sawyer, 2015). Instructors should also consider incorporating team-building and/or direct instruction and guidance about forming and managing successful teams (Hurst & Thomas, 2004). Online collaboration offers students a different experience than on-campus collaboration. It empowers student voices by creating time to think and respond. It mirrors the working environment of global teams. Tackling the potential challenges and promoting metacognition can help students understand themselves better and promote deeper learning.

Questions for Reflection

- Which pedagogical approach do you plan to take in your course? Which components should your collaborative activity have to help you fully implement your pedagogical approach?
- Is your activity cooperative or collaborative? How will your students practice skills such as negotiation and argumentation?
- For which aspects of collaboration do you need to provide direct instruction?
- Beyond standard civility guidelines, how can you help students think about communication and collaboration?
- How is collaboration authentic for your discipline and/or for your students' future professions? How and when can you best communicate this authenticity?
- How can you provide students with a low- or no-stakes opportunity to practice using the tools they will need in their collaborative activity?
- How will you manage problems such as students who fail to participate in a timely manner?
- For your course, which aspects of the collaborative activity are most important to assess? Will you assess students individually or as a group? Which criteria will be most important?

Key Takeaways

- Well-designed collaborative projects and assignments can provide more authentic learning experiences than traditional assessments, such as exams.
- Instructors of online asynchronous courses should provide guidance and direct instruction about online asynchronous collaboration prior to launching a primary group project.
- Reflecting on a chosen pedagogy can help instructors design a collaborative project that aligns with beliefs, ensuring more consistent and coherent guidelines to students.
- Finding ways to emphasize authenticity of collaboration by making the value of the activity more apparent, such as creating assessments that students can perceive as skill-building for future professional practice, can increase student motivation.

References

Anderson, T., & Dron, J. (2011). Three generations of distance education pedagogy. *The International Review of Research in Open and Distributed Learning, 12*(3). Retrieved from http://www.irrodl.org/index.php/irrodl/article/view/890/1663

Hegarty, B. (2015, July–August). Attributes of open pedagogy: A model for using open educational resources. *Educational Technology.* Retrieved from https://upload.wikimedia.org/wikipedia/commons/c/ca/Ed_Tech_Hegarty_2015_article_attributes_of_open_pedagogy.pdf

Hurst, D., & Thomas, J. (2004). Developing team skills and accomplishing team projects online. In T. Anderson (Ed.), *Theory and practice of online learning.* Retrieved from http://cde.athabascau.ca/online_book/ch8.html

Kuh, G. (2008). *High-impact educational practices: What they are, who has access to them, and why they matter.* Washington DC: Association of American Colleges & Universities.

Miyake, N., & Kirschner, P. A. (2015). The social and interactive dimensions of collaborative learning. In R. K. Sawyer (Ed.), *The Cambridge handbook of the learning sciences* (pp. 418–438). Cambridge, UK: Cambridge University Press.

Nathan, M., & Sawyer, R. (2015). Foundations of the learning sciences. In R. Sawyer (Ed.), *The Cambridge handbook of the learning sciences* (pp. 21–43). Cambridge, UK: Cambridge University Press.

Stahl, G., Koschmann, T., & Suthers, D. (2014). Computer-supported collaborative learning. In R. Sawyer (Ed.), *The Cambridge handbook of the learning sciences* (pp. 479–500). Cambridge, UK: Cambridge University Press.

Wiley, D. (2013). What is open pedagogy? *Iterating Toward Openness.* Retrieved from https://opencontent.org/blog/archives/2975

Windham, C. (2007). Why today's students value authentic learning. *Educause Learning Initiative (ELI Paper 9).* Retrieved from https://net.educause.edu/ir/library/pdf/ELI3017.pdf

6

UNDERGRADUATE RESEARCH IN THE HUMANITIES

Ellen Holmes Pearson and Jeffrey W. McClurken

To help students learn fundamental research skills, one common experience in undergraduate classrooms involves a faculty member assigning a research paper, the student completing the assignment (with the faculty member as sole audience), the faculty member thoughtfully crafting comments and suggestions for that student's work, and the student carefully reviewing that feedback before placing it in some cherished place to be referred to in the future. Or at least that is what many faculty members tell themselves about the process. In this idealized world, the work of the undergraduate researcher typically remains written for a single person (with a grade as motivation), and that work is rarely shared beyond that assignment. Although learning and writing in isolation are important academic skills, the common focus on that process wastes valuable undergraduate research potential every semester. How much more powerful would it be to transcend that closed system of undergraduate knowledge production to make students' writing and projects available to all and enable their work to be created not just for a narrow audience of one faculty member but for the larger public world?

In that context, we have been exploring undergraduate research aimed at a broader audience that takes advantage of digital tools, such as those used in distance education in the digital liberal arts. We wanted our students to share and present their hard-won knowledge in public venues that would represent an important alternative to a traditional undergraduate research paper. In this chapter, we will review the current literature on undergraduate research, with specific emphasis on how undergraduate research is applied in the liberal arts context. Additionally, we focus on the benefits of collaborative online learning and the use of digital tools for undergraduate research projects. We also survey some of the more creative approaches to course-embedded undergraduate research in online education and share a case study of our consortium's collaborative online learning course, in which we combined traditional undergraduate research with experience in the digital liberal arts.

Review of the Scholarly Literature

For quite some time, undergraduate instructors have recognized the importance of experiential learning opportunities, such as undergraduate research, because they allow students to wrestle with problems and find their own way toward solutions. These high-impact practices (HIPs) are crucial to student retention and success because they give students the autonomy and permission to fail while also helping them reflect on what happened and move toward solutions (Finkel, 2000). Undergraduate research, one commonly used variety of experiential learning, allows students to conduct research using primary and secondary sources, grapple with the ideas and problems they encounter in these sources, and then communicate their findings, typically in the form of a research paper that is evaluated by their professor. Scholarship on teaching and learning that focuses on undergraduate research addresses the value of those experiences for students as they develop research skills and a sense of intellectual independence (Gilmore, Vieyra, Timmerman, Feldon, & Maher, 2015; MacLachlan & Caplan, 2015; Moran, Wells, & Smith-Aumen, 2015).

Scholarship on undergraduate research has also emphasized the successful impact of such research on graduation rates and graduate school work (Kilgo & Pascarella, 2016). Other scholarship on teaching and learning has focused on close research partnerships between faculty and students as an effective way to build collaborative skills (Boyer Commission, 1998; for more on collaboration as a HIP, see chapter 5, this volume). Although some educators think of undergraduate research as occurring outside of typical coursework, many institutions, especially liberal arts schools, often incorporate undergraduate research into existing courses. When undergraduates engage in research in their traditional classrooms, they have the opportunity to support one another in their independent research, thus promoting teamwork through peer collaboration and providing undergraduates at all levels access to research experiences (Karukstis & Elgren, 2007).

Research has also shown that online education provides similar collaborative experiences while also offering students effective undergraduate research practice. Research conducted over the last 15 years endorses the effectiveness of online and distance learning, even when compared with face-to-face classes. In 2009, the U.S. Department of Education analyzed 51 separate studies as part of a literature review and "found that, on average, students in online learning conditions performed better than those receiving face-to-face instruction" (Means, Toyama, Murphy, Bakia, & Jones, 2009, p. ix). Studies in science, technology, engineering and mathematics (STEM) fields in particular have endorsed online-based undergraduate research using synchronous video or a combination of local and distance supervision of undergraduate research projects (Shaw & Kennepohl, 2013; Tomechko et al., 2004; for more on undergraduate STEM research as a HIP, see chapter 7, this volume).

Still, despite the existing literature and as recently as 2016, the majority of faculty (55%) surveyed by *Inside Higher Ed* and Gallup in their "Faculty Attitudes on Technology Survey" disagreed with the following statement: "Online courses can achieve student learning outcomes equivalent to those of in-person courses at any institution" (Jaschik & Lederman, 2016). Although the survey showed that faculty who had taught online classes were more willing to support its potential, the answers reflected long-standing mistrust about online education and the ways that faculty understand their roles. At the same time, the survey revealed that academic technology administrators supported online education's potential to produce learning outcomes equivalent to face-to-face (63% in general and 87% at their own schools), suggesting that whatever the concerns of faculty are, online courses will continue to be an important piece of higher education going forward (Jaschik & Lederman, 2016; Straumsheim, 2016; Ubell, 2016).

In this environment of faculty resistance, years of work in online education, and rapidly changing technology, it is not surprising to see calls for new ways to think through teaching in the digital age. Most notably, Bass and Eynon's (2016) publication, *Open and Integrative: Designing Liberal Education for the New Digital Ecosystem*, points to a variety of ongoing innovative approaches to teaching in general, several of which allude to new directions for undergraduate research and include an emphasis on student use of digital tools. These new pedagogical approaches take seriously the role of students as creators, not just consumers, of knowledge, and they recognize that the most effective learning happens when students pursue their interests and connect their academic achievements with a broader audience (Major, 2015). The connections now transcend campus boundaries as students use blogs, wikis, audio/video creation, maps and time lines, text-mining, or network visualizations and/or videoconferencing technologies or to engage with peers and mentors on other campuses and in other nations. Whether the field is referred to as digital humanities, digital studies, or the digital liberal arts (Pannapacker, 2013a, 2013b, 2013c), research suggests that such tools allow students to express their ideas in new ways and to more people than the traditional research paper. Entire journals, such as the *Journal of Interactive Technology and Pedagogy*, have emerged to discuss the use of technology in teaching. Such work clarifies the value of using digital tools for group research projects, to increase interaction among students in online courses, and to facilitate the creation of online scholarly digital identities with initiatives such as the "Domain of One's Own" program, begun at the University of Mary Washington and now at more than 40 institutions (Boyd, 2013; Burtis, 2016; Marlow, 2012; Negash & Powell, 2015).

Consortia of institutions are also beginning to leverage digital tools and means of online communication to improve their students' undergraduate research opportunities. The Council of Public Liberal Arts Colleges, for example, has attempted to combine resources and match students with faculty on other campuses for research in a variety of fields (Albuja & Greenlaw, 2014). A recent initiative undertaken by the Council of Undergraduate Research supported sharing resources among members of state systems and public and private consortia to build capacity among member institutions (Malachowski, Osborn, Karukstis, & Ambos, 2015). Participants in this initiative explored a variety of challenges and advantages to collaboration to enhance their students' experiential learning. Among the issues addressed were the unique challenges that public institutions face in regard to meeting the needs of their students with limited resources. These challenges can, at least in part, be overcome with employment of online learning and open-source digital resources.

Putting It All Into Practice

Over the past decade, colleges and universities have devised new ways to blend undergraduate research, online education, the tools of the digital liberal arts, and consortial approaches to reinvent quality liberal learning for the twenty-first century. Institutions have invested in the development and staffing of digital scholarship centers, library-based labs and archives, and curricular concentrations, all in an effort to advance new forms of undergraduate research, publishing, and broad dissemination through online projects and exhibits. Understandably, many of these projects have focused on local issues, often rooted in the history of a community. West Chester University's "Goin' North" (n.d.), for example, brought graduate and honors undergraduate students together to tell the stories of the first Great Migration of African Americans into Philadelphia between 1910 and 1930. The hybrid "Teaching Hidden History" course has involved cross-campus partnerships among graduate students as they examined historical objects, conducted research, and created modules to teach the history that was "hidden" behind the sources (Center for History and New Media, 2016). Undergraduate seminars, such as the University of Richmond's "The Historian's Workshop," have also produced fine scholarship showcased on websites. For example, "Dear Congressman Abbitt" tells the story of a Virginia representative in the mid-twentieth century through his papers. The list of such worthwhile, campus-based student research projects is expanding at a remarkable rate (Sackley & University of Richmond, n.d.).

Case Study: A Consortial, Collaborative, Online, Digital Approach to Undergraduate Research

More recently, the authors created a new "distance" seminar model, "Century America," which taught undergraduates the theory and techniques behind digital scholarship in the humanities. The "Century America" online seminar, supported by the Teagle Foundation of New York, marked the centenary of the outbreak of World War I in Europe and the War and the subsequent influenza pandemic's impact on campuses and local communities in the United States. The collaborative "Century America" initiative involved undergraduates from 15 different member campuses of the Council of Public Liberal Arts Colleges (COPLAC), which integrated research about their own campuses during the period from 1914 to 1919 with the findings of other student scholars to produce an overarching digital portrait of the war on the home front. With this project, we successfully leveraged the COPLAC consortium to create a unique multicampus seminar whose student learning outcomes included experience in collaborative archival research and website design and that journeyed well beyond the traditional classroom setting. Moreover, this initiative expanded undergraduate research options on each campus and afforded students the opportunity to study under scholars from a range of disciplines while also preparing them for careers where liberal arts thinking is essential.

Goals and Organization of the Seminar

The seminar combined the traditional benefits of a liberal arts classroom, high-impact undergraduate research, online teaching of digital skills, and the creation, sharing, and preservation of new knowledge in a digital environment. In addition to learning important archival research and digital skills, the learning goals for our students included the development of competency in critical thinking, oral communication, and writing, as well as collaborative skills. All of these skills boost students' ability to succeed in the postgraduation job market and/or in graduate school.

The student researchers involved in "Century America" worked with special collections librarians on their home campuses to digitize primary source materials for the project website, create interactive maps and time-lines, incorporate video and audio clips, and consult with and offer advice to one another through blog comments and via Twitter. In addition to students' research into their home campuses and local communities, the team built the overarching site where common themes and features were agreed on and illustrated in narrative and photographic text. This blending of the particular with the more general was enriched by the online format of the seminar, allowing students to refine their abilities to synthesize disparate information from multiple sources and geographical settings.

Our teaching strategy throughout was to provide support and mentoring, but we did not want to overly structure the course. It was important that the students take ownership of their sites to make them their own. Our role was to introduce students to digital tools, provide some historical context, and then let them go. It was also important to allow students the freedom to play in and with the technology and to discover the opportunities and limitations of digital tools on their own. We required that students use WordPress for their site, but beyond that students could choose their themes and any other software or Web-based tools they used for the "bells and whistles" on their site. Timeline JS, Vimeo, and Audacity were popular choices for user-friendly—and free—technologies that enabled media-rich projects.

Teaching the Class: Adapting Undergraduate Research to the Digital and Online Environment

A synchronous online learning environment requires a different kind of pedagogy. The videoconference technology used for "Century America" allowed the instructors to see one another (which is important) and five or six of the students at a time in small squares at the bottom of the screen (note, videoconferencing technology continues to evolve rapidly, and technology is now available that allows all participants in a class of as many as 25 people to be seen in one window). Because of the distance, we could not rely on body language and other typical signals to tell us whether the students were engaged, confused, or simply not paying attention. Online technology does not lend itself to lectures, and although some traditional methods work, we found that we had to tailor our discussion tactics to the online format. We tried to keep students engaged with frequent "round-robin" responses, making sure that each student voiced an opinion or gave an update. Because of the distance between professor and students, some participants might feel a bit more invisible than they would in a brick-and-mortar classroom.

However, because the environment requires more flexibility and considerable participation from the students, the format also lends itself naturally to independent research and reflection. We used this feature to our advantage, requiring students to reflect on their work by producing a weekly blog post.

The first seminar included students from nine campuses, and the second featured two-person student teams from six-member institutions. "Century America" students were all undergraduates, primarily of third- and fourth-year standing. In the early weeks of the seminar, we met with students twice weekly via teleconference to introduce the theory and practice of digital scholarship across the humanities and to explore the military and home-front context of the Great War. These meetings incorporated readings such as Cohen and Rosenzweig (2006) and Kennedy (2004) to provide students with a broad contextual foundation for their local research. Students prepared a list of questions and comments on the assigned reading material and videos to explore any similarities or parallels they found with other historical events. They also reflected on any places where the readings or videos troubled or resonated with them. They made connections between the events of the Great War and other historical events, and these reflections served as the basis for blog reflections and group discussion during the videoconference class periods.

A few weeks into the semester, students also began to conduct archival research on their respective institutions and surrounding communities. They worked with the assistance of university special collections librarians and archivists from local and regional public collections to gather materials that were relevant to their campus and community's experiences during the Great War. They also connected with community members who were willing to share private materials, such as letters, photographs, and objects that enhanced the students' projects. In one instance, a student's Facebook inquiry connected her with a local man whose grandfather served in World War I. She was able to photograph his collection of memorabilia, including dog tags, war medals, and photographs, to create a gallery of these objects on her website (Marks, 2014).

Unlike research that students may have done for a traditional paper, we continued to remind them that this research needed to be outward-facing. Instead of finding documents and other objects that would help them to "prove" a thesis, students were charged with locating materials that would help them to tell a larger story that would appeal to the general public. We began to prepare students for this different approach early in the semester by asking them to read and discuss Cohen and Rosenzweig's (2006) chapter on audience. We stressed the importance of being mindful about the communities that they wanted to appeal to—and, yes, they would want to be in conversation with multiple communities. In many ways, this consciousness of community is similar to historians' considerations as they frame traditional research. We are always entering into conversations with particular communities of scholars. However, a website's communities contain different kinds of populations. As Cohen and Rosenzweig (2006) put it, "the most important step in building an audience for your site is having a clear idea of its purposes, who precisely you want to speak to, and why." We also asked students to look at specific digital history sites and to blog about their impressions, what they liked about the websites, what they did not like, what worked, and what did not. We asked them to think about the elements of these sites that they would like to incorporate or avoid in their own projects. We asked them to consider their own Web-surfing habits, how they navigate online, and how their own practices might help them to design their website.

Building the Sites: Facilitating Structured, Collaborative, Digital, Public History

Armed with these ideas and the beginnings of their archival research, as well as guest-lecture sessions on copyright and technology tools, the students began to develop website content for their individual schools and communities. Remaining mindful of the necessity for public appeal, we stressed the importance of organizing a site so that visitors could move through it in an intuitive, logical manner. For some sites, that might mean a chronological organization, but for these sites, the best arrangement tended to be topical. Each student team made those decisions independently of one another. They also had to think about the layout of the site. How could they make each page visually appealing to casual viewers? What would make those casual viewers want to move deeper into the site? What was the right mix of text and image? We left decisions about individual project sites up to the students so they could tailor the content of their websites to the members of their target communities.

To reinforce the importance of intentional planning for each site, student participants developed a project contract with a mission statement, archives to be used and digital tools to be employed, and a schedule of milestones when critical pieces of the individual project would be ready to present. So that they were mindful of the planning and layout process from the beginning, we asked them to start mapping a rough site plan or outline only a few weeks into the semester. The iterative process of drafting and editing a vision for their project helped to keep their goals in front of them throughout the rest of the term. The contract empowered students to own their project and their learning, and to craft it in distinct and personally relevant ways, while still allowing faculty to shape the project to ensure disciplinary relevance. The contract also provided both student and faculty a shared agreement about what work needed to be done.

The individual campus and community histories were then incorporated into the larger "Century America" site. This larger project site provided not only a gateway into all the individual student sites but also a way to frame the projects as one larger contribution to the history of the Great War and the influenza pandemic. Students and professors collaborated on the elements they would include on the overarching site, including a "Century America" logo that we could use on all of the project sites. The map showed the range of locations of the participating COPLAC schools (and the range of areas that the students had studied), and the time line placed national and international events in parallel with the local issues affecting those towns and campuses. Ultimately, the larger "Century America" site provided a way for the public, and for the students themselves, to see how the local, national, and international events of the day fit together in a way that no single undergraduate research paper ever could.

Results

Twenty-three students participated in the "Century America" seminar over the course of two semesters. In addition to the anticipated learning outcomes—improving research, writing, oral communication, and critical thinking skills—our students grew in a variety of other less-tangible ways. All expressed a strong sense of accomplishment in the fact that this centennial commemoration of the first world war is widely accessible thanks to digital technology. Becoming published scholars whose work is available to academic and nonacademic audiences strengthened everyone's sense of public purpose, as well as knowing that their work contributed to filling in unknown or overlooked portions of community and national history. Minnesota-Morris student Britta Buchanan (2015) noted, "It's amazing to think that people from the Morris community will be reading this and, hopefully, learning something from it. It's an incredibly rewarding feeling to know I'll be teaching people about this historically rich community through this website." Similarly, University of Alberta, Augustana Campus student Summer Roasting (2015) contrasted her experience composing traditional research papers that were read and evaluated by one professor before being "filed away" with her contributions to "Century America," where her scholarly work is now "out there" permanently for the public. The students understood that what they created mattered—not only for their college transcripts but also for a larger historical narrative to which they all contributed.

Students also observed that the interactive seminar format, together with the peer-to-peer blog post feedback, contributed to a greater sense of engagement and collective purpose. Joy Feagan (2015) of the New College of Florida commented that instead of viewing one's own campus as operating in an intellectual bubble, it was helpful to interact with students and professors from other campuses, mentors, and peers who cared about the collective implications of the scholarly work they were doing. Along the same lines, Laura Galbraith (2015) of Midwestern State University described the seminar experience as akin to "going to a conference twice a week," where the sharing and critiquing of ideas with other scholars is a matter of course. Another student from the first seminar remarked that working with peers from different campuses was one of the highlights of the project: "The encouragement, helpful hints, and feedback that I received from the other students was invaluable" (Nimer, 2014). Because the seminar takes place in an online environment, it also developed student researchers' independence and collaborative instincts (not to mention technical proficiencies), which are so highly valued in a wide range of professional areas.

It is worth pointing out that the fields of digital humanities/digital liberal arts acknowledge, and even enshrine, the notion of struggle and failure as critical pieces of the creation process. "Century America" embraced that notion, and the students appreciated that we gave them the "freedom to fail." As Jennifer Marks (2014) of Truman State University put it, the best way to teach students how to do digital studies is to "let your students flounder," at least for a little bit. She felt discomfort with the new technology but admitted that "the most useful process in learning how to make this website and to write for a digital history project was to be really bad at it at the beginning." Starting from nothing, being really lost, and then finding her own way out was, for Marks, a more valuable learning experience than being told exactly how to build her site.

"Century America" students also recognized that this sort of trial-and-error process was a way to grow and test the resilience required in the workforce. Joseph Hadwal (2015) of Midwestern State University stated that in confronting the obstacles he and his partner met in the construction of their site, "I became a better historian. I learned how to conduct community research and efficiently organize my time. More importantly, I gained an understanding of the skills required to present history to a wider audience." Victoria Carter (2015) of the University of Virginia at Wise agreed, stating that historical research practices and the digital world are both constantly evolving and

can bring joy, heartache, and frustration. And yet, even with all the days I wanted to pull my hair out or throw my pencil down, I would go back and do it all over again. Century America has taught me lessons I know I will use in both my academic and future careers.

Additional Benefits for the Students: Broadening Career Path

The skills that students acquired paid off for many of the "Century America" alumni on a scale that we simply did not anticipate. We knew that the research, writing, digital, and collaborative skills that our students cultivated would help them in the job market or in graduate school—or both. For many of these students, participation in the "Century America" course has helped them land prestigious internships or graduate school posts at places like the London School of Economics and the University of Iowa. Leah Tams (n.d.-a) interned at the Smithsonian Institution, where she researched and created an online object group—really an exhibit—of items from across the Smithsonian related to women and their experiences during the Great War, "Women in World War I," which is now available to the public. Tams has gone on to assist us as program associate for our current Digital Liberal Arts at a Distance Initiative, which is outlined in the following section. Tams (n.d.-b) states that "'Century America' was my first introduction to digital history/humanities, and it is where I cultivated the vast majority of my digital skills. This knowledge of DH tools, practices, and skills directly informs (and allows me to excel at) my work in digital humanities/liberal arts."

Other "Century America" alumni work as librarians, national park service rangers, geographers, and archivists. Christopher Hightower received a Master of Library and Information Science degree at the University of Alabama, and he is now a records manager at the University of Washington Medical. Hightower (n.d.) states that his experiences with "Century America" "directly inform my understanding of the evidential, informational, and historical value of the records I work with each day, and the skills I gained building my Century America website continue to help me in my work as an information professional." Julia Wood (n.d.), currently working for a federal government contractor in Washington DC, states that, although she is not working in a history field, "much of what I learned in the Century America project relates to my everyday work in the technology industry and [I] am incredibly grateful for the experience." Wood's duties include considerable writing as she documents a variety of processes,

> and I have been able to apply what I learned about using appropriate language for the audience at hand. Additionally, since I manage many of my projects' databases, I have referenced what I experienced regarding the function of historical archives to more effectively organize our digital files.

Although we anticipated that this unique opportunity would distinguish our students as they sought employment or applied for graduate school, we did not realize how quickly we would begin to see these results. Perhaps the most unexpected outcome was the publication of a book—not by us—but by one of our alumni, James Horn. Horn (2017) currently works as a park ranger at Cedar Creek and Belle Grove National Historical Park and authored the book, *World War I and Jefferson County, West Virginia*. This work builds on research that Horn began in the "Century America" course. He states, "I can't emphasize enough how important the Century America project was in leading me down the path toward this book" (J. Horn, personal communication, 2017).

Going Forward

One significant sign of the model's success is that the Andrew W. Mellon Foundation agreed to fund the expansion of these distance-mentored digital liberal arts courses to more COPLAC schools and faculty. In the resulting "Digital Liberal Arts at a Distance" project, following a convening of 75 faculty, instructional technologists, and archivists at the University of North Carolina, Asheville, and faculty workshops at the University of Mary Washington, 12 team-taught courses will be offered in 2017 and 2018 on a variety of interdisciplinary topics. Students from any COPLAC school across North America will be eligible to take the class as we attempt to replicate the best parts of the digital liberal arts-infused undergraduate research experience at a distance seen in "Century America."

Conclusion

The "Century America" project and the subsequent "Digital Liberal Arts at a Distance" initiative expand the horizons of undergraduate research in a variety of ways. The project and initiative take an interdisciplinary approach to learning beyond the boundaries of single institutions to engage students from multiple campuses on research topics with distinct campus- and community-based dimensions. Their work allowed students to cultivate their critical thinking and oral and written communication skills while also stretching their capacity for critical thinking and collaboration beyond the boundaries of their campuses. Moreover, these digital projects have democratized access to new knowledge for a wider public audience while setting local issues and stories in the context of similar developments elsewhere.

The "Century America" digital scholarship project, in combining the virtual and the local, online teaching and personalized mentoring, single-campus resources with consortium-wide faculty expertise, provides a useful model for how undergraduate researchers can engage in collaborative research with peers and faculty experts from across the country. The potential for expanding theme-based undergraduate research opportunities in the area of digital scholarship is enormous, especially at small to medium-sized colleges that can leverage their membership in consortia to advance interinstitutional learning opportunities. As technology-driven digital scholarship takes its place among the major forms of actively engaged or "hands-on" learning, online mentoring of multicampus collaborative undergraduate research projects opens up exciting possibilities for the creation and publication of student work on global issues with important but often overlooked local dimensions.

Key Takeaways

- Combining the traditional benefits of a liberal arts classroom; high-impact undergraduate research; online teaching of digital skills; and the creation, sharing, and preservation of new knowledge in a digital environment can boost a student's ability to succeed in the postgraduation job market and/or graduate school.
- Digital projects in undergraduate research can provide an interdisciplinary approach to learning beyond the boundaries of single institutions, engaging students from multiple campuses on research topics with campus- and community-based dimensions.
- There is enormous potential for expanding theme-based undergraduate research opportunities in the area of digital scholarship.

References

Albuja, A., & Greenlaw, S. A. (2014). Distance-mentored undergraduate research. *Change: The Magazine of Higher Learning, 46*(5), 44–51. Retrieved from https://doi.org/10.1080/00091383.2014. 941771

Bass, R., & Eynon, B. (2016). *Open and integrative: Designing liberal education for the new digital ecosystem.* Washington DC: Association of American Colleges & Universities.

Boyd, P. (2013). Online Discussion Boards as Identity Workspaces: Building Professional Identities in Online Writing Classes. *The Journal of Interactive Technology & Pedagogy,* (4). Retrieved from https://jitp.commons.gc.cuny.edu/online-discussion-boards-as-identity-workspaces-building-professional-identities-in-online-writing-classes/

Boyer Commission on Educating Undergraduates in the Research University, Stoney Brook, NY. (1998). *Reinventing Undergraduate Education: A Blueprint for America's Research Universities.* Retrieved from https://eric.ed.gov/?id=ED424840

Buchanan, B. (2015, May). Century America final presentations. Videoconference.

Burtis, M. (2016, August 19). Making and breaking domain of one's own [Web log post]. Retrieved from http://www.digitalpedagogylab.com/hybridped/making-breaking-rethinking-web-higher-ed/

Carter, V. (2015, May 2). Final reflection [Web log post]. Retrieved from http://course.centuryamerica.org/author/victoria/

Center for History and New Media. (2016). Teaching hidden history [Webpage]. Retrieved from http://edchnm.gmu.edu/teachinghiddenhistory/

Cohen, D. J., & Rosenzweig, R. (2006). *Digital history: A guide to gathering, preserving, and presenting the past on the web*. Philadelphia, PA: University of Pennsylvania Press. Retrieved from http://chnm.gmu.edu/digitalhistory/

Feagan, J. (2015). Final reflection [Web log post]. Retrieved from http://course.centuryamerica.org/author/feagan/

Finkel, D. L. (2000). *Teaching with your mouth shut*. Portsmouth, NH: Heinemann.

Galbraith, L. (2015, May). Century America final presentations. Videoconference.

Gilmore, J., Vieyra, M., Timmerman, B., Feldon, D., & Maher, M. (2015). The relationship between undergraduate research participation and subsequent research performance of early career STEM graduate students. *Journal of Higher Education, 86*(6), 834–863.

Hadwal, J. (2015). Century America reflection [Web log post]. Retrieved from http://course.centuryamerica.org/author/joseph/

Hightower, C. (n.d.). Where are they now? [Webpage]. Retrieved from http://coplacdigital.org/faq/where-are-they-now/

Horn, J. (2017). *World War I and Jefferson County, West Virginia*. Charleston, SC: History Press.

Jaschik, S., & Lederman, D. (Eds.). (2016, October 24). 2016 Inside Higher Ed survey of faculty attitudes on technology. *Inside Higher Ed*. Retrieved from https://www.insidehighered.com/news/survey/doubts-about-data-2016-survey-faculty-attitudes-technology

Karukstis, K. K., & Elgren, T. E. (Eds.). (2007). *Developing and sustaining a research-supportive curriculum: A compendium of successful practices*. Washington DC: Council of Undergraduate Research.

Kennedy, D. M. (2004). *Over here: The First World War and American Society* (25th anniversary ed.). New York, NY: Oxford University Press.

Kilgo, C. A., & Pascarella, E. T. (2016). Does independent research with a faculty member enhance four-year graduation and graduate/professional degree plans? Convergent results with different analytical methods. *Higher Education, 71*(4), 575–592. Retrieved from https://doi.org/10.1007/s10734-015-9925-3

MacLachlan, E. S., & Caplan, A. J. (2015). Fostering resources for undergraduate research at the City University of New York: Fostering resources for undergraduate research. *New Directions for Higher Education, 2015*(169), 73–83. Retrieved from https://doi.org/10.1002/he.20124

Major, C. H. (2015). *Teaching online: A guide to theory, research, and practice.* Baltimore, MD: Johns Hopkins University Press.

Malachowski, M., Osborn, J. M., Karukstis, K. K., & Ambos, E. L. (2015). Realizing student, faculty, and institutional outcomes at scale: Institutionalizing undergraduate research, scholarship, and creative activity within systems and consortia: Realizing student, faculty, and institutional outcomes at scale. *New Directions for Higher Education, 2015*(169), 3–13. Retrieved from https://doi.org/10.1002/he.20118

Marks, J. (2014). No man's land: Kirksville, Missouri and the Great War. A Century America Digital History Project [Webpage]. Retrieved from http://truman.centuryamerica.org/galleries/the-earl-l-stahl-collection/

Marlow, J. (2012). Wiki wars: Conversation, negotiation, and collaboration in online spaces. *The Journal of Interactive Technology & Pedagogy, 2.*

Means, B., Toyama, Y., Murphy, R., Bakia, M., & Jones, K. (2009). *Evaluation of evidence-based practices in online learning: A meta-analysis and review of online learning studies.* Washington DC: U.S. Department of Education. Retrieved from https://eric.ed.gov/?id=eD505824

Moran III, J. D., Wells, M. J., & Smith-Aumen, A. (2015). Making undergraduate research a central strategy in high-impact practice reform: The PASSHE journey. *New Directions for Higher Education, 2015*(169), 61–71. Retrieved from https://doi.org/10.1002/he.20123

Negash, S., & Powell, T. (2015). Increasing student engagement and assessing the value of an online collaboration tool: The case of VoiceThread. *The Journal of Interactive Technology & Pedagogy.* Retrieved from https://jitp.commons.gc.cuny.edu/increasing-student-engagement-and-assessing-the-value-of-an-online-collaboration-tool-the-case-of-voicethread/

Nimer, C. (2014). Veterans of WWI: The B.A.C. and Cedar City. A Century America Digital History Project [Webpage]. Retrieved from http://suu.centuryamerica.org/veterans-of-wwi/

Pannapacker, W. (2013a, February 18). Stop calling it "Digital Humanities." *The Chronicle of Higher Education.* Retrieved from http://www.chronicle.com/article/Stop-Calling-It-Digital/137325/

Pannapacker, W. (2013b, September 3). "Hacking" and "yacking" about the Digital Humanities. *The Chronicle of Higher Education.* Retrieved from http://www.chronicle.com/article/HackingYacking-About/141311/

Pannapacker, W. (2013c, November 18). No more digitally challenged liberal-arts majors. *The Chronicle of Higher Education.* Retrieved from http://www.chronicle.com/article/No-More-Digitally-Challenged/143079/

Roasting, S. (2015, May). Century America final presentations. Videoconference.

Sackley, N., & University of Richmond. (n.d.). Dear Congressman Abbitt [Webpage]. Retrieved from http://abbitt.richmond.edu/

Shaw, L., & Kennepohl, D. (2013). Student and faculty outcomes of undergraduate science research projects by geographically dispersed students. *The International*

Review of Research in Open and Distributed Learning, 14(5). Retrieved from https://doi.org/10.19173/irrodl.v14i5.1551

Straumsheim, C. (2016). Doubts about data: 2016 Survey of Faculty Attitudes About Technology (essay). *Inside Higher Ed.* Retrieved from https://www.insidehighered.com/news/survey/doubts-about-data-2016-survey-faculty-attitudes-technology

Tams, L. (n.d.-a). Women in World War I [Webpage]. Retrieved from http://americanhistory.si.edu/collections/object-groups/women-in-wwi

Tams, L. (n.d.-b). Where are they now? [Webpage]. Retrieved from http://coplacdigital.org/faq/where-are-they-now/

Tomechko, S., Leigh, A. M., Oommen, A., Burns, A. E., Holland, L. A., & Bradford, A. (2004). Real-time distance research with IP network videoconferencing: Extending undergraduate research opportunities. *Journal of Chemical Education, 81*(8), 1224. Retrieved from https://doi.org/10.1021/ed081p1224

Ubell, R. (2016). Advice for faculty members about overcoming resistance to teaching online (essay). *Inside Higher Ed.* Retrieved from https://www.insidehighered.com/advice/2016/12/13/advice-faculty-members-about-overcoming-resistance-teaching-online-essay

West Chester University History 601 and Honors 452 classes. (n.d.). Goin' North: Stories from the first great migration to Philadelphia [Webpage]. Retrieved from https://goinnorth.org/

Wood, J. (n.d.). Where are they now? [Webpage]. Retrieved from http://coplacdigital.org/faq/where-are-they-now/

7

UNDERGRADUATE RESEARCH IN THE SCIENCES

Kevin F. Downing and Jennifer K. Holtz

Undergraduate research (UR) in the United States has been championed as a vital component of science education for at least 100 years through the early efforts of the scientific research honor society, Sigma XI, the journal *Science*, UR honors such as the University of Chicago's Rickett's Award, and advocacy groups such as Indiana's Scientech club (Kinkead, 2012). In science, technology, engineering, and mathematics (STEM) education, significant strides have broadened student involvement in the high-impact practice (HIP) of UR, the so-designated Undergraduate Research Experiences in Science (URES). Engagement in URES varies by subject and is highest in the physical and biological sciences, with more than 40% of seniors having been involved in research, although first-year participation is closer to 5% (Hu, Scheuch, & Gayles, 2009). The more competitive and selective schools have greater levels of student engagement in UR (Hu et al., 2009), suggesting inequality in institutional opportunity and implementation, as well as a participation bias toward more affluent STEM academic environments. Providing access to the "real world" as a platform for research is hard for institutions to support, particularly through regular classes (Thiry, Laursen, & Hunter, 2011), highlighting that a commitment to UR regularly comes with elevated logistical, financial, and faculty resource costs.

Undergraduate research was first identified as a HIP by Kuh (2012), who connected it to the liberal learning outcomes of fostering knowledge of culture and the natural world, improving intellectual and practical skills, and preparing for integrative and applied learning. HIPs have been characterized as those that have a "significantly beneficial impact on student learning and success in college" (Kezar & Holocombe, 2017, p. 34). Their legitimacy can be statistically verified by such measures as improvement in grade point average (GPA), retention, and advanced degree aspirations (Kuh, 2012; Locks & Gregerman, 2008). In a longitudinal study of 17 institutions, UR was recognized as one of the two most effectual practices for advancing liberal arts learning objectives (Kligo, Sheets, & Pascarella, 2014).

Undergraduate research has largely been viewed and advanced through the prism of learning activities, students, and faculty physically situated at a college with UR experiences taking place in an on-campus lab or supervised field area. In light of the rapid and continuing growth of online learning in the United States, now with more than six million students taking at least one online course and about five million of those at the undergraduate level (Allen & Seaman, 2017), there is an emerging need to devise and advance curricula, classes, and other research experiences for online students pursuing STEM instruction. Enormous attention and resources have been devoted to supporting UR in traditional settings. However, consideration of Online Undergraduate Research Experiences in STEM (OURES) is largely a vacuum in terms of concept, practice, and strategies.

We define an *OURES* as an undergraduate research experience in a STEM area that is facilitated entirely online not only using the best applicable practices for undergraduate research experiences but also combining and employing the affordances and best practices of online learning. This chapter reviews the current issues, efforts, and practices in UR to conceptualize how UR can be extended using OURES with the emerging student body that chooses to take online science courses or chooses to pursue a complete science degree through a fully online degree program.

Benefits of Undergraduate Research Experiences

The literature has pointed to several benefits of URES. First, research indicates that students involved in URES benefit in the process of becoming a professional scientist. For students who plan to become practicing scientists, the UR experiences promote broader awareness of discipline and career opportunities to help formulate student career choices (Barker, 2009; Laursen, Hunter, Seymour, Thiry, & Melton, 2010). Likewise, well-designed URES experiences foster thinking like a scientist, becoming a scientist, and promoting personal-professional gains through contact and exchange with practicing professionals (Hunter, Laursen, & Seymour, 2008). The process of working on UR projects and the typical intense interaction with graduate students and professors also contributes to lifting a student's graduate degree aspirations (Eagan et al., 2013; Kilgo & Pascarella, 2016). It also has a societal impact through the production of domestic scientific expertise and the nurturing of rising scientists (Eagan et al., 2013), as well as building scientific capital (Holtz & Downing, 2009).

Second, beyond the disciplinary skills gained through the URES experiences, extensive literature documents the cognitive and lifelong learning benefits of these experiences for students. In a meta-analysis of student gains coalesced from numerous studies, Laursen and colleagues (2010) identify two main groupings of benefits, the first including undergraduate learning outcomes in science, social development, and acquisition of universal skills. The second group of benefits centers on a student's aspirational growth for postbaccalaureate graduate work and insight on career choice. Some of the chief URES benefits and learning outcomes include improved competence in information literacy, communication skills, reading improvement, writing skills, data collection and analysis, intellectual and practical understanding of science research, independent thinking, research design, technical skills, and acquisition of disciplinary skills (George et al., 2014; Laursen et al., 2010; Lopatto, 2010; Zee, de Boer, & Jaarsma, 2014). There is strong concurrence on the benefits of UR experiences based on faculty and student interviews (Hunter, Laursen, & Seymour, 2006; Lei & Chuang, 2010). Students participating in UR experiences also show higher GPAs, retention rates, and engagement in college leadership activities than peers (Schneider, Bickel, & Shetlar, 2015).

Third, students involved in UR experiences also grow in psychological dimensions. Affectual development from UR experiences is observed in capacities such as confidence in conducting research, satisfaction conducting research, fostering collegial relationships, viewing the rest of required science activities as more meaningful, becoming a stronger student, and growing in appreciation of knowledge (George et al., 2014; Harsh, Maltese, & Tai, 2011; Laursen et al., 2010; Lopatto, 2010). Similarly, URES experiences positively affect a student's self-efficacy, which enhances acquisition of knowledge and research skills (Adedokun, Bessenbacher, Parker, Kirkham, & Burgess, 2013).

URE Types: CURES, SUREs, ALUREs, and GERP

There are several established designations for UR experiences, ranging from those based on the teaching unit, such as Course-Based Undergraduate Research Experiences in Science (CURES), to those based on calendar timing and format of the offering, such as Summer Undergraduate Research

Experience (SURE). Some URES are based on the class scale, such as an Authentic Large-Scale Undergraduate Research Experience (ALURE); a discipline, such as the Geoscience Education Research Project (GERP); and the delivery format of the learning, such as the OURES discussed in this chapter.

CURES are course-based undergraduate experiences, distinguished from research internships by involving many students, having one instructor, where instruction occurs in a lab setting with all students undertaking research and student time investment being primarily during class (Auchincloss et al., 2014). The distinguishing dimensions that characterize a CURE when combined are: (a) use of scientific practices, (b) discovery of new knowledge or insights where the outcomes are not known to the instructor or student and novel questions are asked, (c) broadly relevant research that has meaning beyond just the course context, (d) collaboration among participants, and (e) revision is permitted on assignments (Auchincloss et al., 2014). One of the strengths of a CURE is the ability to scale research opportunities broadly to a large class (Curenet, n.d.).

A SURE is often structured as an internship. This acronym also refers to the Survey of Undergraduate Research Experiences, which has been used as a standard assessment tool to evaluate a student's experience in SURE programs (Lopatto, 2003, 2010). The distinct summer timing of a SURE is a potential benefit for some students because there are few competing academic interests, so attention is directed principally to the research endeavor. Mentoring (e.g., peer and instructor) and communities of practice are intensified during SUREs and are supportive of professional development toward careers (Lopatto, 2010; Sanford, n.d.).

ALUREs allow UR to take place in class settings of 30 or more students in a timeframe that would normally be devoted to a lab, or about 30 to 36 hours (Rowland, Pedwell, Lawrie, Toon, & Hung, 2016). The Biochemistry and Molecular Biology course, which was the basis of the ALURE concept (Rowland et al., 2016), applies a more liberal definition of *research authenticity*, centering on a student answering a question with no known answer and communicating the answer to an applicable audience (Allure Project, n.d.).

GERP is tailored to the distinctiveness of a particular discipline—in this case, geology. A GERP is a form of CURE intended to provide students in an introductory geology course with the opportunity to go through the research cycle from formulating a question to presenting results (Kortz & van der Hoeven Kraft, 2016). It does not require an original contribution to geology and uses prompting questions and regular checkpoint assignments culminating in a final presentation devoted to the steps of the scientific process. (See details at https://serc.carleton.edu/NAGTWorkshops/undergraduate_research/workshop_2014/activities/88699.html)

Best Practices and Quality Considerations: URES Versus OURES

Formulating strategies for online URES requires consideration of established best practices. The best practices in the literature for URES include the key areas of promoting research, implementing URES, instructional design, mentoring, assessment, and institutional support. These are each considerations for online URES, and OURES, as well. With few differences (e.g., those in the area of design) the challenges are the same.

Promoting Research

An incoming undergraduate student may have little understanding of or experience with authentic research beyond having written a research paper or carried out laboratory experiments as part of a high school course. Therefore, programs must introduce students immediately to what research is, the research cycle, and the value of URES (Wilson, Howitt, Roberts, Åkerlind, & Wilson, 2013). Likewise, students may be unaware of the power that honed research skills can provide to them as lifelong learners, so it is essential to promote research as a universal and marketable skill (Wilson et al., 2013). In addition, students should be made aware of how UR experiences and the competencies developed through them impact employability (Healey & Jenkins, 2009). Still, URES are not for everyone. Thus, despite the strong benefits for participants in UR experiences—including faculty—programs should identify and differentiate both faculty and students for which research is not a good fit because research done voluntarily has more positive outcomes (Chmielewski & Stapleton, 2009; Russell, 2008). How to do so without relying on self-reported interest is a latent area for research, as is readiness for URES as compared to OURES.

Implementation

Providing early research experiences is vital to ensure the success of more comprehensive UR experience efforts in upper division studies (Schneider et al., 2015). Supportive early research experiences (i.e., freshman and sophomore levels) can include introduction to research courses and introductory science courses that incorporate regular activities to create and solve problems (Graham, Frederick, Winston, Hunter, & Handelsman, 2013). An example of this strategy is provided by the University of Central Florida's Learning Environment and Academic Research Network (LEARN, see http://learn.fau.edu) where students take two semesters of research methods early on, tour working laboratories, write a proposal, and are involved in a lower division research apprenticeship (Schneider et al., 2015). Providing a steady amplification of research competence is an important scaffolding strategy. Departments should consider multiple-year strategies for UR experiences with increasing degrees of complexity and expectations for students (Healey & Jenkins, 2009). An example of this coordinated curricular planning strategy is the ecology curriculum at the University of Ontago. In this program, students are trained as researchers from the initial stages, with research expectations increasing each year capped by a third-year project that is potentially publishable (Wald & Harland, 2017). Each of these best practices can be as readily introduced in OURES as in URES.

Quality URES experiences at all levels and in both onsite and online formats is essential because poor research experiences can negatively affect a student's interest (Peters, Howard, & Sharp, 2012; Thiry et al., 2011). A critical element is appropriate engagement of students by the student's year, with corresponding research expectations, and clearly defined roles (e.g., colleague, technician, etc.) (Kremer & Bringle, 1990; Walkington, 2015). Healey and Jenkins' (2009) flexible framework has the following four categories demarcated in part by whether the learning around research is passive or active:

1. Research-led, passive learning about current research in the discipline by reading research articles and being exposed to staff research
2. Research-oriented, passive learning where research and inquiry skills focus on development of a hypothesis around a question
3. Research-based, active research involving final projects, capstone research, virtual conferences, or contributing to a website
4. Research-tutored, active engagement with faculty in analysis of current research articles or group research projects

In addition, for active research projects, students should develop a sense of ownership through their engagement, which can be evaluated by surveys designed for that purpose (Hanauer & Dolan, 2014).

As discussed, learning formats including CURES, SUREs, ALUREs, and GERPs are comparatively flexible, lending themselves to essential scaffolding in online and onsite environments (Laursen et al., 2010). Critical to each is a learning space for regular interaction with instructors and supervisors (Elsen, Wijnveen, Rijst, & Driel, 2008). Online-based research platforms have been implemented effectively, as with the eBiolabs system at Bristol University

(Healey & Jenkins, 2009) and the University of Adelaide's Web 2.0-based interventions system that facilitates quality research supervision by including discussion starters and resources on best practices (Laursen et al., 2010; Picard, Wilkinson, & Wirthensohn, 2011).

Although most of the focus and staging for STEM UR occurs in the confines of an institution's own facilities, abundant resources and platforms for research are also available off-campus and at a distance. For example, natural history collections in museums are becoming an important source of data for research as collections become digitized. Cook and colleagues (2014) describe how high-quality data representing hundreds of millions of specimen observation records in the Global Biodiversity Information Facility can be used for student-centered research on niches, habitat specialization, community composition, adaptation, species distribution, host-parasite dynamics, and so on (Global Biodiversity Information Facility, n.d.). Likewise, they describe the National Science Foundation (NSF)-sponsored program Advancing Integration of Museums Into Undergraduate Programs, which bridges collections, museum scientists, and educators to support student research on regional topics such as Florida flora and Alaskan archipelago island biogeography using specimen data and corresponding genomic information (Aim-Up!, n.d.).

Another promising online learning strategy to engage undergraduate students in authentic research is involving them in citizen science projects with opportunities to collect and analyze data. For instance, Citizen Scientists volunteering with the Monarch Larva Monitoring Project (MLMP) (University of Minnesota, 2016) monitor residential and natural areas during the monarch breeding stage to determine their densities per milkweed plant, and those contributing to the Great Sunflower Project plant sunflowers and record bee pollinator information through the growing season (Oberhauser & LeBuhn, 2012; see also Great Sunflower Project, n.d.). Hence, citizen science projects provide excellent opportunities for faculty to design data-driven and low-cost field learning experiences where students can develop and test hypotheses.

Remotely conducted research is another strategy for engaging students in UR at a distance. Remote research typically involves a student's use and control of a research institute's instruments, often in the context of an ongoing research project sponsored by the organization. Pallant, McIntyre, and Stephens (2016) report an example of undergraduate students conducting authentic oceanographic research through the NSF-funded Transforming Remotely Conducted Research through Ethnography, Education, and Rapidly Evolving Technologies (TREET) program (Concord Consortium, 2017).

The University of Rhode Island's Inner Space Center provides telepresence to deep ocean research being conducted by remotely operated underwater vehicles from the research vessel *Nautilus*, which allows students to develop their own research questions and data collection methods (Inner Space Center, 2018). The drawback of this type of remote research is that it is expensive and significantly limited in participation (e.g., eight undergraduates from three select universities) attributable to the functional capacity of the telepresence facility. In contrast, other remote experimentation undertakings have been designed to accommodate much greater numbers of student researchers. An example of an online lab and microscope environment that permits students to conduct research on the impact of light on living *Euglena* cells has been integrated with cloud computing and is highly scalable (Hossain, Bumbacher, Blikstein, & Riedel-Kruse, 2017).

Problem Identification, Learning Approaches, and Time Frames

Students should have sound guidance from their mentor on the field of research and initiation of a feasible topic that is valuable and centered on a research hypothesis (Peters et al., 2012). Likewise, students should also be assisted in the determination of research approach (e.g., field, lab, case study, or survey) and project dimensions (Peters et al., 2012), including time to become familiar with online or remote access equipment. Research activities should be modest in scope and able to produce results in the requisite time frame to complete the regular elements of the research cycle from data collection to dissemination (Laursen et al., 2010; Peters et al., 2012). Conversely, longer duration UR experiences have been demonstrated to be more beneficial for accomplishing student learning outcomes (Coker, Heiser, Taylor, & Book, 2017), so instructional design should emphasize depth of the experience and realistic proficiency expectations (Feldman, Divoll, & Klyve, 2013) regardless of technology employed.

Multilevel Entry Scaffolding

As with any well-constructed learning activity, scaffolded instruction in URES and OURES is an important best practice. The entry point for research should be the level at which the learner is capable of understanding, building on the skills a student already has acquired or can acquire during the research (Laursen et al., 2010). Students are adversely affected when faculty do not structure and scaffold activities well, when they assume too much about a student's abilities, or when they do not take a student's UR experiences effort seriously (Barker, 2009). An example of scaffolded instruction for UR using problem-based learning is described by Keebaugh, Darrow,

Tan, and Jamerson (2009) for an interdisciplinary UR methods course. The diverse learning employed through the course involved the following: (a) group study of a research article to identify the hypothesis, variables, and methods; (b) professors' explanations of their own research process; (c) class debate over research issues; (d) minilectures; (e) workshop days where groups collaborate on aspects of the assignments; and (f) group involvement in a final research proposal. The four modules of the research methods course are built with increasing levels of analysis, with each module structured to instill aspects of the scientific process.

Good Dissemination Options

Essential to authentic research in URES is that students complete the research cycle and disseminate their findings, a step for which the online environment is ideal. Dissemination can occur throughout the research cycle and can be framed around the concept of exposure, with measures of the level of publicness from the classroom to the world, the extent to which the dissemination goes beyond the taught curriculum, and the potential sphere of influence or impact the research may have on the discipline (Spronken-Smith et al., 2013). An abundance of dissemination formats can be employed in the instructional design of URES and OURES, including journal clubs, poster sessions, blogs, podcasts, online conferences, simulations, displays, wikis, guides, Web pages, standard publication options such as journals, and product launches common to engineering education (Spronken-Smith et al., 2013; Walkington, 2015). Undergraduate research journals are another emerging way for students to disseminate their research, as in the geography examples GEOverse and Geoversity (Walkington, 2015).

Communities of Practice and Collaboration

A community of practice is a group of people "who share a concern or a passion for something they do and learn how to do it better as they interact regularly" (Wenger, 2006, p. 1) and is a structure that thrives in the online environment (e.g., see the organization Association of Science-Technology Centers). Numerous studies have highlighted the importance and positive impact of engaging students in communities of practice while carrying out URES. Students report greater gains if coursework is supplemented with participation and membership in professional communities of practice (Graham et al., 2013; Hunter et al., 2006; Thiry et al., 2011; Vandermaas-Peeler, 2016). Likewise, the use of peer UR groups is another beneficial means to engage students successfully in scientific research, accelerate learning through collaboration, and promote gains in methodological and intellectual proficiency (Feldman et al., 2013; Laursen et al., 2010). A well-constructed OURES should facilitate collaboration opportunities for online undergraduate researchers through available virtual communities of practice (see more about online collaboration as a HIP in chapter 5, this volume).

Mentoring

Quality mentoring is indispensable in the UR experience process because it facilitates an efficient research cycle for students. Mentors are particularly impactful because of their disciplinary expertise and ability to guide students toward meaningful scientific questions that are unsolved, open-ended, and well defined (Laursen et al., 2010). Preferably, this is accomplished in a Socratic style to draw out the concept from the student. Mentors are also critical in assessing a student's learning development through the UR experience. Although the typical model for mentoring is for an undergraduate student to be linked to a subject compatible mentor when they undertake a UR experience, a stronger mentoring system is progressive, such as that described by Santora, Mason, and Sheahan (2013). In this example, mentoring support is provided from novice through expert level with corresponding and changing mentor responsibilities and activities. Research mentors for URES can come from a variety of sources, including faculty, graduate students, industry and scientific institution researchers, and student peers (Gentile, Brenner, & Stephens, 2017). Ideally, an OURES model will also incorporate an advanced collaboration between student researcher and support disciplinary mentors.

Assessment

Some studies suggest that the effectiveness of URES in meeting stated learning objectives requires additional study with different methodologies because previous research relied too heavily on self-reporting data rather than actual measures of student learning (Feldon, Maher, Hurst, & Timmerman, 2015), a position with which the authors agree. The general point of these critiques is that the assessment of URES should be multifaceted to examine the spectrum of desired student learning outcomes. Wilson, Howitt, and Higgins (2015) conclude there is often a misalignment between desired outcomes and assessment by faculty because of the strong emphasis on grading the final product of research rather than assessing student learning during the process. Therefore, programs and mentors should build URES and OURES assessment tools that evaluate the process of research, the components of science competence developed, a student's affectual development, in addition to the product of research. A useful list of measurement tools for URES and the domains they evaluate is provided in Gentile and colleagues (2017).

Institutional Support

Developing and supporting URES and OURES for large numbers of students is implausible without significant institutional and faculty buy-in as well as directed resources. For instance, faculty research needs to be supported internally and externally because faculty funding for research has a positive relation to student participation in research (Hu et al., 2009). This is not to say that it is unworkable to engage students in URES on a budget. In fact, Robertson (2016) describes how miniresearch proposals paralleling a grant were used to engage students in authentic research. The strategy was to use observations in a basic biology lab as preliminary data for a miniresearch proposal following the structure of a National Institutes of Health grant. Many faculty participate in mentoring in UR experience programs for personal satisfaction or a sense of obligation (i.e., stewards of the profession), even more than their own tenure and professional success (Barker, 2009). Nevertheless, numerous barriers affect faculty participation in URES and require attention by universities and departments, including faculty load, capacity, intensity, interest, rewards (i.e., credit for mentoring), student entry-level knowledge, administrative barriers, and funding and space issues (Hu et al., 2008; Lei & Chuang, 2010). College consortium efforts to support URES are another form of emergent institutional support. Gagliardi, Martin, Wise, and Blaich (2015) discuss how consortiums of college systems can work together to pool resources in support of undergraduate research, and Moran, Wells, and Aumen (2015) review how the Pennsylvania State System of Higher Education is coordinating efforts and the corresponding driving factors behind the effort that include cost savings. OURES may be a useful complementary approach to extend and economize UR opportunities, but they too will require strategic institutional support.

Conclusion

Although differences exist between online and onsite learning environments, there are extensive similarities between the best practices for URES and OURES. The major distinction between the two is the conventional presence of a local laboratory infrastructure for URES. The professional and personal benefits of URES and OURES are identical, as are mentoring, scaffolding, and dissemination best practices. Design and implementation vary the most, but even that variance is minimized as an increasing variety of research experiences are made possible through Web-based interfaces such as remote labs, online data sets (e.g., National Oceanic and Atmospheric Administration, National Aeronautics and Space Administration), and situating UR at local museums or through citizen science projects. Further, communities of practice collaborations reduce costs for onsite learning work as well as for online learning environments.

Current research clearly supports the effectiveness of UR experiences in STEM in promoting learning, retention, and promotion of STEM careers. Determining students and faculty who are best suited for OURES, assessing the effectiveness of such innovations for those persons, and assessing the process of learning beyond research outcome are areas awaiting investigation. Universities have begun to respond to the student desire for online learning in STEM areas and should now plan to make the most of OURES.

Key Takeaways

- Several different models of UR experiences can translate into the online environment.
- Involving students in citizen science projects as part of OURES in the sciences can be an excellent way for faculty to design data-driven and low-cost field learning experiences.
- Institutional support is critical to create successful OURES that are complementary to traditional UR opportunities.

References

Adedokun, A. O., Bessenbacher, A. B., Parker, L. C., Kirkham, L. L., & Burgess, W. D. (2013). Research skills and STEM undergraduate research students' aspirations for research careers: Mediating effects of research self-efficacy. *Journal of Research in Science Teaching, 50*(8), 940–951.

Aim-Up! (n.d.). *Advancing integration of museums into undergraduate programs.* Retrieved from http://aimup.unm.edu/

Allen, I. E., & Seaman, J. (2017). *Digital learning compass: Distance education enrollment report 2017.* Babson Park, MA: Babson Survey Research Group.

Allure Project. (n.d.). *The Allure Project.* Retrieved from http://www.alure-project.net/

Auchincloss, L. C., Laursen, S. L., Branchaw, J. L., Eagan, K., Mark Graham, M., Hanauer, D. I., Lawrie, G., McLinn, C. M., Pelaez, N., Rowland, S., Towns, M., Trautmann, N. M., Nelson, P. V., Weston, T. J., & Dolan, E. L. (2014). Assessment of course-based undergraduate research experiences: A meeting report. *CBE—Life Sciences Education, 13*(1), 29–40.

Barker, L. (2009). Student and faculty perceptions of undergraduate research experiences in computing. *ACM Transactions on Computing Education, 9*(1), n.p.

Chmielewski, J. G., & Stapleton, M. G. (2009). The undergraduate research experience: It's really not for everyone, students and faculty alike. *The Biologists' Forum, 80*(2), 53–58.

Coker, J. S., Heiser, E., Taylor, L., & Book, C. (2017). Impacts of experiential learning depth and breadth on student outcomes. *Journal of Experiential Education, 40*(1), 5–23.

Concord Consortium. 2017. *About us.* Retrieved from https://concord.org/about/

Cook, J. A., Edwards, S. V., Lacey, E. A., Guralnick, R. P., Soltis, P. S., Soltis, D. E., Welch, C. K., Bell, K. C., Galbreath, K. E., Himes, C., Allen. J. M., Heath, T. A., Carnaval, A. C., Cooper, K. L., Hanken, M. L. J., & Bond, S. I. (2014). Natural history collections as emerging resources for innovative education. *BioScience, 64*(8), 725–734.

Curenet (n.d.). *Welcome to Curenet.* Retrieved from https://curenet.cns.utexas.edu/)

Eagan, M. K., Hurtado, S., Chang, M. J., Garcia, G. A., Herrera, F. A., & Garibay, J. C. (2013). Making a difference in science education: The impact of undergraduate research programs. *American Educational Research Journal, 50*(4), 683–713.

Elsen, M. G. M. F., Wijnveen, G. J. V., Rijst, R. M. V. D., & Driel, J. H. V. (2008). How to strengthen the connection between research and teaching in undergraduate university education. *Higher Education Quarterly, 63*(1), 64–85.

Feldman, A., Divoll, K. A., & Klyve, R. A. (2013). Becoming researchers: The participation of undergraduate and graduate students in scientific research groups. *Science Education, 97*(2), 218–243.

Feldon, D. F., Maher, M. A., Hurst, M., & Timmerman, B. (2015). Faculty mentors', graduate students', and performance-based assessments of students' research skill development. *American Educational Research Journal, 52*(2), 334–370.

Gagliardi, J. S., Martin, R, R., Wise, K., & Blaich, C. (2015). The system effect: Scaling high-impact practices across campuses. *New Directions for Higher Education, 2015*(169), 15–26.

Gentile, J., Brenner, K., & Stephens, A. (2017). *Undergraduate research experiences for STEM students: Successes, challenges, and opportunities.* Washington DC: National Academies Press.

George, P. P., Papachristou, N., Belisario, J. M., Wang, W., Wark, P. A., Cotic, Z., Rasmussen, K., Sluiter, R., Sasco, E. R., Car, L. T., Musulanov, M. E., Molina, J. A., Heng, B. H., Zhang, Y., Wheeler, E. L., Shorbaji, N. A., Majeed, A., & Car, J. (2014). Online eLearning for undergraduates in health professions: A systematic review of the impact on knowledge, skills, attitudes and satisfaction. *Journal of Global Health, 4*(1), n.p.

Global Biodiversity Information Facility. (n.d.). *Free and open access to biodiversity data.* Retrieved from http://www.gbif.org/

Graham, M. J., Frederick, J., Winston, A. B., Hunter, A, B., & Handelsman, J. (2013). Increasing persistence of college students in STEM. *Science, 341*(6153), 1455–1456.

Great Sunflower Project. (n.d.). *The great sunflower project.* Retrieved from https://www.greatsunflower.org/

Hanauer, D. I., & Dolan, E. L. (2014). The project ownership survey: Measuring differences in scientific inquiry experiences. *CBE-Life Sciences Education, 13*(1), 149–158.

Harsh, J. A., Maltese, A. V., & Tai, R. H. (2011). Undergraduate research experiences from a longitudinal perspective. *Journal of College Science Teaching, 41*(1), 84–91.

Healey, M., & Jenkins, A. (2009). Developing undergraduate research and inquiry. *The Higher Education Academy.* Retrieved from https://www.heacademy.ac.uk/system/files/developingundergraduate_final.pdf

Holtz, J. K., & Downing, K. F. (2009). Valuing science and science learning as global capital. In G. Strohschen (Ed.), *Handbook of blended shore education: Adult program development and delivery* (pp. 89–102). New York, NY: Springer.

Hossain, Z., Bumbacher, E., Blikstein, P., & Riedel-Kruse, I. (2017). Authentic science inquiry learning at scale enabled by an Interactive Biology Cloud Experimentation Lab. In C. Urrea, J. Reich, & C. Thille (Eds.), *Proceedings of the Fourth Annual Meeting of the ACM Conference on Learning at Scale* (pp. 237–240). Cambridge, MA: MIT Press.

Hu, S., Scheuch, K., & Gayles, J. G. (2009). The influences of faculty on undergraduate student participation in research and creative activities. *Innovative Higher Education, 34*(3), 173–183.

Hunter, A., Laursen, S. L., & Seymour, E. (2006). Becoming a scientist: The role of undergraduate research in students' cognitive, personal, and professional development. *Science Education, 91*(1), 36–74.

Hunter, A., Laursen, S. L., & Seymour, E. (2008). Benefits of participating in undergraduate research in science: Comparing faculty and student perception. In R. Taraban, & R. L. Blanton (Eds.), *Creating effective undergraduate research programs in science* (pp. 135–171). New York, NY: Teachers College Press.

Inner Space Center. (2018). *Welcome to the Inner Space Center.* Retrieved from http://innerspacecenter.org/

Keebaugh, A., Darrow, L., Tan, D., & Jamerson, H. (2009). Scaffolding the science: Problem based strategies for teaching interdisciplinary undergraduate research methods. *International Journal of Teaching and Learning in Higher Education, 21*(1), 118–126.

Kezar, A., & Holcombe, E. (2017). Support for high-impact practices: A new tool for administrators. *Liberal Education, 103*(1), 34–39.

Kilgo, C. A., & Pascarella, E. T. (2016). Does independent research with a faculty member enhance four-year graduation and graduate/professional degree plans? Convergent results with different analytical methods. *Higher Education: The International Journal of Higher Education Research, 71*(4), 575–592.

Kilgo, C. A., Sheets, J. K. E., & Pascarella, E. T. (2014). The link between high-impact practices and student learning: Some longitudinal evidence. *Higher Education: The International Journal of Higher Education and Educational Planning, 69*(1), 509–525.

Kinkead, J. (2012). What's in a name? A brief history of undergraduate research. *CUR Quarterly, 33*(1), 20–29.

Kortz, K. M., & van der Hoeven Kraft, K. J. (2016). Geoscience education research project: Student benefits and effective design of a course-based undergraduate research experience. *Journal of Geoscience Education, 64*(1), 24–36. Retrieved from https://doi.org/10.5408/15-11.1

Kremer, J. F., & Bringle, R. G. (1990). The effects of an intensive research experience on the careers of talented undergraduates. *Journal of Research & Development in Education, 24*(1), 1–5.

Kuh, G. D. (2012). High-impact educational practices: What they are, who has access to them, and why they matter. *Peer Review, 14*(3), 19–29.

Laursen, S., Hunter, A., Seymour, E., Thiry, H., & Melton, G. (2010). *Undergraduate research in the sciences: Engaging students in real science.* Hoboken, NJ: John Wiley & Sons.

Lei, S. A., & Chuang, N. K. (2010). Undergraduate research assistantship: A comparison of benefits and costs from faculty and students' perspectives. *Education, 130*(2), 232–240.

Locks, A. M., & Gregerman, S. R. (2008). Undergraduate research as an institutional retention strategy: The University of Michigan model. In R. Taraban, & R. L. Blanton (Eds.), *Creating effective undergraduate research programs in science: The transformation from student to scientist* (pp. 11–32). New York, NY: Teachers College Press. Retrieved from https://www.scienceopen.com/document?vid=49174227-f0e1-4955-965f-48da5369ed54

Lopatto, D. (2003). The essential features of undergraduate research. *Council on Undergraduate Research Quarterly, 24,* 139-142.

Lopatto, D. (2010). Undergraduate research as a high-impact student experience. *Peer Review, 12*(2), 27–30.

Moran III, J. D., Wells, M. J., & Aumen, A. S. (2015). Making undergraduate research a central strategy in high-impact practice reform: The PASSHE journey. *New Directions for Higher Education, 2015*(169), 61–71.

Oberhauser, K., & LeBuhn, G. (2012). Insects and plants: Engaging undergraduates in authentic research through citizen science. *Frontiers in Ecology and the Environment, 10*(6), 318–320.

Pallant, A., McIntyre, C., & Stephens, L. A. (2016). Transforming undergraduate research opportunities using telepresence. *Journal of Geoscience Education, 64*(2), 138–146. Retrieved from https://doi.org/10.5408/15-118.1.

Peters, J., Howard, K., & Sharp, J. A. (2012). *The management of a student research project.* Aldershot, UK: Gower Publishing, Ltd.

Picard, M. Y., Wilkinson, K., & Wirthensohn, M. (2011). An online learning space facilitating supervision pedagogies in science. *South African Journal of Higher Education, 25*(5), 954–971.

Robertson, K. (2016). An authentic research experience for undergraduates on a budget: Using data from simple experiments to develop mini-research proposals. *Journal of College Science Teaching, 46*(2), 32–36.

Rowland, S., Pedwell, R., Lawrie, G., Toon, J. L., & Hung, Y. (2016). Do we need to design course-based undergraduate research experiences for authenticity? *CBE-Life Sciences Education, 15*(4), ar79.

Russell, S. H. (2008). Undergraduate research opportunities: Facilitating and encouraging the transition from student to scientist. In R. Taraban & R. L. Blanton (Eds.), *Creating effective undergraduate research programs in science: The transformation from student to scientist* (pp. 53–80). New York, NY: Teachers College Press.

Sanford. (n.d.). *Summer undergraduate research program.* Retrieved from http://www.sanfordresearch.org/education/undergraduates/sure/

Santora, K. A., Mason, E. J., & Sheahan, T. C. (2013). A model for progressive mentoring in science and engineering education and research. *Innovative Higher Education, 38*(5), 427–440.

Schneider, K. R., Bickel, A., & Shetlar, A. M. (2015). Planning and implementing a comprehensive student-centered research program for first-year STEM undergraduates. *Journal of College Science Teaching, 44*(3), 37–43.

Spronken-Smith, R., Brodeur, J., Kajaks, T., Luck, M., Myatt, P., Verburgh, A., Walkington, H., & Wuetherick, B. (2013). Completing the research cycle: A framework for promoting dissemination of undergraduate research and inquiry. *Teaching and Learning Inquiry: The ISSOTL Journal, 1*(2), 105–118.

Thiry, H., Laursen, S. L., & Hunter, A. B. (2011). What experiences help students become scientists? A comparative study of research and other sources of personal and professional gains for STEM undergraduates. *The Journal of Higher Education, 82*(4), 357–388.

University of Minnesota. (2016). *Monarch larva monitoring project.* Retrieved from https://mlmp.org/default.aspx

Vandermaas-Peeler, M. (2016). Mentoring undergraduate research: Student and faculty participation in communities of practice. *Transformative Dialogues: Teaching & Learning Journal, 9*(1), 1–10. Retrieved from http://eds.b.ebscohost.com/eds/pdfviewer/pdfviewer?vid=0&sid=8a1d2c12-4cdc-46f0-98d6-aecdef38bac5%40sessionmgr104

Wald, N., & Harland, T. (2017, February 7). A framework for authenticity in designing a research-based curriculum. *Teaching in Higher Education*, pp. 1–15. Retrieved from http://dx.doi.org/10.1080/13562517.2017.1289509.

Walkington, H. (2015). Students as researchers: Supporting undergraduate research in the disciplines in higher education. Retrieved from https://www.heacademy.ac.uk/knowledge-hub/students-researchers-supporting-undergraduate-research-disciplines-higher-education

Wenger, E. (2006). Communities of practice: A brief introduction. Retrieved from http://www.ewenger.com/theory/index.htm

Wilson, A., Howitt, S., & Higgins, D. (2015). A fundamental misalignment: Intended learning and assessment practices in undergraduate science research projects. *Assessment & Evaluation in Higher Education, 41*(6), 869–884.

Wilson, A., Howitt, S., Roberts, P., Åkerlind, G., & Wilson, K. (2013). Connecting expectations and experiences of students in a research-immersive degree. *Studies in Higher Education, 38*(10), 357–370. Retrieved from http://dx.doi.org/10.108 0/03075079.2011.633163.

Zee, M., de Boer, M., & Jaarsma, A. D. (2014). Acquiring evidence-based medicine and research skills in the undergraduate medical curriculum: Three different didactical formats compared. *Perspectives on Medical Education, 3*(5), 357–370.

8

DIVERSITY AND
GLOBAL LEARNING

Jesse Nelson and Nelson Soto

The higher education online learning environment is an increasingly important and relevant domain for students to engage critical studies of diversity and global learning. In the United States, more than 5.75 million students are now enrolled in online education courses at degree-granting postsecondary institutions. Remarkably, more than one in four postsecondary students are enrolled in at least one online education course, with half of online learners engaged exclusively in online education (U.S. Department of Education, 2016). With the percentage of online postsecondary students rising at about 4% annually, online education is now a significant teaching and learning modality for postsecondary education (Allen & Seaman, 2015).

The normalization of digital teaching modalities in postsecondary education has occurred while institutions of higher education have increasingly pursued inclusive teaching and learning practices. Inclusive courses are characterized by curricular, pedagogical, and assessment strategies that incorporate diversity of content and acknowledge diversity among learners. Inclusive pedagogy is largely supported in the literature as encounters with diversity, be they through collaborative coursework, classroom discussions, or casual interactions with peers who are different from one other. Regular encounters with difference are shown to lead to stronger outcomes in leadership skills and cultural and social understanding, critical elements for success in today's economy and society (Antonio, 1998). Notwithstanding the benefits associated with inclusive course transformations, the effort to develop inclusive classrooms often requires a new perspective on the traditional disciplinary canon and courage to attempt less comfortable teaching strategies.

Transformations of online courses face unique challenges, often related to distance and asynchronicity.

Although technology and diversity are two of the most salient postsecondary themes to emerge in the past 20 years, efforts to understand the interactive impact of these two themes have been limited. In essence, the current era of higher education could be considered the age of digital and diversity transformation; however, the lack of teaching and learning scholarship related to online diversity strategies is particularly noteworthy (Delahunty, Verenikina, & Jones, 2014; Hughes, 2007). To more fully understand the interaction of digital and diversity transformation in higher education, this chapter will explore the application of diversity and global learning within the context of online coursework. After reviewing the literature on diversity and global learning and online education as distinct domains, this chapter will explore specific strategies for successfully incorporating diversity and global learning in the online environment. Attention will be paid to common challenges inhibiting this work, with related solutions for successfully overcoming the challenges and facilitating high-impact learning.

Diversity and Global Learning as a High-Impact Practice

Within Kuh's (2008) often-cited work on high-impact practices (HIPs), the concepts of diversity and global learning are identified as significant components of a strong undergraduate experience. The intentional incorporation of diversity in a course has been shown to improve both learning outcomes and attitudes toward learning. Seifert, Gillig, Hanson, Pascarella, and Blaich (2014) found that interaction with diversity was associated with positive critical thinking gains and attitudes toward literacy outcomes. The findings were especially pronounced for students entering postsecondary education with lower critical thinking levels and less positive attitudes toward literacy. For online students returning to formal education after a significant break in their studies, positive gains in learning efficacy are fundamental to academic success.

In fact, encouraging findings link student success to inclusive online classrooms. Using National Survey of Student Engagement data limited only to a population of online students, Lundberg and Sheridan (2015) found that a supportive campus environment and the encouragement to engage with students different from oneself were the strongest predictors of positive learning outcomes. Outcomes included skill development improvements in areas such as writing, speaking, analysis, and problem-solving, as well as attitudinal gains in self-awareness, civic responsibility, and community development. Impressively, a supportive campus environment and engagement with diverse others accounted for about one-third of the learning gains.

Compelling connections between HIPs and student success have motivated many faculty and institutions to develop innovative approaches for expanding diversity and global learning opportunities. The Association of American Colleges & Universities (AAC&U) recently acknowledged such efforts:

> Many colleges and universities now emphasize courses and programs that help students explore cultures, life experiences, and world views different from their own. These studies—which may address U.S. diversity, world cultures, or both—often explore "difficult differences" such as racial, ethnic, and gender inequality, or continuing struggles around the globe for human rights, freedom, and power. Frequently, intercultural studies are augmented by experiential learning in the community and/or by study abroad. (Kuh, 2008)

Of particular interest in the AAC&U statement is the recognition that faculty and institutions can employ a variety of approaches when developing diversity and global learning opportunities; there is not a one-size-fits-all approach.

The AAC&U statement also highlights the expansive array of concepts incorporated under the umbrella of diversity and global learning. Beyond the traditional focal points of race, class, gender, and sexual orientation, diversity and global learning encompasses all types of difference, including religious, neurodiverse, and geographic identities.

Understanding how diversity and global learning as a HIP can be successfully incorporated into an online environment is critical to effective online teaching and learning. Considering the collective momentum to more fully understand best practice approaches to diversity and global learning initiatives, it is perhaps somewhat surprising that most scholarship on the topic continues to focus on the traditional classroom. Before reviewing inclusive strategies for online environments, it is important to consider what we know about online learners.

Considering Online Learners

Research affirms common perceptions of difference between online and face-to-face students. Within the context of continuing professional education programs, and applicable to many for-credit undergraduate online programs, online students tend to be older, enroll more frequently part time, and possess more life and work experience (Dabbagh, 2007). As a result, these students are more likely to be motivated by specific professional advancement pursuits (Dabbagh, 2007). Therefore, when considering the implementation of diversity and global learning in online courses, it may be helpful to build learning experiences with students' specific life/work experience and career connections in mind.

Patterns for effective online teaching and development of inclusive, online learning environments clearly emerge in the literature. Just as in traditional classrooms, active learning strategies, including student presentations, interactive discussion forums, and experiential learning opportunities, were directly associated with courses that exposed students to difference (Phillips, 2005; Reason, Cox, Lutovsky-Quaye, & Terenzini, 2010). Extending this line of inquiry, Ukpokodu (2008) explored the impact of pedagogical approaches that online students perceived as meaningful. After analyzing student feedback, five transformative pedagogical strategies emerged:

1. Written pre- and postnarrative inquiries. Written reflections not only provided an opportunity for students to apply course content to their own lives but also gave students voice while honoring life experience.

2. Written reading response papers. Having students synthesize course readings had the added benefit of facilitating engagement with course content.

3. Threaded discussions. Discussion, whether synchronous or asynchronous, enhanced the development of community and facilitated peer learning.

4. Partner-shared learning. Intentionally creating diverse partnerships helped students approach and make meaning of course content with multiple lenses.

5. Relationship, rigor, and relevance. Qualitative feedback confirmed the importance of relationship building, high expectations, and the ability to find personal meaning in course content.

Ukpokodu's (2008) research provides an important student perspective to our understanding of effective online learning and affirms the impact of community, student voice, and multiple perspectives. Similar to their on-campus peers, online students benefit from active learning strategies and academic support resources (Sandeen, 2012). Whether online or face-to-face, the key lies in providing pedagogical variety.

Liu, Liu, Lee, and Magjuka's (2010) study of online international students also highlights the importance of multiple engagement strategies. International students reported a desire for balance between synchronous and asynchronous activities and greater diversity in the content of case studies and methods of student assessment. In terms of communication channels, audio and video aids and the use of early term student informational surveys were highly recommended. Early term information surveys or discussion board posts can also meaningfully encourage community development and model inclusive pedagogy.

Challenges to Diversity and Global Learning in Online Courses

Notwithstanding higher education's general commitment to digital and diversity transformation, sizable challenges to these pursuits remain. Within an online environment, peer interaction, faculty interaction, and curricular transformation present, arguably, the most common and impactful impediments to high-impact learning. Unaddressed, these challenges will significantly inhibit the ability of postsecondary institutions to meaningfully improve the facilitation of online student learning.

Interaction among students is a critical element to encouraging cross-cultural dialogue and understanding of difference. Without frequent opportunity to engage with other learners, students may miss out on the types of interaction that have been shown to strengthen the higher education experience (Delahunty et al., 2014). If interaction with others is indeed fundamental to diversity and global learning, then the primary challenge facing online instructors may be facilitating student-to-student and student-to-faculty interactions. Beyond the typical instructional design concerns associated with asynchronous interaction, students may struggle to arrange their schedules to align with availability of instructors and peers. Online students may also have lower affiliation needs, making it less likely for peer learning to evolve spontaneously (Lundberg & Sheridan, 2015).

Dixson (2010) recognized these obstacles and sought to better understand how successful online students perceived their "in-class" interactions. Not surprisingly, the need for multiple methods of interaction and varied communication channels emerged as a fundamental finding. Interestingly, the students classified as "highly engaged," via Dixson's (2010) methodology, were twice as likely to view discussion forums as a means for interacting with their classmates. Instructor intentionality around student-to-student interaction and transparency about the pedagogical strategy may facilitate greater levels of peer learning and the formation of a vibrant learning community (LC).

Modes of peer and instructor interaction often differ considerably between face-to-face and online courses. Online learning environments are highly dependent on written communication while being nearly void of nonverbal communication (Andresen, 2009). Even in cases where synchronous video is incorporated, nonverbal communication is either entirely or mostly nonexistent. One result is that student participation can more easily be interpreted out of context or simply misunderstood. Students are more acutely at the mercy of their peers for latitude regarding the intent and meaning of their written comments.

Charitable classmate interpretations, however, may actually be less likely to occur because students have fewer opportunities to get to know their peers. Additionally, relationship building in those moments before and after class is less likely to occur, and visual cues (i.e., Do you bike to class? Do we have the same phone? What style of clothes do you like?) are significantly diminished. The lack of visual and auditory cues regarding the class community may also lead to deracialized and degendered discourse, as students strive to present as nonprejudiced (Durrheim, Greener, & Whitehead, 2015). With limited community and social cues, students may engage within a perceived safe zone of normatively acceptable interaction. When this occurs, instructors can acknowledge the phenomenon and provide curricular content that requires students to engage in critical reflection.

Although the availability of visual and auditory cues regarding one's LC may be limited in an online environment, the online environment may also increase the degree to which social media cues are sought. In instances where social media is explored to better understand one's classmates, students may have to process an overwhelming amount of information regarding their peers. Perceived or real statements of bias on social media can quickly become influential factors in how an online LC develops. Class discussion about this fact, as well as perceptions regarding professional etiquette in social media, may be educational and support the development of an LC.

With limited access to get to know one's classmates, in most online programs, and fewer opportunities to view their humanity, charitable assumptions for one's peers and a healthy recognition of the diversity of the class may not occur without intentional facilitation on the part of the instructor. Skillful instruction can address each of these potential challenges, but the instructor faces the additional obstacle of not being physically present. Not unlike a face-to-face classroom, a couple key steps can make all the difference when attempting this type of instructor facilitation. First, faculty can model the community values by transparently articulating the metacognitive process they employ. Metacognitive modeling may include a discussion board response such as, "I'm intrigued by your comments. I'm thinking I'd like to more fully understand your perspective and experience before commenting too much about what you've written. Please tell me more." In addition to metacognitive modeling, faculty can incorporate and encourage awareness-building into both synchronous and asynchronous activities. As students learn more about one another, they will be more apt to engage one another as a community. Often, asking students to communicate "why" they came to a particular conclusion and/or "how" their own lived experience applies to the content will build the desired awareness.

Second, through their own regular contribution to discussion boards, chats, and group work, instructors can also facilitate an inclusive community. Faculty can encourage students to be slow to judge and quicker to employ a practice of inquiry. This may be particularly helpful for peer interaction. Regular contribution further provides the opportunity to guide difficult conversations, prompt different lenses for considering a topic, address microaggressions as they occur, and mediate should differences of opinion become adversarial. Ultimately, these suggested facilitation strategies seek to give students voice, honor diverse student identities, model how to appropriately engage in difficult conversation, and build community. Some might simply call these strategies effective universal design, for they apply to on-campus as well as online classrooms, and they establish a foundation for transformational diversity and global learning for all students.

In light of higher education's commitment to online modalities and the need to infuse the postsecondary experience with diverse and global dimensions, creating diverse online experiences is of vital importance. Previous research has demonstrated that although diversity and global learning may appear in portions of some online courses, it is rarely integrated across the curricula of a course and almost never intentionally integrated throughout an online degree program (Sandeen, 2012). Reflective online instructors would be wise to ask why facilitating the development of inclusive online environments can be challenging.

Difficulty around community-building and class interaction contributes to the challenges surrounding inclusive online course design. These challenges may be more pronounced in online settings, where physical distance, unfamiliarity with technology, and overreliance on asynchronous interaction directly impact the LC. Fortunately for online educators, meaningful and highly accessible options are available for weaving diversity and global learning into the online classroom.

Faculty Development and Training

Without question, the role of the faculty member in facilitating digital and diverse transformation is paramount. Support and traning for faculty as they design curricular and pedagogical strategies and engage students throughout the term are critical to the success of online learning and cannot be emphasized enough. Few faculty will have prior experience with how to facilitate online community development, respond to microaggressions, or structure effective online peer learning. Institutional commitment to online teaching and learning will include faculty development and training prior to and throughout the academic term.

In her review of high-impact online strategies, Sandeen (2012) identified a number of institutional strategies for enhancing online teaching and learning. Because many online programs employ adjunct instructors, Sandeen (2012) highlighted the importance of ensuring accessible faculty training oriented toward all faculty groups. Among the suggested training topics, institutions would do well to provide faculty with a review of the research on HIPs, strategies for integrating all students into the online community, release time or additional funding to participate in training or program reviews, and a commitment to supporting regular program reviews.

Other recommendations for developing a meaningful culture of faculty support include cultural sensitivity and cross-cultural training (Liu et al., 2010), training on discourse facilitation skills (Hughes, 2007), and experience facilitating student interaction across differences (Reason et al., 2010). In short, faculty will benefit from enhanced awareness of good teaching and learning practices and corresponding opportunities to practice effective evidence-based strategies. Institutional commitment to comprehensive faculty training is foundational to faculty capacity to facilitate a transformative online learning experience.

In Practice: Diversity and Global Learning in Online Education

When considering some of the challenges facing effective implementation of diversity and global learning in online courses, the reflex may be to solve all the problems with online cohorts and/or hybrid models. Certainly, online courses structured around a cohort and/or hybrid model have enhanced opportunity to provide students longitudinal experiences with their classmates, multiple common experiences, and greater opportunity for developing relationships of trust (Nye, 2015). Cohort and hybrid approaches merit consideration whenever possible; however, they are not compatible approaches with a significant portion of online education. Many online educational programs and opportunities are developed with the desire to expand access to students who may be place-bound or in need of flexibility around the scheduling of classes. Cohort and hybrid models fundamentally reduce access because they require some face-to-face time and/or adherence to specific degree plan schedules. For that reason, this section focuses on effective teaching and learning strategies that can be adapted and applied to nearly all online course types.

Like other online teaching and learning objectives, diversity and global learning outcomes can be readily achieved through adaptation of evidence-based, face-to-face strategies. The following three online activities are ones we have personally used with success or witnessed their success in the hands of colleagues.

Community Scavenger Hunt

Our first introduction to this approach came in a hybrid geography course. As a capstone for each unit, students explored their local community in search of specific architectural artifacts. They uploaded photos of their discoveries, which prompted vibrant asynchronous discussion. Adaptation options for this strategy are endless. Students could interview small business owners in ethnic neighborhoods, delve into the history of a specific city lot, or search for graphical evidences of bias in their communities. The ability to upload photographs, GPS coordinates, and immediate reflections directly into the online classroom make this strategy highly accessible to an online educational environment. An important reminder is to consider student safety in the design of this activity; risk management considerations must be thoughtfully considered and addressed prior to launching the assignment.

International Partner Class

Feedback on international partner classes range from amazingly transformational to logistically nightmarish. Current technology tools allow online courses to engage university students at institutions across the globe in synchronous or asynchronous interaction (Buchanan, Wilson, & Gopal, 2008). We have seen some courses connect with an international classroom weekly, whereas others came together once or twice a term.

Videoconferencing with an international class, including a guest presentation from an international faculty member, streaming an international panel, or sharing a discussion board with an international class, has strong potential for providing the online student meaningful global learning experiences. In Kan's (2011) research, international partner classes effectively generated transformational interglobal (akin to intergroup) dialogue. The most pronounced positive outcomes occurred when synchronous videoconference experiences were structured around preparatory asynchronous learning activities.

The most frequent challenge to the implementation of international class partners relates to logistics. Finding an international partner, coordinating faculty and class schedules, accommodating time zone differences, and counting on the technology to work all add a new level to professorial angst. When successful, however, international partner classes can provide a global experience for students who otherwise may not be able to participate in traditional international education opportunities. Instructors can work with their institution's International Studies office to identify possible international partners where relationships already exist.

Jigsaw

In many ways, asynchronous learning is optimal for a jigsaw activity. The jigsaw concept requires each student to independently learn about a specific piece of a larger content puzzle (Aronson, Blaney, Stephan, Sikes, & Snapp, 1978). When students share what they have learned with the entire class, a more holistic view of the puzzle is formed. This strategy is excellent for exposing students to diverse content. Rather than drawing from a minimal number of sources, jigsaws allow faculty to incorporate readings and content from multiple perspectives. Jigsaw groups may be designed around only a few students at a time (each student would complete a jigsaw once or twice a term), or they may be focused on one or two specific topics during the term, in which all students participate concurrently.

The presentation of multiple perspectives provides students the opportunity to wrestle with multiple realities and supports their development beyond a dualistic worldview. The jigsaw approach has been most successful when we have created space for significant discussion (either synchronous or asynchronous) following the initial postings. Although it can be meaningful for a single student to study a narrow piece of the content, the greatest degree of critical thinking occurs when students grapple collectively with the diversity of content supplied by their classmates.

Conclusion

Higher education finds itself in the midst of a digital and diversity transformation. College students are increasingly turning to online courses, programs, and institutions to support their educational and professional goals. Additionally, the student body is becoming increasingly diverse, and postsecondary institutions are expected to provide for diversity and global learning as part of their educational outcomes.

Incorporating diversity and global learning into an online environment is a HIP, but it is not always easy to achieve. In her exploratory analysis of diversity within an online learning environment, Hughes (2007) identified three important paradoxes. Each of these paradoxes poses challenges to instructors seeking to integrate diversity and global learning within the online course. First, course structure (i.e., assignments, timing) provides the framework for students to develop a true LC; however, a strong community may come at the expense of individual diversity. Second, the development of social presence, through making one's identities explicit, may ultimately serve to create a feeling of identity incongruence for some students. Third, the rhythm of an online course may enhance inclusion for some while excluding others (e.g., timing of discussion board responses).

Although addressing these paradoxes is not easy, viewing diversity and global learning as a process, more than an outcome, is a helpful first step. Instructors can be transparent about the paradoxes and their orientation to the process. Additionally, students can engage in (and faculty can model) reflection regarding the LC and individual student identities.

A nuanced and flexible approach to online teaching and learning is more feasible when faculty-student interaction is an expectation of the course and when the LC is committed to a constructivist approach. Alternatively, courses where content is pushed unidirectional to the student will struggle to effectively incorporate diversity and global learning. Postsecondary institutions may be faced with having to choose between a course structure that allows for HIPs or that maximizes the scalability of a course.

Another potential challenge to diversity and global learning lies in the evolving norms surrounding online communication. Should it become increasingly acceptable to communicate prejudiced and discriminatory perspectives, instructors may face a more difficult challenge striking a balance between the development of a community and the presentation of individual identities. Inherent in this potential challenge is that the meaning associated with diversity and global learning may evolve to a point where instructors find it difficult to move the students beyond political rhetoric and deeply divisive culture wars.

Notwithstanding the paradoxes and potential challenges associated with the integration of diversity and global learning in online coursework, the impact on student learning is well worth the effort. As increasing numbers of students turn to online education as a means to support lifelong learning and professional development, inclusive online educational experiences will enhance equitable access to higher education and equip students to positively impact the world. Indeed, diversity and global learning has the power to transform the online educational experience as well as the communities in which students live.

Key Takeaways

- Faculty capacity to facilitate a transformative online learning experience relies on an institutional commitment to comprehensive faculty training.
- Diversity and global learning outcomes can be readily achieved online through adaptation of evidence-based, face-to-face strategies (e.g., see "Community Scavenger Hunt," "International Partner Class," and "Jigsaw").
- Diversity and global learning should be viewed as a process as opposed to an outcome.
- Inclusive online educational experiences can enhance equitable access to higher education and positively equip students to impact their surroundings.

References

Allen, I. E., & Seaman, J. (2015). *Grade level: Tracking online learning in the United States.* Wellesley, MA: Babson Survey Research Group and Quahog Research Group, LLC.

Andresen, M. A. (2009). Asynchronous discussion forums: Success factors, outcome, assessments, and limitations. *Educational Technology & Society, 12*(1), 249–257.

Antonio, A. (1998, April 13–17). *Student interaction across race and outcomes in college.* Paper presented at the annual conference of the American Educational Research Association, San Diego, CA.

Aronson, E., Blaney, N., Stephan, C., Sikes, J., & Snapp, M. (1978). *The jigsaw classroom.* Thousand Oaks, CA: Sage.

Buchanan, J., Wilson, S., & Gopal, N. (2008). A cross cultural virtual learning environment for students to explore the issue of racism: A case study involving the UK, USA and SA. *Social Work Education, 27*(6), 671–682.

Dabbagh, N. (2007). The online learner: Characteristics and pedagogical implications. *Contemporary Issues in Technology and Teacher Education, 7*(3), 217–226.

Delahunty, J., Verenikina, I., & Jones, P. (2014). Socio-emotional connections: Identity, belonging and learning in online interactions. A literature review. *Technology Pedagogy and Education, 23*(2), 243–265.

Dixson, M. D. (2010). Creating effective student engagement in online courses: What do students find engaging? *Journal of the Scholarship of Teaching and Learning, 10*(2), 1–13.

Durrheim, K., Greener, R., & Whitehead, K. (2015). Race trouble: Attending to race and racism in online interaction. *British Journal of Social Psychology, 54*(1), 84–99.

Hughes, G. (2007). Diversity, identity, and belonging in e-learning communities: Some theories and paradoxes. *Teaching in Higher Education, 12*(5–6), 709–720.

Kan, K. H. (2011). Meeting face to face = seeing eye to eye? Inter global dialogue via video conference. *International Journal of Education & the Arts, 12*(10), 1–24.

Kuh, G. D. (2008). *High-impact educational practices: What they are, who has access to them, and why they matter.* Washington DC: Association of American Colleges & Universities.

Liu, X., Liu, S., Lee, S., & Magjuka, R. J. (2010). Cultural differences in online learning: International student perceptions. *Educational Technology & Society, 13*(3), 177–188.

Lundberg, C. A., & Sheridan, D. (2015). Benefits of engagement with peers, faculty, and diversity for online learners. *College Teaching, 63*(1), 8–15.

Nye, A. (2015). Building an online academic learning community among undergraduate students. *Distance Education, 36*(1), 115–128.

Phillips, J. (2005). Strategies for active learning in online continuing education. *The Journal of Continuing Education in Nursing, 36*, 77–83.

Reason, R. D., Cox, B. E., Lutovsky-Quaye, B. R., & Terenzini, P. T. (2010). Faculty and institutional factors that promote student encounters with difference in first-year courses. *The Review of Higher Education, 33*(3), 391–414.

Sandeen, C. (2012). High-impact educational practices: What we can learn from the traditional undergraduate setting. *Continuing Higher Education Review, 76*, 81–89.

Seifert, T. A., Gillig, B., Hanson, J. M., Pascarella, E. T., & Blaich, C. F. (2014). The conditional nature of high impact/good practices on student learning outcomes. *The Journal of Higher Education, 85*(4), 531–564.

Ukpokodu, O. N. (2008). Teachers' reflections on pedagogies that enhance learning in an online course on teaching for equity and social justice. *Journal of Interactive Learning, 7*(3), 227–255.

U.S. Department of Education, National Center for Education Statistics. (2016). *Digest of Education Statistics, 2015.* Retrieved from https://nces.ed.gov/programs/digest/d15/

9

eSERVICE-LEARNING

Jean Strait and Katherine Nordyke

In the last 10 years, online teaching and learning have matured greatly, especially through the use of technological innovations. If educators can imagine a learning situation, then models, tools, and resources can be created to make it a reality. As we know, one of the ways student engagement can be enhanced is through the use of service-learning and more recently through a more specialized form of service-learning known as electronic service-learning or eService-learning (eSL).

eSL combines service-learning and online learning to enable the delivery of the instruction and service to occur partially or fully online (Strait & Sauer, 2004; Waldner, McGorry, & Widener, 2012). eSL allows students anywhere, regardless of geography, physical constraints, work schedules, or other access limitations, to participate in service. In addition to providing powerful technological tools for global community engagement, the core components of service, learning, and reflection may take a different form in eSL due to the online implementation. The service can occur through many possibilities that connect students with communities across the globe or in their own backyard. Many uses of technology for instructional purposes in eSL are emerging. The purpose of this chapter is to examine essential questions regarding eSL, highlight the four types of eSL, discuss technologies that can be used in eSL, and provide starting points for those who seek to use eSL as a teaching tool. However, before we can discuss eSL, we need to understand service-learning.

What Is Service-Learning?

The National Service-Learning Clearinghouse (2014) defines *service-learning* as a teaching and learning strategy that integrates meaningful community service with instruction and reflection to enrich the learning experience and contribute in a positive way to the community. Both the learner and community partner benefit equally from experiential learning that connects content to hands-on, real-world experience. Research shows that students involved in experiential learning are more likely to retain and use that information once they enter the workforce (Kuh, 2008). Furthermore, research conducted over the past three decades indicates a number of benefits and positive outcomes for students who completed service-learning-based courses, such as higher grade point averages, increased retention rates, increased critical thinking and problem-solving skills, and long-term commitment to community (Nordyke, 2015).

Although each service-learning experience is uniquely tailored to meet specific learning goals and community needs, several common elements are critical for success. Preiser-Houy and Narrete (2006) noted that high-quality service-learning contained each of these elements:

- Integrated learning
- High-quality service
- Collaboration
- Student voice
- Civic responsibility
- Reflection
- Evaluation

Service-learning provides students with real-world experiences that are frequent and meaningful while applying academic knowledge and skills in a variety of situations: civic responsibility, where students learn how they impact their community; collaboration, where students and community partners work together to solve real-world problems; and reflection, where students have the ability to connect their service experiences to the academic curriculum. In service-learning, reflection occurs before, during, and after the service-learning project. Service-learning is similar to other field-based practices and is considered one of the six pedagogies of community engagement (see Table 9.1).

Service-learning, characterized by deep interaction and hands-on engagement, is identified as one of the Association of American Colleges & Universities high-impact practices (HIPs) (Kuh, 2008). Service-learning can be both transformational (long-term sustained interaction partnerships are deeper and longer lasting) and transactional (completing a short-term task). Traditional service-learning experiences can be integrated into a course, offered as a course component, or delivered as a stand-alone component.

TABLE 9.1
Pedagogies of Community Engagement

Pedagogy	Examples
Community-based research	Researching and gathering information on areas of need as defined by a community
Service-learning	Connecting real-world experiences with academic goals; service benefits the community partner and the learning benefits the student
Deliberative dialogue	Well-planned, thoughtful discussions with topics and agendas; can be workshops, community meetings, even online open discussions
Internships	Practical application of theory learned in an academic setting but provided in a controlled setting for students to "try on" the profession
Activism	Increasing community awareness with advocacy through both public and media avenues
Volunteerism/ Community Service	Usually a one-time experience working on an important issue or need

Note: Copyright 2015 by Stylus Publishing, LLC. Adapted with permission.

Four kinds of service-learning implementation are prevalent (University of Arkansas, 2017). The first is direct service-learning, where students work face-to-face with community partners and directly impact those who receive services from them. As an example, nursing students and biomedical science preoptometry and premed students at Missouri State University (MSU) provide vision screenings for youths and adults whom might not otherwise have access to vision care. In the fall of 2015, these service-learning students screened more than 8,000 children, youths, and adults, of whom 11% were identified as having significant or potentially significant vision problems.

The second is indirect service-learning which focuses on larger community issues that show clear benefit to the community rather than the individual. Examples of this second kind of service-learning might include removing buckthorn as part of a science class or building low-income housing.

The third kind of service-learning is research based. Here, students might map traffic flow or translate important legal documents into other languages. They also learn how to conduct surveys and report results. Occasionally, indirect service-learning might be combined with research-based service-learning. At MSU, for example, students use their knowledge of software applications to assess and evaluate identified red flag issues in the community; through analysis with this software, they provide recommendations back to the City of Springfield, Missouri, to assist in addressing the problems/issues identified as red flags.

The fourth kind of service-learning is advocacy-based service-learning. This is where the student takes on the role of an advocate, educating community members about issues or needed resources. A powerful example of this type of service comes from a group of sixth graders one of the authors worked with who studied a particular area in Minneapolis with a high homeless rate. The students determined that an immediate need existed for public restrooms so the homeless population could care for their needs without getting arrested for public urination. They lobbied the city council and worked with a local sanitation department to get port-a-potties placed in high-traffic areas. The arrest rate dropped by 99% in a single month!

What Is eSL and What Does it Look Like?

Just as online learning can have many variations, so too can eSL. Implementation of eSL is more complex; both the content and delivery can vary. For example, with eSL, the instruction and service may be online, face-to-face, or a mixture of both. Waldner and colleagues (2012) developed a chart that shows traditional service-learning and Hybrids I, II III, and IV, also known as extreme eSL (see Figure 9.1).

Figure 9.1. Four emerging types of eService-learning.

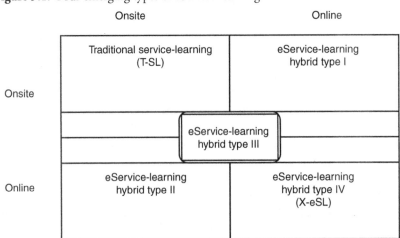

Note: Modified from Waldner et al., 2012.

Hybrid I

The key to Hybrid I is the intensive hands-on service experience, whether locally or globally paired with online delivery of the course content. As you look at Figure 9.1, you can see that traditional service-learning offers both the instruction and service on site. When eSL started at both Bemidji State University in 2004 and MSU in 2011, most of the work fell within the Hybrid I realm, where the instruction was online and the service-learning was still provided in real time at a face-to-face site. Students were all over Minnesota or Missouri and/or beyond and would individually set up service in their local area. Each student had a different location and a different community partner. Originally, that was quite hard to manage. Other examples of Hybrid I include offering an online course as part of a traditional program and having a local partner where students all come together to do service.

Nordyke (2015) describes a first-year experience course at MSU that is also a Hybrid I model. Students complete an online course with a 15-hour service-learning placement in their community addressing a need of their choosing. In this example, the local community is the community in which MSU resides.

Burton (2003) created a Hybrid I field experience model where the course was offered online and the experience was offered internationally for 10 days in Guatemala. Students created a product in the online course and then implemented that product on the trip.

Hybrid II

When defining a Hybrid II eSL experience, the content instruction is onsite (as in a traditional classroom), and the service is offered online. Often in a Hybrid II model, both the community partner and students reside in the same local community. One of the best examples of this model was created by Pauline Mosley at Pace University. Mosley teaches Web design courses in the Seidenberg School of Computer Science and Information Technology. She created a Hybrid II model that uses civic-based, problem-based, consulting-based, community-based action research (Mosley, 2015). Mosley taught Web design courses face-to-face while having students create websites for potential clients online. Students were required to meet online with community partners in a lab design format for one hour once a week for the duration of the 14-week semester. Students worked in teams of three or four with a community partner. Interestingly, more than 87% of the students were nontechnology majors. Over the course of five years, Mosley (2015) reports that 43 Westchester, New York, nonprofit organizations took part in the Web design process and benefitted from student service.

Hybrid III

The Hybrid III model integrates a combination of online and face-to-face instruction and service. Because it overlaps with each of the other four quadrants, it is perhaps the most common hybrid. What makes this model unique is the setup. One program at Bemidji State University, Distributed Learning in Teacher Education, met for face-to-face weekend classes with professors twice per semester, and the rest of the instruction was online. Students were responsible for arranging their own service placement and could individualize where they served. In this case, the instruction was both face-to-face and online, but the service was face-to-face only (Strait & Sauer, 2004).

The Each One, Teach One model created at Hamline University in 2006 is another example of Hybrid III. Hamline University students received face-to-face and online instruction. The Hamline students provided online tutoring and then later face-to-face instruction when the group traveled to New Orleans over the spring break and summer sessions (Strait & Jones, 2009).

Hybrid IV

Dubbed *extreme eSL* by Waldner and colleagues (2012), the Hybrid IV model has both service-learning and instruction completely online. What makes this model unique is the delivery and purpose. Often this model is designed to work more intensively with community partners and provides some type of tangible product that the community partner can use once the course is complete. Absolutely nothing happens face-to-face. With continued advances in technology, we are sure to see a growth in the implementation of this model.

Sue McGorry, chair of Business Administration at Desales University, teaches courses on marketing, research, and data mining. McGorry has been teaching online since 1996, and that depth of experience has led her to design several courses using extreme eSL. In her recommendations for using eSL, McGorry (2015) recommends four critical factors that need to be addressed when planning: length of course, student and partner availability, technology available to support the project (from both the institution and community partner), and partner logistics. Instructors will need to map out how they will direct the project and how to manage it online.

Mixed-Hybrid Studies

Sometimes eSL encompasses more than just one hybrid type. At the University of Georgia (UGA), for example, Paul Matthews (2015) used an existing service-learning course in education and transferred the instruction to an online format. He kept the onsite service for the course. This course is considered a Hybrid I.

In 2010, Matthews moved from education to UGA's office of service-learning. Now having access to more data, Matthews compared outcomes among Hybrid I, Hybrid III, and traditional face-to-face service-learning courses. He examined student growth in academic learning, moral reasoning/critical thinking, personal and professional skills development, and commitment to service. He found students in the Hybrid III models had significantly better outcomes than face-to-face in all four categories, and students in Hybrid I models outperformed those in face-to-face settings in three areas: academic learning, moral reasoning/critical thinking, and commitment to service (Matthews, 2015). In addition, when comparing Hybrid I and Hybrid III students, Hybrid I narrowly outperformed Hybrid III in moral reasoning/critical thinking. Waldner and colleagues (2012) note that with each of the structural differences of eSL, it is difficult to make comparisons with such radically different course or service outcomes. As eSL matures, the body of research around each of the hybrid models will grow and deepen.

What Are the Strengths and Barriers of eSL?

eSL already possesses the ability to offer all the HIPs that regular service-learning does. Research shows that eSL is a great way to teach twenty-first-century skills and make service-learning accessible to underserved populations. In many cases, eSL can eliminate costs normally associated with traditional service-learning for things such as travel or meeting space, reducing the overall carbon footprint of the population. Another benefit of eSL is that it can be specifically designed to optimize the learning and service of a specific content area, class, and community partner. In addition, eSL has the potential to outperform traditional service-learning because of its digital delivery, and eSL will enable service-learning to expand on a global level in a way that traditional service-learning has not. As technology continues to improve and our ability to find ways to use it increases, learning will not be confined to a single program or university, and student learning will be far more individualized through the multiple ways eSL will be utilized.

Little research has been conducted around the supplemental considerations for the creation and implementation of eSL practices, including technology challenges; difficulties sustaining three-way communication among the instructor, community partner, and students; and added workload. Although the number of colleges and universities that offer online and hybrid learning continues to increase rapidly, little is being done to determine the impact this growth will have on community engagement and service-learning. Some potential questions include the following:

1. What exactly is eSL and what does it look like?
2. How do I use eSL in my teaching/course?
3. What makes eSL different from other instructional approaches?
4. What are the strengths and barriers of eSL?
5. What essential technologies should be considered when constructing an eSL experience?
6. How does eSL affect the global expansion of community engagement to partners in countries where the instruction is not taking place?

Potential barriers do exist for eSL. When considering faculty, experienced online instructors may not know how to incorporate service-learning into their existing courses. Traditional service-learning instructors may be new to online learning and cannot translate what they do face-to-face to an online format. When instructors look for institutional help, they find that many institutions are not even thinking about any kind of systematic undertaking of eSL. In addition, technology could be a barrier. Different technologies and delivery/virtual systems may actually impede course delivery and collaboration with community partners. Institutions with limited technology will not be able to keep pace with larger institutions using eSL and thus will either not offer it or, worse, remove themselves from eSL opportunities altogether.

What Essential Technologies Should Be Considered When Constructing an eSL Experience?

Most traditional face-to-face service-learning experiences use some kind of technology component. From online readings to video chats with community partners, the options appear to be limitless. In online courses, what differs is communication; technology is the means of communication for the content and service. In traditional classes, the technology is more of a tool for completing tasks. Mihalynuk and Seifer (2003) examined service-learning activities and suggested uses for technologies (see Table 9.2). Examining this process in more depth, Table 9.3 reflects a hardware/software list that could be utilized in stages of the eSL process (Strait & Nordyke, 2015). Hardware is changing dramatically. It is envisioned that this list would be updated frequently to reflect newly available items.

TABLE 9.2
Service-Learning Activities and Technology Usage

Service-Learning Task or Activity	Example of Technology
Program management	Databases and course platforms
Community partner participation	Communication, discussion board
Curricular tools	Blackboard course platform, books
Community service	Posting on websites, communication
Reflection	Discussion boards, group work
Program evaluation	Online or paper evaluation

Note: Copyright 2015 by Stylus Publishing, LLC. Reproduced with permission.

TABLE 9.3
Technology Use in the Stages of eService-Learning

Stages of the eService-Learning Process	Hardware	Software or Function
Content delivery	Desktop computer, laptop, netbook, and tablet	Videos, e-books, YouTube, Internet, Blackboard, podcasts
Service delivery	Phone, desktop computer, laptop, netbook, and tablet	Creating digital media product for community partners
Communication	Phone, netbook, and tablet	E-mail, texting, videoconferencing, and social media
Data collection	Phone, camera, netbook, and tablet	Online surveys, mapping software, pubic surveys
Data analysis	Phone camera, netbook, and tablet	SPSS, free/open software application
Participant reflection	Phone camera, netbook, and tablet	Written journals, blogs, videos, podcasts

Note: Copyright 2015 by Stylus Publishing, LLC. Reproduced with permission.

How Do I Use eSL in My Course?

There is no doubt that taking on service-learning in an online class can be a daunting task. If you have never taught an online course, then you may want to teach it once or twice before you implement eSL so you are comfortable with the changes in your teaching. If you have taught online previously, then we encourage you to look at the purpose, standards, and community you wish to serve as you begin planning eSL. We would offer the same advice for instructors who are familiar with the online format but have never used service-learning. We would suggest checking with your service-learning or community engagement office on campus for ideas and suggestions. At MSU, a dedicated service-learning office works with faculty members to assist them in navigating design, development, and implementation, including needed resources, to assist in creating eSL courses. If your higher education institution does not have a dedicated service-learning center, you may want to consider partnering with a face-to-face instructor who uses service-learning so you can bounce ideas off him or her and get suggestions you may have never considered.

If you are someone who knows online teaching and has experience with service-learning, then we suggest reading *eService-Learning: Creating Experiential Learning and Civic Engagement Through Online and Hybrid Courses* (Strait & Nordyke, 2015). This edited collection includes tips and models that can serve as a template to get you started with eSL.

We often use the following steps to plan for eSL in our teaching:

Start small. Before you start an entire online service project, consider experimenting with ways in which students in your class could serve online. Sometimes students have full schedules and need to volunteer when they have time. Sites such as the United Nation's http://onlinevolunteering.org let students volunteer anywhere around the world online. The Community Corps also has availability for technology-savvy students to help non profits with their technology online. Visit at www.serviceleader.org/virtual for more virtual volunteering resources.

Consider service and delivery mode. What kind of service do you want students to do? Is it embedded in the course (integrated), is it a separate project linked to the course (component), or is the service independent (stand-alone)? Your institution may offer one or more of these methods of delivery. Next, evaluate your institution's course management tools. Do you have what you need to deliver the class the way you want to? Remember, you also have to consider Americans with Disabilities Act guidelines so your students can access everything. Also consider whether everyone can get to the community partner and access the building or electronic site.

Review the goals, skills, and abilities you want for your students. What skills and abilities do you want students to develop as a result of the eSL? Are you looking at twenty-first-century goals or are you looking at content or licensure standards that will be met as a result of taking your course? What are the goals of your course and how does eSL tie directly to those goals? Identify professional standards for your course and then clearly show students how those standards are met through eSL.

Determine the geographic location and then select community partner(s). Before students start anything, you need to have clear expectations from the community partner. What will students be doing? How long will it take? Do students have the time and skills to complete what the partner needs? Creating clear lines of communication and expectations up front will head off problems before they have a chance to begin.

Identify the number of service hours and project(s) students will be required to complete. List them in the syllabus and hold firm on this commitment. Research shows that for service-learning to be meaningful, students should complete at least 20 hours per term. You and the community partner should set these and agree on tracking and completion of student hours during the term.

Reflect, reflect, reflect. Whatever project or service you put in place, the key to a successful service-learning experience is providing ways to have students reflect and think critically about what service they are completing. Reflection is not limited to writing. Can students perform something? Can they do an oral report? Think outside the box to develop ways in which your students can show what they have learned. Most importantly, what will you grade? What meets a professional standard? What will deepen student skills and knowledge?

Consider conduct and liability. We all try to teach our students professional conduct. Be clear up front about what the community partner, university or institution, and academic program require of students in terms of behavior. We also like to address potential plagiarism here. Google is not a source! It is a tool used to find references and resources. Once found, that information needs to be referenced appropriately. None of us wants problems, but this will help address potential issues from the start. Liability is another important consideration. Are the students covered if something goes wrong with the community partner? What can and cannot be posted on live electronic sites, social media, or other course tools?

Conclusion

eSL is in its infancy, and we believe we have yet to fully realize its potential. We are excited to see what new ideas and programs will develop as more educators use it. Perhaps the most important feature of eSL is its ability to enable people to stay connected to issues and communities they are passionate about and want to contribute to. It gives people a way to serve when and where they want. We believe this gives new meaning to the term *local* in a global community. We look forward to helping this innovative new pedagogy grow and develop, and we hope you will consider giving it a try.

Key Takeaways

- eSL, associated with academic coursework, allows students anywhere, regardless of geography, physical constraints, work schedules, or other access limitations, to participate in experiential service-learning experiences, engage in opportunities to further career choices, and have an impact in communities.
- eSL has the potential to outperform traditional service-learning because of its digital delivery, and it will enable service-learning to expand on a global level in a way that traditional service-learning has not.
- eSL has the ability to enable people to stay connected to issues and communities they are passionate about and in which they want to contribute.

References

Burton, E. (2003). Distance learning and service-learning in the accelerate format. *New Directions for Adult and Continuing Education, 2003*(97), 63–72.

Kuh, G. D. (2008). *High-impact educational practices: What are they, who has access to them, and why they matter.* Washington DC: Association of American Colleges & Universities.

Matthews, P. (2015). Mixed hybrid: Hybrid I and Hybrid III eService-learning: Investigating the influence of online components on service-learning outcomes at the University of Georgia. In J. Strait & K. J. Nordyke (Eds.), *eService-learning: Creating experiential learning and civic engagement through online and hybrid courses.* Sterling, VA: Stylus.

McGorry, S. (2015). Hybrid IV: Extreme eService-learning. In J. Strait & K. J. Nordyke (Eds.), *eService-learning: Creating experiential learning and civic engagement through online and hybrid courses.* Sterling, VA: Stylus.

Mihalynuk, T. V., & Seifer, S. D. (2003). *Risk management and liability in higher education service-learning.* Scotts Valley, CA: National Service-Learning Clearing-house.

Mosley, P. (2015). Hybrid II: A model design for web development. In J. Strait & K. J. Nordyke (Eds.), *eService-learning: Creating experiential learning and civic engagement through online and hybrid courses.* Sterling, VA: Stylus.

National Service-Learning Clearinghouse. (2014, September 12). *A definition of service-learning.* Retrieved from https://gsn.nylc.org/clearinghouse

Nordyke, K. J. (2015). Developing an eService-learning experience for online courses. In J. Strait & K. J. Nordyke (Eds.), *eService-learning: Creating experiential learning and civic engagement through online and hybrid courses.* Sterling, VA: Stylus.

Preiser-Houy, L., & Narrete, C. J. (2006). Exploring the learning in service-learning: A case of community-based research project in web-based systems development. *Journal of Information Systems Education, 17*(3), 273–284.

Strait, J., & Jones, J. (2009). *Each One, Teach One program.* Retrieved from http://www.eric.ed.gov/ERICPortal/detail?acco=EJ853211

Strait, J., & Nordyke, K. J. (2015). *eService-Learning: Creating experiential learning and civic engagement through online and hybrid courses.* Sterling, VA: Stylus.

Strait, J., & Sauer, T. (2004). Constructing experiential learning for online courses: The birth of e-service. *EDUCAUSE.* Retrieved from http://www.educause.edu/EDUCAUSE+QuarterlyMagazineVolume/ConstructingExperientialLearning/157274

University of Central Arkansas. (2017, June 17). *Service-learning types.* Retrieved from https://uca.edu/servicelearningtypes

Waldner, L. S., McGorry, S. Y., & Widener, M. C. (2012). E-service-learning: The evolution of service-learning to engage a growing online student population. *Journal of Higher Education Outreach and Engagement, 16*(2), 123–150.

10

INTERNSHIPS

Pamela D. Pike

From a pedagogical standpoint, internships help advance students' abilities to synthesize, apply, and hone skills introduced during coursework that would otherwise be missed with the time and environmental limitations of classroom settings. The terms *internship* and *practicum* are interchangeable in some fields but imply that a student will practice what he or she has learned in a real or applied professional setting. Internships are required in some curricula and may serve as capstone experiences in fields such as education, medicine, engineering, and business. In 1993, George D. Kuh identified 14 categories of personal development in which students developed competency outside of the classroom. Internships can address outcomes in several of these domains. For example, well-designed internships help students to apply knowledge by relating theory to practice, develop vocational competence, and clarify a sense of purpose with respect to professional life beyond the formal educational experience (Kuh, 1993).

In reality, internships vary greatly between fields and institutions. Maertz, Stoeberl, and Marks (2014) identified 11 dimensions of internships that are frequently discussed in the literature. It should be noted that several of these components would provide students with different, dichotomous experiences depending on how the internship is structured. These dimensions include the following: graduate or undergraduate; paid or unpaid; full time, limited-term part time, or part time concurrent with coursework; academic credit or not; institutional or student-arranged internship; clarity in duties and evaluation or more opaque, with evolving expectations; project- or job-based format; faculty mentor or not; and implied opportunity for continued employment or not. Although the types of internships and experiences of students can vary greatly, researchers suggest that the most effective internships feature (a) a faculty mentor/

internship coordinator who sets parameters for the learning experience and evaluates student outcomes; (b) a site supervisor who provides regular feedback; (c) clearly defined learning goals; and (d) a means for the student to reflect, with guidance, on the internship, practicum, or fieldwork experiences (Dobratz, Singh, & Abbey, 2015; Gault, Redington, & Schlager, 2000; Goldsmith & Martin, 2009; Ruggiero & Boehm, 2016). The faculty adviser, site supervisor, and student are often referenced as the internship team (Goldsmith & Martin, 2009), suggesting that all parties must communicate and work together for optimal student development. Traditional internships, where students physically leave campus and work in a professional setting, have existed in the United States since 1906 (Thiel & Hartley, 1997).

Best Practices for Effective Online Internships and Student Outcomes

Online or virtual internships differ from traditional face-to-face programs. Presently, there is diversity in how online internships are structured. Some occur entirely online, whereas others use a hybrid approach. As technology and Internet speeds improve, more virtual internships are taking place completely online, where the student intern works from a computer at a remote location and communicates with the internship team via videoconferencing and the Internet (e.g., Pike, 2015a, 2017; Ruggiero & Boehm, 2016). Other online internships still require interns to complete fieldwork in person (face-to-face), but make use of an extensive online component that permits discussion and reflection with faculty or peers (e.g., Goldsmith & Martin, 2009; Low, 2008). In this chapter, I explore a range of online internships, from those that occur entirely in the online environment to those that include online components for the requisite coursework.

Although online internships are frequently discussed in the popular media, they are still in the exploratory stage in many professional programs throughout the world. Preliminary research findings regarding online internships suggest that as with traditional internships, faculty and professional supervisors (DeWitt & Rogers, 2009; Dotson & Bian, 2013), clearly defined goals (Conroy & Khan, 2009; Goldsmith & Martin, 2009), regular feedback (Goldsmith & Martin, 2009; Pike, 2017), and self-reflection (Goldsmith & Martin, 2009; Pike, 2015a) are important. Depending on the type of online internship, additional factors may need to be addressed to cultivate successful internship programs.

As noted, a rewarding internship experience depends on setting up effective learning experiences, including creating well-defined learning objectives, recognizable outcomes, time for the student to reflect, and clear communication among members of the internship team. Research about online internships (at both the undergraduate and graduate levels) has been published in fields as diverse as biotechnology, business, educational leadership, teacher education, music education, and physical therapy (see Table 10.1). Yet common threads or best practices that may be transferable to other fields have emerged. For a comparison of benefits, drawbacks, and other considerations of the best practices identified in literature prior to this publication, see Table 10.1. Best practices include

- activities for student interns (including orientation and preparation for the internship, and skill development through communication, reflection, collaboration, and projects);
- faculty teaching techniques (e.g., internship design, student evaluation, feedback techniques, and coordination with site supervisors); and
- general internship team needs (related to training for intern supervision, creating meaningful projects, or availing of appropriate technology).

In the following sections, I elaborate on each area. First, I explore best practices related to students' development and needs. These practices include the creation of online learning communities (LCs), development of communication and collaboration skills, and display of mastery through capstone or other internship projects. Second, I look at best practices from the perspective of faculty and intern supervisors, such as assessment, rubrics, feedback, and recommended institutional support so the internship team can learn about technology and maintain effective online LCs.

Student Development and Needs in Online Internships

Online Learning Communities: Reflecting and Co-Constructing Knowledge

Interns should expect to receive regular feedback from supervisors, faculty advisers, and even professional peers. However, it can be challenging for interns to make meaning of the evaluations and make connections between previous coursework and application in the field. Further, a fully online internship, or even an online component of a conventional face-to-face internship, may lead some interns to feel isolated from their academic LCs. Thus, it is critical that the faculty adviser, site supervisor, and

TABLE 10.1
Overview of Best Practices in Online Internships as Reported in the Literature

Best Practice	Benefits	Drawbacks	Tools/Support Required	Academic Field/ Educational Level	Author/Date
Online Support for Conventional Internships					
• Student reflection • E-journals • Discussion groups • Live virtual office hours	• Communicating with peers and finding answers to questions • Feedback from faculty (based on e-Journals and discussions)	• Interns did not avail themselves of office hours	• Faculty training to moderate discussions • Faculty time to monitor and respond to discussions	• Physical Therapy (Undergraduate)	Low, 2008
Online Internships					
• Student orientation and preparation	• Students understand expectations and objectives • Students understand how work will be graded or assessed	• May not be feasible outside of regular semester (or prior to internship)	• Space (in person or virtual) for orientation sessions • Technology for training sessions	• Leadership in Ed Admin (Graduate) • Business (not faculty supervised) • Music Education (Undergraduate) (Graduate) • Learning Design (Grad)	Goldsmith & Martin, 2009; Jeske & Axtell, 2016; Pike, 2015a, 2017; Ruggiero & Boehm, 2016

Best Practice	Benefits	Drawbacks	Tools/Support Required	Academic Field/ Educational Level	Author/Date
Student Skill Development					
• Communication with supervisor and faculty (video conference and phone)	• Student receives regular and specific feedback • Student has opportunities to ask questions • Student develops weaker skills and communication skills	• Scheduling with all internship team members can be challenging	• Faculty need release time or load credit for frequent communication • Site supervisor may need some incentive or compensation for extra work	• Leadership in Ed Admin (Graduate) • Marketing (Graduate) • Music Education (Undergrad/Grad) • Learning Design (Graduate) • Biotechnology (Graduate)	Goldsmith & Martin, 2009; Jeske & Axtell, 2014; Pike, 2015a, 2017; Ruggiero & Boehm, 2016; Conroy & Khan, 2009
• Peer/team collaboration	• Students learn to collaborate with superiors and colleagues	• Some projects do not lend themselves to teamwork	• Resources and time to train students to collaborate	• Marketing (Graduate) • Biotech (Grad)	Jeske & Axtell, 2014, 2016; Conroy & Khan, 2009
• Self-reflection • e-Journals • Discussion groups/boards • Pre and post internship self-assessment	• Communicating with peers • Finding answers • Feedback from faculty (based on e-Journals and discussion threads) • Personal growth	• Requires time for faculty to monitor discussions, respond to e-Journals, and guide development	• Faculty release time or load credit for preparation and work	• Biotechnology (Graduate) • Leadership in Ed Admin (Graduate) • Music Education (Undergrad/Grad)	Conroy & Khan, 2009; Goldsmith & Martin, 2009; Pike, 2015a, 2017

(Continues)

Table 10.1. (*Continued*)

Best Practice	Benefits	Drawbacks	Tools/Support Required	Academic Field/ Educational Level	Author/Date
• ePortfolios and capstone projects • Demonstrate development of discipline-specific skills	• Students work on long-term projects where they develop and assimilate professional skills	• Can consume a lot of time and take away from other coursework opportunities	• Several faculty may be required to oversee larger student projects deliver regular specific feedback	• Educational Leadership (Graduate) • Leadership in Ed Admin (Graduate) • Biotechnology	DeWitt & Rogers, 2009; Goldsmith & Martin, 2009; Conroy & Khan, 2009
Internship Team Preparation & Needs for Online Internships					
• Required online course concurrent with internship	• Students make connections between coursework and application of skills	• Not always feasible within the curriculum • Not possible with full-time internship	• Communication opportunities between supervising faculty and course instructors	• Leadership in Ed Admin (Graduate) • Music Education (Undergrad/Grad) • Biotech (Graduate) • Learning Design (Grad)	Goldsmith & Martin, 2009; DeWitt & Rogers, 2009; Pike, 2015a, 2017; Conroy & Khan, 2009; Ruggiero & Boehm, 2016

Best Practice	Benefits	Drawbacks	Tools/Support Required	Academic Field/ Educational Level	Author/Date
• Assessment guidelines and rubrics • Create and clearly communicate	• Students, faculty, and supervisors know objectives, goals, and how each will be measured	• Not all supervisors comfortable with giving formal and frequent feedback in this manner	• Requires pre-internship planning and preparation among internship team	• Biotech (Graduate) • Music Ed (Ugrad/Grad) • Learning Design (Grad) • Ed Leadership (Grad) • Library Ed (Grad)	Conroy & Khan, 2009; Pike, 2015a, 2017; Ruggiero & Boehm, 2016; DeWitt & Rogers, 2009; Dotson & Bian, 2013
• Regular and specific feedback online • Provided by faculty and internship supervisor	• Students know what needs improvement and can work on identified weaknesses	• Not all supervisors comfortable giving formal and frequent feedback • Time consuming	• Training for supervisors in appropriate feedback techniques • Time for faculty and supervisor to communicate	• Leadership in Ed Admin (Grad) • Biotech (Graduate) • Marketing (Graduate) • Music Ed (Ugrad/Grad) • Library Ed (Grad)	Goldsmith & Martin, 2009; Conroy & Khan, 2009; Jeske & Axtell, 2014; Pike, 2015a, 2017; Dotson & Bian, 2013

(Continues)

Table 10.1. (Continued)

Best Practice	Benefits	Drawbacks	Tools/Support Required	Academic Field/Educational Level	Author/Date
Technology and Other Support Provided by Institution					
• Institutional support for faculty • Time to build rapport with off-site team • Formalize communication • Prepare all work before internship • Communicate regularly with team throughout internship	• Team members prepared for internship experiences • Communication channels developed prior to and throughout internship • Better/more effective learning experience for students	• Requires substantial time prior to and during internship • May not be compensated or practical • May require special training to help parties learn to communicate effectively	• Release time for faculty members or appropriate load given to faculty for overseeing internship team • Appropriate trainers and resources for communication training	• Biotechnology (Grad) • Educational Leadership (Graduate) • Music Education (Undergraduate) • Learning Design (Graduate) • Marketing/Business (Grad)	Conroy & Khan, 2009; DeWitt & Rogers, 2009; Pike, 2015a; Pike, 2017; Ruggiero & Boehm, 2016; Jeske & Axtell, 2016
• Institutional support for site supervisor • Clear guidelines and expectations • Training seminar (for assessment and technology)	• All team members understand expectations • All have technological support for essential to the internship	• Not all team members have time for training	• Institution must have professionals and resources who can support training and technology maintenance	• Biotechnology (Grad) • Educational Leadership (Graduate) • Library Education (Graduate) • Business (not faculty supervised)	Conroy & Khan, 2009; DeWitt & Rogers, 2009; Dotson & Bian, 2013; Jeske & Axtell, 2016

program director work together to create online LCs where interns can reflect and make meaning of new learning and experiences during the internship. Best practices from effective online LCs can be transferred to online internship settings. For example, Palloff and Pratt (2005, 2007) suggest that effective online LCs are built when the people involved have effective guidelines about individual responsibilities to the group and access to technology appropriate for the task. Additionally, participants share goals, engage in collaborative learning where they co-construct knowledge, and critically reflect on and evaluate their work.

Online internship leadership teams (faculty advisers, site supervisors, and program directors), therefore, can design effective internships by clearly articulating goals, objectives, and evaluation methods for each student, socializing interns into working with the group, availing technology to increase communication between interns and other group members, and following through with evaluative procedures and effective feedback throughout the internship (Wade, Cameron, Morgan, & Williams, 2016). In addition to preparing and facilitating appropriate learning experiences online, the effective instructor actively evaluates student work, responds to discussions and reflections, creates new ways for students to scaffold material and elaborate on concepts, and encourages deeper student learning (Bowman, 2014). In short, online student outcomes are better if instructors and supervisors are actively engaged in guiding student learning, knowledge generation, and reflection (Conrad & Donaldson, 2011; Tallent-Runnels et al., 2006; Wade et al., 2016).

Communication and Collaboration

In addition to discipline-specific skills, internships often help students to develop collaboration, communication, and interpersonal skills (Dobratz et al., 2015). Students should be encouraged to improve competency in these areas regardless of the internship medium (online or face-to-face). However, designing effective online collaboration and communication can be challenging. Creating an online LC is one way to improve collaboration and communication. Using other online tools, such as those available in learning management systems (LMSs), has been helpful in fostering collaboration among students (Hanna, Glowacki-Dudka, & Conceição-Runlee, 2000). For example, during physical therapy and educational leadership internships, faculty recognized that having students contribute to common topics on discussion boards permitted them to communicate more frequently, share ideas, corroborate experiences, and pose questions raised during their internships with peers whom they no longer encountered daily (Goldsmith & Martin, 2009; Low, 2008). Those who participated in online discussion groups made more meaningful connections between prior coursework and internship experiences than those who did not. Additionally, faculty advisers have found e-journal reflections to be helpful in assessing student learning, assessing individual reflection, and addressing issues that students experience during internships (Low, 2008; Pike, 2015a, 2017).

In addition to discussion and online forum contributions, Conroy and Khan (2009) describe how they had interns complete weekly group projects online. Prior to the internship experience, they also created clear objectives for individual student work, rubrics for individual assessment of the online group projects, and discussion topics that encouraged students to develop effective reflection and peer interaction strategies. The interns experienced success in applying discipline-specific knowledge in both the internship and associated online work. Similar positive results were reported following preinternship and group project orientations for students (Goldsmith & Martin, 2009).

Comparatively, Jeske and Axtell (2014) found there were fewer positive outcomes for a graduate student involved in an unstructured internship without academic credit, where there were no group projects or regular communication among team members. In general, research from the fields of teacher education (Pike, 2015a, 2017), leadership development (DeWitt & Rogers, 2009; Goldsmith & Martin, 2009), design learning (Ruggiero & Boehm, 2016), and biotechnology (Conroy & Khan, 2009) reveals that online student interns who participate in well-structured internships with clear objectives, frequent feedback, and well-designed group projects learn to collaborate and communicate effectively. Students who collaborate effectively online demonstrate improved self-efficacy, knowledge elaboration, and critical thinking skills (Tseng, Gardner, & Yeh, 2016).

Capstone Projects and ePortfolios

Virtual internships or courses that integrate online learning and visible outcomes through the creation of ePortfolios or capstone projects have also proven effective in helping student interns develop requisite professional skills (Conroy & Khan, 2009; DeWitt & Rogers, 2009; Goldsmith & Martin, 2009; Pike, 2017). When such projects are connected with a concurrent course or requirement in the curriculum, they become more significant for students, which can improve learning. Although some projects may be overseen by the intern supervisor, they are ultimately evaluated by the faculty member. Projects and ePortfolios can be shared with peers through an electronic exhibition or other online forum (for more information on capstone experiences and ePortfolios as high-impact practices, see chapters 11 and 12, this volume).

Faculty and Supervisor Roles and Needs in Online Internships

As noted, in effective virtual internships, the internship team mentors guide the student to transfer classroom knowledge to real-world applications, develop skills associated with professional standards in the field, create meaningful projects, and reflect on learning. Careful planning before the internship begins and effective evaluation (including sharing feedback among all team members) throughout the internship leads to more trust among the internship team and more successful outcomes (DeWitt & Rogers, 2009). Conroy and Khan (2009) suggest that developing a personal rapport with off-site supervisors prior to the start of the semester should become a standard procedure for online internship programs. Both on- and off-campus stakeholders need time to establish guidelines for the internship, agree on evaluation procedures, and foster effective communication between themselves and, eventually, the intern.

Another design feature of online internships relates to students' engagement when they are not physically present but working with others online. It can be difficult for faculty and students to pick up on subtle visual, verbal, and other cues, particularly if communication is not synchronous. Scholars have suggested that to create online presence, online courses need to be designed to intentionally create a "dynamic interplay of thought, emotion, and behavior" (Lehman & Conceição, 2010, p. 7). There is some indication that learning becomes more poignant when online interns experience novel situations that require them to use their skills to engage with people from different places, from different cultures, or in different contexts (Pike, 2015a, 2017; Ruggiero & Boehm, 2016). When faculty advisers pose and respond to carefully sequenced discussion and reflection questions via the LMSs, students can process these new experiences, both individually and with peers. If students engage with others emotionally and build rapport during the internship, there can be a vibrant and creative interplay of ideas, and profound learning can occur.

Finally, student outcomes and the synergy between interns and off-campus agencies are better when faculty advisers carefully consider the placement of interns. Faculty might contemplate the virtual internship requirements and compare these with each student's strengths, weaknesses, and ability to work independently, as well as share work with peers, instructors, and the client online (Ruggiero & Boehm, 2016). When working in the online medium, successful interns are highly motivated, are effective communicators, and employ prior training with technology during the internship (Jeske & Axtell, 2016; Pike, 2017).

Recommended Institutional Support for Online Internships

Faculty and Supervisor Training and Support

Supervisors report that their ability to use the technology required for online internships and effective communication skills was important for positive virtual internship outcomes (Dotson & Bian, 2013). Faculty and off-campus supervisors who have not experienced working in the online medium may need support with developing internships that use appropriate technology effectively, designing projects that make the best use of the intern's time, and employing best practices in online learning and internships. Recommendations in the literature include improving communication between the site supervisors and supervising faculty; providing mandatory training for site supervisors; and creating clearer guidelines for the goals, procedures, and outcomes of the internships (Conroy & Khan, 2009). When the university supports the site supervisor and faculty in these activities, better outcomes have been reported.

Program coordinators, faculty mentors, and internship supervisors need time to agree on shared goals and objectives for the internship and to design suitable assessment rubrics that support student learning. Supervisors may complete some ongoing project evaluations, whereas faculty advisers provide follow-up feedback and assign grades associated with coursework or university credit. Ideally, objectives and evaluation procedures are agreed on in advance of the virtual internship experience, and these components relate to the stated goals for the project. Preplanning meetings provide opportunities for the on- and off-campus stakeholders to develop rapport, which leads to better communication among team members and more effective student feedback throughout the internship (Conroy & Khan, 2009; DeWitt & Rogers, 2009; Dotson & Bian, 2013). Effective communication can occur in various forms, including online videoconference, teleconference, informal video chats, written electronic messages, and even in person if possible.

Infrastructure and technological support are also important for the success of interns and their project assignments. Typically, this is implemented at the institutional level, but compatibility with off-site partners will need to be considered. Faculty, supervisors, and interns may require training with technology specific to the online internship, to the field, or to the campus

LMS (Pike, 2015a, 2017; Ruggiero & Boehm, 2016). Some universities have technology centers that support faculty, whereas others do not. However, there are many ways to provide technological tools and training for team members. For example, at one institution where specific technology is used in teaching synchronous online music lessons, instructors may choose from several options to increase their skills and knowledge about teaching in the online medium. They may participate in observation and evaluation of expert online teachers, test teaching strategies with peer-to-peer online teaching, avail themselves of information technology support during online teaching, use video and written materials created by the online teaching support staff and colleagues, and/or solicit support (through videoconferences) from expert online teaching colleagues across the country (Pike, 2015b). Note that faculty need not be physically on campus to take advantage of some of these training options.

Offering faculty and supervisors alternatives for their training allows them to choose an option that will make the most of their valuable preparation time while also meeting their specific internship needs. Once faculty have become adept at using the technology, they will need time to facilitate use of the tools by students (and possibly intern supervisors) prior to the start of the internship (Pike, 2015a, 2017). Some supervisors need to become familiar with student feedback and assessment models commonly employed in academia.

Faculty Recognition for Time Associated With Managing Online Learning

Instructors and supervisors might consider using emerging software and tools that could assist interns in meeting with peers online to assess and process their experiences (Jeske & Axtell, 2016). Regardless, many faculty advisers appear to use discussion boards, blogs, online forums, e-journals, and other tools available in LMSs to help students reflect, collaborate with peers, and make the most of their internship experiences (Bender, 2003). It has been noted, however, that daily or weekly management and oversight of these online tools requires more time than associated with preparation for traditional face-to-face classes, and this time may not always be compensated or accounted for in faculty loads (Conroy & Khan, 2009; Low, 2008; Ruggiero & Boehm, 2016).

Beyond online discussions and providing feedback on assignments, additional videoconferences and meetings with the internship team may be required to ensure effective communication (DeWitt & Rogers, 2009). In some instances, faculty members volunteer to serve as mentors during the internship, which may not be tenable at all institutions (Ruggiero & Boehm, 2016). Often virtual internships need to be piloted, on a smaller scale, before being integrated into the broader curriculum. The preparation, implementation, and evaluation of pilot programs require time and effort on the part of faculty and community partners. When working with individuals from different countries or cultures, additional time may be required to create understanding and develop effective virtual internships.

As program directors and faculty consider including virtual internships or adding online components to existing internships, they should communicate with administrators about additional preparation time and ongoing workload that such assignments present. Hopefully, administrators will thoughtfully consider and address how individuals will be recognized for such efforts. When these recommendations are shared through published literature, eventually there may be more consistency across institutions concerning faculty roles and rewards associated with virtual internships.

Conclusions: Best Practices for Online Internships

As with all aspects of distance teaching and learning, the most effective principles from traditional internships should be applied in the online environment. Additionally, it is important to embrace the emerging set of best online practices that is evolving as increased access to new technology and more remote locations make online internships viable. At present, we know that effective online internships are created and overseen by internship teams consisting of the faculty mentor, the site supervisor, and the student intern. Student placement in virtual internships should be considered by faculty who are familiar with each student's strengths and weaknesses, and by comparing these with the skill sets required by each potential site supervisor. Thus, communication between the site supervisor and faculty mentor should begin well in advance of the actual internship, and it should continue for the duration of the practicum.

Clear guidelines for the internship and evaluative procedures, including frequent, honest feedback, are critical for the intern's engagement, learning, growth, and success. These guidelines also contribute to the satisfaction of all parties involved. Creating efficient and effective communication pathways through various forms, such as online chat, e-mails, phone, and videoconference, is crucial. Communication among the intern, supervisor, and faculty mentor must occur regularly both before and throughout the internship.

The online platform and LMS used to facilitate an online internship should be selected to ensure that it meets the needs of all constituents. Ideally, interns, site supervisors, and faculty mentors can share files and engage in multiple forms of communication via the platform. Universities that offer technological resources and support for the internship team provide a critical service that has an immense impact on the overall experience and success of virtual internships. University administrators who recognize the increased workload and time demands placed on faculty members who oversee online courses and internships, and who make accommodations to teaching load, add value to the program because faculty will be able to engage with interns more effectively throughout the internship.

Many internships occur concurrently with a corresponding course, allowing the faculty member to ensure that the intern is remaining accountable, creating appropriate learning attributions, and synthesizing concepts correctly. The site supervisor and work-group members verify that knowledge and skills are being applied correctly. Ideally, interns can turn to peers, colleagues within the profession (with whom they meet and work during the internship), the site supervisor, and the faculty mentor to reflect on their learning, ask questions about issues that arise, develop skills required for work in the field, increase critical thinking, and begin to understand their potential roles within the profession. If such a course is not possible, then a preinternship seminar or training that outlines expectations and prepares students to use the requisite technology is advisable. A capstone project or ePortfolio, for which the student receives a grade at the conclusion of the internship, can also be beneficial.

Because internships provide students with opportunities to develop, elaborate on, synthesize, and generate skills and techniques that they will be required to use throughout their careers, more institutions and faculty members may implement online internships into their academic programs. Although the practice of engaging students in online internships is nascent, and much of the research has taken place with relatively small numbers of participants, the field will likely grow. Best practices should be shared within and across academic disciplines. If internships are thoughtfully planned, created, and executed, all stakeholders involved (institutions, community agencies, students, faculty members) enjoy positive experiences and reap benefits that will continue to impact the professional and broader community for many years.

Key Takeaways

- Effective online internships should be created and overseen by internship teams consisting of the faculty mentor, site supervisor, and student intern.

- Placement of interns in virtual internships should be carefully considered to ensure effective student outcomes and synergy between interns and agencies.
- Clear guidelines and frequent, honest feedback are critical for an intern's engagement, learning, growth, and success.

References

Bender, T. (2003). *Discussion-based online teaching to enhance student learning: Theory, practice and assessment.* Sterling, VA: Stylus.

Bowman, J. (2014). *Online learning in music: Foundations, frameworks, and practices.* Oxford, UK: Oxford University Press.

Conrad, R.-M., & Donaldson, J. A. (2011). *Engaging the online learner: Activities and resources for creative instruction.* San Francisco, CA: Jossey-Bass.

Conroy, R., & Khan, R. (2009). Integrating virtual internships into online classrooms. *Journal of Commercial Biotechnology, 15*(2), 97–112.

DeWitt, D. M., & Rogers, C. (2009). Online internships: A successful model. *International Journal of Educational Leadership Preparation, 4*(4), 1–6. Retrieved from http://www.eric.ed.gov/contentdelivery/servlet/ERICServlet?accno=EJ1071408

Dobratz, C. L., Singh, R. P., & Abbey, A. (2015). Using formal internships to improve entrepreneurship education programs. *Journal of Entrepreneurship Education, 18*(1), 96–110.

Dotson, K. B., & Bian, H. (2013). Supervision on site: A critical factor in the online facilitated internship. *The Quarterly Review of Distance Education, 14*(2), 51–62.

Gault, J., Redington, J., & Schlager, T. (2000). Undergraduate business internships and career success: Are they related? *Journal of Marketing Education, 22*(1), 45–53.

Goldsmith, L., & Martin, G. E. (2009). Developing and implementing an effective online educational leadership internship. *International Journal of Leadership Preparation, 4*(1), 1-12. Retrieved from http://www.eric.ed.gov/contentdelivery/servlet/ERICServlet?accno=EJ1068484

Hanna, D. E., Glowacki-Dudka, M., & Conceição-Runlee, S. (2000). *147 practical tips for teaching online groups: Essentials of web-based education.* Madison, WI: Attwood Publishing.

Jeske, D., & Axtell, C. M. (2014). E-internships: Prevalence, characteristics and role of student perspectives. *Internet Research, 24*(4), 457–473.

Jeske, D., & Axtell, C. M. (2016). Going global in small steps: E-internships in SMEs [small and medium-sized organizations]. *Organizational Dynamics, 45,* 55–63. Retrieved from http://dx.doi.org/10.1016/j.orgdyn.2015.12.007

Kuh, G. D. (1993). In their own words: What students learn outside the classroom. *American Educational Research Journal, 30*(2), 277–304.

Lehman, R. M., & Conceição, S. C. O. (2010). *Creating a sense of presence online: How to "be there" for distance learners.* San Francisco, CA: Jossey-Bass.

Low, S. (2008). Supporting student learning during physical therapist student internships using online technology. *Journal of Physical Therapy Education, 22*(1), 75–82.

Maertz, C. P., Jr., Stoeberl, A., & Marks, J. (2014). Building successful internships: Lessons from the research for interns, schools, and employers. *Career Development International, 19*(1), 123–142.

Palloff, R. M., & Pratt, K. (2005). *Collaborating online: Learning together in community.* San Francisco, CA: Jossey-Bass.

Palloff, R. M., & Pratt, K. (2007). *Building online learning communities.* San Francisco, CA: Jossy-Bass.

Pike, P. D. (2015a). Using a synchronous online teaching internship to develop pedagogical skills and explore teacher identity: A case study. *Journal of Music, Technology & Education, 8*(3), 227–242.

Pike, P. D. (February 4–7, 2015b). *Dismantling barriers to quality music instruction for retirees in rural America: A collective case study of six octogenarians taking music lessons.* Paper presented at the Suncoast Music Education Symposium, Tampa, FL.

Pike, P. D. (2017). Improving music teaching and learning through online service: A case study of a synchronous online teaching internship. *International Journal of Music Education, 35*(1), 107–117.

Ruggiero, D., & Boehm, J. (2016). Design and development of a learning design virtual internship program. *International Review of Research in Open and Distributed Learning, 17*(4), 105–120.

Tallent-Runnels, M. K., Thomas, J. A., Lan, W. Y., Cooper, S., Ahern, T. C., Shaw, S. M., & Liu, X. (2006). Teaching courses online: A review of the research. *Review of Educational Research, 76*(1), 93–135.

Thiel, G. R., & Hartley, N. T. (1997). Cooperative education: A natural synergy between business and academia? *SAM Advanced Management Journal, 62*(3), 19–24.

Tseng, H., Gardner, T., & Yeh, H.-T. (2016). Enhancing students' self-efficacy, elaboration, and critical thinking skills in collaborative educator preparation program. *The Quarterly Review of Distance Education, 17*(2), 15–28.

Wade, C. F., Cameron, B. A., Morgan, K., & Williams, K. C. (2016). Key components of online group projects: Faculty perceptions. *The Quarterly Review of Distance Education, 17*(1), 33–41.

11

CAPSTONE COURSES AND PROJECTS

Zapoura Newton-Calvert and Deborah Smith Arthur

C apstone courses and projects are high-impact educational practices, and although they take various forms and structures, they are
being employed at many colleges and universities nationally, often
as a culminating educational experience for undergraduates (Kuh, 2008).
Whether offered in departmental or general education programs, capstones
involve the integration of students' prior learning with an application of
that learning, employing a student-centered pedagogy, and resulting in
an individual or a group final project. These courses and projects can be
difficult and time-consuming, for both the faculty member and students,
with many moving parts to negotiate, facilitate, and manage. Add to those
difficulties the efforts and technological aptitude required for the creation
of and participation in an engaging and successful online learning environment, and many faculty and students may be reluctant to enter the
world of online capstone courses. However, the benefits of online capstone
courses are plentiful, as we will discuss, and provide outcomes that are
well worth the effort. Increased critical thinking skills, the ability to apply
one's education to real-world situations and problems, and increased problem-solving and communication skills are some of the benefits of effective
online capstone courses. Additionally, converting capstone courses to an
online format begins to address equity concerns, ideally allowing more
students access to this high-impact educational practice. After a review of
the literature, we will look closely at best practices and the various benefits
and challenges of online capstone courses.

The Landscape of Capstone Courses

Capstone courses are now a prominent feature of an undergraduate education. The capstone course grew in popularity as a culminating educational experience in the 1990s (Kinzie, 2013; Starr-Glass, 2010). Plentiful existing scholarly literature describes the history, development of, and use of the capstone in higher education (Hauhart & Grahe, 2015; Hunter, Keup, Kinzie, & Maietta, 2012; Kilcommins, 2015; Kinzie, 2013; Kuh, 2008; Starr-Glass, 2010). Currently, a large percentage of U.S. higher education institutions offer some type of capstone experience. Based on a review of 3 research studies, Hauhart and Grahe (2015) estimate that 81.1% of U.S. higher education institutions offer a capstone experience. Capstone courses are much more likely to be utilized in smaller liberal arts and private institutions, although some larger universities also utilize and even require capstone courses (Kinzie, 2013; Rhodes & Agre-Kippenhan, 2004).

The format of capstone courses can vary widely across institutions (Shaffer, 2013). However, some commonalities among capstones can be extracted and highlighted. Most capstone courses are designated as "culminating experiences" (Kuh, 2008, p. 11) of an undergraduate education, usually taken in the final year of undergraduate study. These experiences can take the form of a final project, performance, or paper; a fieldwork experience; or other culminating event (Kuh, 2008). Capstones, as culminating courses and experiences, are often used as an assessment of a student's undergraduate education (Berheide, 2007; Hartmann, 1992; van Acker & Bailey, 2011); they are used to assess student knowledge and capabilities, as well as being used for larger programmatic review (Berheide, 2007; Kerrigan, 2015; Kerrigan & Jhaj, 2007; van Acker & Bailey, 2011).

In many cases, capstone courses and projects provide opportunities for faculty and students to work together as *co-investigators of knowledge* (Baker, 1997; Holdsworth, Watty, & Davies, 2009). The majority of capstone courses are developed as disciplinary, project-based courses, whereas a smaller number of institutions have developed interdisciplinary capstone courses (Hauhart & Grahe, 2015; Kinzie, 2013). Discipline-specific capstone courses and experiences allow students to integrate and synthesize the knowledge gained in their fields of study and develop connections between their academic fields of study and the larger work world beyond college (Kinzie, 2013). Thus, capstones can be both a "cap" on an undergraduate education and a "bridge" to graduate school and employment (Starr-Glass, 2010). Interdisciplinary capstone courses, naturally, in addition to the integration of disciplinary knowledge, allow for building intellectual connections across various fields of study (Henscheid, 2008; Kerrigan, 2015).

Many senior capstone experiences encourage students to develop and practice "soft skills," such as critical thinking, communication, high-level organization and planning, presenting their work, and the skills to work with a teams across difference; all of which are important for success beyond college, in both graduate school and employment (Britton, 2013; Kuh, 2008; Thomas, Wong, & Li, 2014; van Acker & Bailey, 2011). Indeed, capstone projects and experiences can help create in students a disposition toward lifelong learning (Schermer & Gray, 2012). Further, capstones are not used only in undergraduate programs, although that is the central focus of this chapter. Many graduate programs also offer capstone courses, particularly in engineering, business, nursing, and even law (Datar, Garvin, & Cullen, 2011; Kilcommins & Spain, 2016; Todd & Magleby, 2005; van Acker & Bailey, 2011).

Literature on Online Capstones

Because the practice of online capstone development and teaching is still relatively rare in the academy, the body of literature dedicated to research on pedagogy and practice in online capstone courses is limited. Most examples in the literature describe courses in technology, science, and business administration programs, disciplines in which capstones in face-to-face courses have been long-standing. A major area of focus in the existing literature is addressing concerns about the ability of instructors or institutions to translate the unique components of capstone courses into online spaces and programs.

Research demonstrates that the primarily asynchronous nature of course delivery and discussion in most current online capstone courses, instead of being a barrier to embracing capstone characteristics, actually leads to positive outcomes in student learning. The inherent delay between instruction and student response allows students sufficient time and flexibility to digest and consider content, reflect deeply, and carefully craft questions and responses within discussion forums (Alstete & Beutell, 2016; Carmichael, Carmichael, & Leber-Gottberg, 2014; Khan & Hill, 2014). Gill and Mullarkey (2015) found that asynchronous online discussions were more complex than their face-to-face iterations and maintained the momentum and energy needed for deeper student learning. Ultimately, the asynchronous aspect of online capstone learning allows students to encounter their learning at a time and place that is most favorable to and accommodating of their own learning style and schedules (Carmichael et al., 2014). The flexibility offered through technology can also facilitate flexible and extended instructor and community partner presence (when capstones contain community partnership). Some research has also shown that online and hybrid capstone students have more positive learning outcomes in a variety of learning areas, including final products, than their face-to-face counterparts (Carmichael et al., 2014). Kilcommins (2015) notes that students in online capstone are allowed—and required—to take greater ownership of their learning than those students in a solely face-to-face classroom.

The ability of an online capstone course to facilitate growth in content knowledge and soft "soft skills," such as connecting with community partners, interpersonal communication, and teamwork, is also examined in the existing literature. De Young and Fung (2004) found that their capstone student math tutors were able to hone their response skills with more time to craft useful feedback for student learners. Britton (2013) also found that students were able to increase soft skill capabilities in online capstone courses.

In addition to interpersonal skills, community partnership can be a component of an experiential capstone experience. Tappert and Stix (2010) showcase a course "working on real computational needs of a community client" (p. 4), while Bojanova and Khan (2010) and Khan and Hill (2014) describe carefully scaffolded, successful pilot industry/client-sponsored projects with long-standing community partners in their online capstone courses. Arthur and Newton-Calvert (2015) also describe success with the community-based learning capstone model online and showcase successful case study models.

As Alstete and Beutell (2016) aptly state, success in online capstones fundamentally occurs when "we are not advocating technology because it is available but rather, technology techniques that are related to cognitive, affective, and behavioral learning outcomes" (p. 187). Although the literature up to this point is primarily optimistic, it is important that practitioners continue to assess and monitor student learning in online capstone models long term to more deeply understand what success looks like in these courses.

Developing and Supporting Online Capstone Courses

Nationally, the demand for online instruction has grown rapidly and consistently (Uijl, Filius, & Ten Cate, 2017). In 2014, the number of higher education students taking at least one online or distance learning course was up 3.9%, and 14% of higher education students were engaging in all of their coursework in a fully online format (Allen, Seaman, Poulin, & Straut, 2016; Uijl et al., 2017). Varied reasons account for this rapid growth in online higher education courses. As the landscape of higher education continues to experience a shift toward more cost-effective and flexible models, online learning can address a variety of student needs (Berger & Wild, 2016).

Rapid technological and digital advances and increasing access to technology are also making online learning more accessible than in the past.

Certainly, online courses can overcome the barriers of space and time (Broadbent & Poon, 2015). However, there is general agreement that simply translating traditional classroom learning models to an online format does not necessarily lead to rich and engaged learning opportunities for students (Carver, King, Hannum, & Fowler, 2007; Kidder, 2015; Verene, 2013). In capstone courses, which are heavily focused on the synthesis and integration of knowledge and on student interaction, the need for creative pedagogies and technologies to engage students is critical to the preservation of online capstone as a high-impact educational practice. Some would argue that it is not possible to create this rich and engaged learning environment using technology, and that, simply but definitively stated, "online education is the passing out of information, like passing out goods in a commissary" (Verene, 2013, p. 304). Although this statement may arguably have some merit when examining large online courses, such as massive open online courses (MOOCs), research indicates that small, student-focused online learning courses, including online capstone courses, can most certainly translate into rich and engaging online learning experiences for students and provide extended benefits beyond traditional classroom teaching and learning (Fox, 2013). Capstone courses—small, student-centered experiences—can provide a helpful model of successful and effective online learning (Carver et al., 2007; Fox, 2013).

Online Capstones at Portland State University

Developed in 1994 as part of a complete redesign of the undergraduate general education model at Portland State University (PSU), the capstone program at PSU is the largest community-based learning capstone program in the country and has been recognized nationally by prestigious organizations such as the Pew Charitable Trust, the Atlantic Foundation, *US News and World Report*, the Kellogg Foundation, and the Corporation for National Service (Kerrigan, 2015; Kerrigan & Jhaj, 2007). Strong institutional support for online teaching and learning, such as we enjoy at PSU, is essential for the success of online capstone courses and experiences (Arthur & Newton-Calvert, 2015; Carmichael et al., 2014). At PSU, on average, 10 capstone courses (small, interdisciplinary, community-based learning courses) are offered in a fully online format per term (Kerrigan, 2015).

The Office of Academic Innovation (OAI), our campus-wide teaching and learning center, provides robust instructional design and best practice assistance for online and hybrid instructors, among myriad other teaching and learning supports and services. Additionally, University Studies, the interdisciplinary general education program at PSU that offers the vast majority of capstone courses on the PSU campus, employs a digital coordinator internal to the department. The digital coordinator (a position currently held by Newton-Calvert, one of the authors of this chapter) provides pedagogical support for online instructors, with a focus on translating the highly engaged course model in University Studies into the online learning environment. In addition, the digital coordinator reviews and promotes the use of innovative technology, serves as liaison with OAI, and provides training to faculty and student peer mentors. This type of institutional support increases the success of these courses in terms of learning outcomes and likewise supports faculty willingness to teach online capstone courses, as well as their satisfaction in doing so (Marzilli, Delello, Marmion, McWhorter, Roberts, & Marzilli, 2014). Faculty attempting this work without that level of support are often left unsatisfied and frustrated, as are the students enrolled in their courses (Bolliger & Wasilik, 2009; Carver et al., 2007; Gilman, 2010).

Best Practices in Facilitation of Online Capstone Courses

The current literature combined with our experiences in PSU's capstone program allow us insight into what works best in online capstone course practice. Much of this simply involves best practices in online teaching and learning overall; other elements are distinctive to the kind of multimodal learning that takes place in capstone experiences. The Community of Inquiry Model (Garrison, Anderson, & Archer, 2010) serves as a useful tool to structure our exploration of best practices in online capstones. The elements of this framework are (a) cognitive presence, (b) social presence, and (c) teaching presence, designed as a model allowing for assessment and understanding of what takes place in student distance learning experiences.

Cognitive Presence

Best practices in cognitive presence include providing space for reflection, critical thinking, and selection or creation of course content (Garrison et al., 2010). Reflective activities are integral for strong asynchronous online learning (Riggs & Linder, 2016) and the integration of learning, a primary objective of the capstone course model. There are many spaces where reflection can take place—in discussion boards, via ePortfolio, or in weekly reflective papers or journals. In many PSU capstones, weekly reflections are an essential course component, with students using them as a space to make connections between their disciplinary learning on course content and their experiences in the community. Modes for weekly reflection range from simple document submission to an assignment Dropbox to PebblePad ePortfolio development over the 10-week term. PSU capstones often also require a culminating reflection that synthesizes and explores all of the learning from the term. In the Social Justice for K–12 Education capstone, for instance, this work takes the form of an ePortfolio page reflective of each student's personal or teaching philosophy related to social justice outcomes (for more about online ePortfolios as a high-impact practice [HIP], see chapter 12, this volume).

Also central to engaging students on the cognitive level is the way the content is chosen and experienced by students. One thoughtful, student-centered approach to this piece of online capstone learning is to use principles of Universal Design for Learning (UDL). Researchers see universal design as holding the ability to refocus away from individual user characteristics and instead toward the ability of the environment to narrow or extend access (Swain, French, Barnes, & Thomas, 2004). Providing multiple means of engagement is one of the UDL principles (Wakefield, 2011). In practice, this can look like giving "options for perception," for "language, mathematical expressions, and symbols," and "provid(ing) options for comprehension" (Wakefield, 2011). Best practice suggests that online instructors implement UDL revisions in their courses to reach multiple kinds of learners.

Framing it in a different way, Horn (2016) argues that student self-regulation of their own thinking is an indicator of persistence and success online: "Rather than increasing a number of external motivators to encourage the retention of online students, institutions should move to increase metacognition" (para. 10). Indeed, in a review of relevant studies examining self-regulated learning in online course success, Broadbent and Poon (2015) mirrored this thinking, finding that the self-regulated learning strategies of time management, metacognition, critical thinking, and effort regulation had a significant positive impact on student success in online courses. For capstone experiences in particular, incorporating opportunities for students to analyze their own learning can be an organic part of reflection activities or small-group discussion, as students integrate various aspects of their learning across their university experience.

Social Presence

For many institutions and faculty, thinking about the social presence in an online capstone course or experience is a formidable challenge. *Social presence* can be defined as the means by which communication happens in a course and how groups of students cohere and function as learning communities (LCs) (Garrison et al., 2010). However, any apprehension about the ability to create this social presence is often misplaced; the key is in the original structuring of the various components of the course (Gill & Mullarkey, 2015). An interactive and engaging learning space requires smart use of tools that allow for connection and engagement. Tools for connection among class members or small-group members, and between teacher and the class, are prolific, but the way in which the tools are utilized is of utmost importance.

To understand how to best structure the course and utilize the various technological tools, effective course assessment is essential. Online capstone faculty at PSU have been provided ample data based on each term's course assessment data and subsequent goal setting by our Assessment Coordinator and Digital Coordinator. In the 2016–2017 academic year, goals for online teaching and learning focused on increasing teacher presence and connection among students. As part of this process, we encouraged instructors to self-assess their interactivity and engagement using an interactivity rubric (Roblyer & Ekhaml, 2000). This type of rigorous assessment and reflection can help ensure that technology tools are being utilized in the most effective way for the creation of a strong social presence in online capstone courses.

In terms of actual tools, due to ongoing technological advances, we can move beyond the practice of using available learning management systems' discussion boards in innovative ways (Riggs & Linder, 2016). Online capstone instructors have experimented with the use of VoiceThread, an asynchronous tool that allows for video or audio discussion. Likewise, Flipgrid is another platform that allows for an asynchronous video presence. Visually connecting with one another and with the instructor, even asynchronously, helps students to feel connected in their online LC. There are also increased opportunities for synchronous discussion utilizing Google Hangouts. Encouraging group members to meet in real time, offering opportunities for small-group or one-on-one consultation with the instructor via video or phone, and meeting as a large group for live discussion on capstone topics or processes immediately and easily increases social presence and utilizes technology for what it does best.

Teaching Presence

Perhaps even more so than in a traditional classroom context, the instructor in an online capstone serves as a guide and mentor throughout the course and has a key role in supporting students as they integrate their learning; collaborate with a community partner or on a case study; and/or develop culminating research, writing, or other projects. Teaching presence is seen as a significant aspect of the online capstone course design and also as the means by which the instructor facilitates student learning in an online capstone course (Garrison et al., 2010). In online learning, successful teaching presence looks slightly different than it does in traditional face-to-face classrooms. This is what Riggs and Linder (2016) call "the architecture of engagement" (p. 1), a way of structuring a course to create clarity around communication and presence, in addition to other factors. UDL can provide a framework for this kind of course development in that it focuses on multiple modes for student learners.

Building rapport and teaching presence in online capstones requires a student-centered pedagogical approach (Kilcommins, 2015). This student-centered model is particularly appropriate at the capstone level because students are near the end of their undergraduate (or graduate) careers and have developed skills that benefit the LC as a whole. This approach can result in faculty feeling a loss of educational control. However, the instructor role remains vital to success in online capstone courses. A deeply engaged and flexible instructor is a fundamental aspect of a successful online learning experience. Much of the literature on instructor engagement focuses on the fact that faculty-student rapport and instructor presence and framing of course materials lead to higher levels of course retention and persistence (Ferdousi, 2016; Glazier, 2016; Songer, 2015).

Teaching presence can be built into online capstone courses in myriad ways. For example, a precourse toolkit containing the syllabus and an introduction from the instructor that is e-mailed to students can set students' minds at ease and prepare them for the course to come (Arthur & Newton-Calvert, 2015). Teacher presence can also be represented by offering multiple modes and clear guidelines around communication. Further, being available via text, instant message, phone, or synchronous video during specific time periods can give students the feeling that their instructor is present even if they do not engage in these points of contact. It is important to note that this type of teacher presence can undoubtedly feel demanding for the instructor. Faculty satisfaction is an important pillar of a quality course, and online capstone faculty who provide this type of access and interaction with students need to be supported by the institution in multiple ways, such as being recognized for the work they are doing, being granted release time to learn and explore supportive technologies and to develop significant online learning experiences, and being assured that their online teaching is fully recognized in the promotion and tenure process (Bolliger & Wasilik, 2009).

Benefits and Challenges of Online Capstone Courses

As mentioned previously in this chapter, online capstone courses provide numerous positive outcomes for students. Flexibility, the opportunity for deep reflection, the ability to take ownership over their own learning experience, and increased academic outcomes are some of the benefits for students (Alstete & Beutell, 2016; Carmichael et al., 2014; Gill & Mullarkey, 2015; Kilcommins, 2015). For faculty, teaching online capstone courses is satisfying for a variety of reasons. Many faculty feel positively that online courses allow for greater access to higher education and HIPs for traditionally underserved students (Bolliger & Wasilik, 2009). Many faculty also appreciate the ability of the online format to allow for rich and deep student-peer and student-faculty interactions (Bolliger & Wasilik, 2009). In a quantitative and qualitative study examining faculty attitudes around incorporating more technology into their teaching, Marzilli and colleagues (2014) found that many faculty agree that, "in general, technology use enhances student engagement and learning, improves instruction and provides convenience in course delivery" (p. 14). However, in this same study, knowledge of technology for both faculty and students was found to be a barrier.

Another significant challenge associated with online capstone courses and experiences is the negative perception that many higher education faculty continue to hold about fully online learning generally. Although student interest and enrollment in online courses continues to grow, many faculty and institutions maintain skeptical attitudes about the value of online learning (Gilman, 2010; Verene, 2013). Unfortunately, the perception remains among some faculty that online learning overall is less rigorous than face-to-face learning (Alstete & Beutell, 2016). These faculty perceptions can lead to a reluctance to do the heavy lifting of becoming savvy with the newest technology that enhances student learning in online courses. Additionally, many faculty perceive that teaching in an online setting will increase their workload beyond what a traditional face-to-face classroom experience requires (Bolliger & Wasilik, 2009). Indeed, development of successful online capstones with strong learning outcomes does require substantial effort around design and interaction with students (Carmichael et al., 2014). Rigorous practice of both formative and summative assessment in online capstone courses is important to keeping these learning spaces as HIPs.

Finally, the primary barrier to increased strategizing around best practices and successful models of fully online capstone courses is the need for a more substantial body of research on this course model and continued research on pilot models (Britton, 2013; Khan & Hill, 2014).

Online Capstones and the Issue of Equity

One of the greatest untapped benefits of online capstone learning is the opportunity to offer equitable access to capstone experiences to all students, regardless of factors such as their current location, family caregiving roles, learning style, or work schedule. Indeed, as mentioned, a strong motivational factor for faculty willingness to take on the workload of engaging online experiences is the fact that it provides access to a wider variety of underrepresented and nontraditional students (Bolliger & Wasilik, 2009). Looking to the small body of literature on social justice issues in online education, we can gather a sense of the practices that will actualize the liberatory possibilities of online capstones for learners facing the greatest barriers. In the in-depth case study, "Moving Applied Learning Online: Creating Engaged and Inclusive Spaces," researchers find the online course to be "a unique opportunity to encourage a greater population of students to engage in applied learning within a larger context. Essentially, [online learning] removed the boundaries and restrictions of the physical classroom in a way that also challenged students to think beyond the confines of the classroom" (DeVita, Lanier, Parker, Boersma, & Hicks, 2016, p. 158).

Across universities, however, the most underserved and underrepresented students often struggle in online courses, including capstones. The research identifies three reasons for this outcome: "technical difficulties," increased "social distance," and a "relative lack of structure inherent in online courses" (Jaggars, 2011, p. iii). Some departments do offer robust support for online learning, including Help Desk access for students; however, issues related to a lack of attention to social and instructor presence can cause a prohibitive sense of social distance. In addition, some of the largest technology gaps for students cannot be surmounted by individual instructors or students. It will require both institutional and instructor support for expanded access to updated technology and course design elements. Instructor/student presence is necessary for deep change to happen so online capstones can fulfill their potential to serve students equitably. Jaggars (2011) notes that providing opportunities for underserved students to bolster their online learning and study skills and to understand what online practices best serve these students are vital next steps in offering real and meaningful access to culminating experiences to all of our near-graduating students.

HIPs, such as capstones, must be expanded to reach underserved students (Kuh, 2008). Research on persistence in online courses supports this idea with a call to the academy to become attuned to the personal, institutional, and circumstantial needs of the online learner (Ferdousi, 2016). Although the community of inquiry model does address the personal level of the learner in some ways, the institutional and circumstantial needs of our potential online capstone students are not directly addressed. Additional research shows that these circumstantial or deeper personal needs of student learners are key to retention and success in online courses. In a recent study examining the global achievement gap among online learners, it was found that precourse social identity activities eliminated the gap and raised completion rates for learners in less-developed countries (Kizilcec, Saltarelli, Reich, & Cohen, 2017). Although the focus of this research was MOOCs, it would be worthwhile to examine these results further, specifically examining whether application of a similar activity would support students in the much smaller online capstone model. Feelings of alienation and decreased social belonging are barriers to equity of access to capstone experiences for all students.

The existing research regarding the means of strengthening support for low-income students, first-generation students, and students of color in online courses, including capstones, indicates that there are some promising practices, most of which require small and targeted prevention/intervention strategies, with strong results. Hiring student advocates to work with a caseload of students whom they support as they participate in their courses online is an excellent practice (Garcia, 2006). These advocates are not technology experts but instead individuals with skills around mentoring, university resources, and relationship building. In addition, Garcia suggests integration of a practice of peer review by instructors of each other's courses prior to teaching their courses and throughout the life of each course (Garcia, 2006). Jantz (2010) advocates for offering instruction on self-regulation for online success and incentives for students, including technology or financial incentives for completing training around success in online learning. Finally, in, "An Exploration of African American Students' Attitudes Toward Online Learning," Okwumabua, Walker, Hu, and Watson (2010) indicate that we must address the roots of the digital divide and lack of confidence in using technology to further academic learning and engage in more work around showing students explicitly how technology can be a tool for research, connection, and even social justice work. Work by Xu and Jaggars (2013) echoes this call to explore adaptability to online learning and to bolster all online students' skills in being online learners so we will see more equitable learning outcomes in these courses.

McNair's and Albertine (2012) review of Kuh's HIPs model sums up the urgency around offering online capstone experiences to our online learners via an equity framework: "Our society can no longer afford to reserve 'islands of innovation' for a select group of students while others, often students traditionally underserved, receive an education more suited to the industrial age" (para. 4). Because we can see enough models of best practices and success in online capstone courses, the call should be to continue to develop promising online capstone teaching strategies and models, as well as truly serve the students who need these online course offerings the most.

Conclusion

Although the research is still evolving, it is clear that capstones taught online can have the same positive high impact as they do in face-to-face classrooms. The asynchronous nature of these courses benefits reflective practice, allows for distinctive student ownership over the capstone learning and synthesis process, and provides space for flexible partnership with community. The literature is predominantly positive about the possibilities for online capstone courses, yet it is important to emphasize the lack of a substantial body of research on this topic and the importance of deeper examination of essential capstone elements (e.g., instructor presence, a sense of an LC, and course organization for diverse learners) as designed for online courses.

Because the practice of offering online capstones holds such great potential, it is important that both instructors and institutions dedicate energy to further research on these topics. If we truly value the significance of experiencing multiple HIPs as part of a successful higher education, it is important that we carefully construct these courses utilizing an equity lens for all learners, especially those most underserved and in need of flexible course offerings.

Key Takeaways

- Converting capstone courses to an online format can address equity concerns by allowing more students to access this high-impact educational practice.
- The need for creative pedagogies and technologies to engage students is critical to the preservation of online capstone as a high-impact educational practice.
- You can build teaching presence into online capstone courses by offering multiple modes and clear guidelines around communication.

References

Allen, I. E., Seaman, J., Poulin, R., & Straut, T. T. (2016). *Online report card: Tracking online education in the United States.* Babson Park, MA: Babson Survey Research Group and Quahog Research Group, LLC.

Alstete, J. W., & Beutell, N. J. (2016). Balancing instructional techniques and delivery formats in capstone business strategy courses. *Quality Assurance in Education: An International Perspective, 24*(2), 173–193.

Arthur, D. S., & Newton-Calvert, Z. (2015). Online community-based learning as the practice of freedom: The online capstone experience at Portland State University. *Metropolitan Universities, 26*(3), 135–157.

Baker, M. P. (1997). *"What is English?": Developing a senior "Capstone" course for the English major.* ERIC Clearinghouse. (ED411512)

Berger, D., & Wild, C. (2016). Turned on, tuned in, but not dropped out: enhancing the student experience with popular social media platforms. *European Journal of Law and Technology, 7*(1).

Berheide, C. W. (2007). Doing less work, collecting better data: using capstone courses to assess learning. *Peer Review, 9*(2), 27–30.

Bojanova, I., & Khan, R. (2010). Restructuring online capstone courses in partnership with industry for professional science master's (PSM) recognition. *Frontiers in Education Conference (FIE), 2010 IEEE,* F1C-1-F1C-3.

Bolliger, D. U., & Wasilik, O. (2009). Factors influencing faculty satisfaction with online teaching and learning in higher education. *Distance Education, 30*(1), 103–116.

Britton, G. S. (2013). *Using online project-based capstone experiences to enhance soft skills development* (Order No. 3566178). Retrieved from ProQuest Dissertations & Theses Global (1415918382). Retrieved from http://stats.lib.pdx.edu/proxy .php?url=http://search.proquest.com/docview/1415918382?accountid=13265

Broadbent, J., & Poon, W. L. (2015). Self-regulated learning strategies & academic achievement in online higher education learning environments: A systematic review. *The Internet and Higher Education, 27,* 1–13.

Carmichael, T. S., Carmichael, J. S., & Leber-Gottberg, R. (2014). Capstone courses: Student learning outcomes indicate value of online learning in pilot study. *Journal ISSN, 2368,* 6103.

Carver, R., King, R., Hannum, W., & Fowler, B. (2007). Toward a model of experiential e-learning. *MERLOT Journal of Online Learning and Teaching, 3*(3), 247–256.

Datar, S. M., Garvin, D. A., & Cullen, P. G. (2011). Rethinking the MBA: Business education at a crossroads. *Journal of Management Development, 30*(5), 451–462.

De Young, M., & Fung, M. G. (2004). Online mentoring with the math forum: A capstone experience for preservice K-8 teachers in a mathematics content problem-solving class. *Contemporary Issues in Technology and Teacher Education (CITE Journal), 4*(3), 363–375.

DeVita, J. M., Lanier, C., Parker, M., Boersma, J., & Hicks, R. (2016). Moving applied learning online: Creating engaged and inclusive spaces. *International Journal for Scholarship of Technology Enhanced Learning, 1*(1), 145–161.

Ferdousi, B. (2016, March 18–19). *Addressing student retention and persistence issue in online classes.* Proceedings of the 2016 ASEE North Central Section Conference. Central Michigan University, Michigan.

Fox, A. (2013). Viewpoint from MOOCs to SPOCs. *Communications of the ACM,* *56*(12), 38–40.

Garcia, M. (2006). *Supporting first generation online students. Online student support services: A best practices monograph.* Retrieved from http://www.onlinestudent support.org/ Monograph/firstgen.php.

Garrison, D. R., Anderson, T., & Archer, W. (2010). The first decade of the community of inquiry framework: A retrospective. *The Internet and Higher Education, 13*(1), 5–9.

Gill, T. G., & Mullarkey, M. T. (2015). Taking a case method capstone course online: A comparative case study. *Journal of Information Technology Education: Research, 14*, 189–218.

Gilman, T. (2010, February 22). Combating myths about distance education. *The Chronicle of Higher Education.* Retrieved from https://www.chronicle.com/ article/Combating-Myths-About-Distance/64299

Glazier, R. A. (2016). Building rapport to improve retention and success in online classes. *Journal of Political Science Education, 12*(4), 437–456.

Hartmann, D. J. (1992). Program assessment in sociology: The case for the bachelor's paper. *Teaching Sociology, 20*(2), 125–128.

Hauhart, R. C., & Grahe, J. E. (2015). *Designing and teaching undergraduate capstone courses.* New York, NY: John Wiley & Sons.

Henscheid, J. M. (2008). Preparing seniors for life after college. *About Campus, 13*(5), 20–25.

Holdsworth, A., Watty, K., & Davies, M. (2009). *Developing capstone experiences.* Melbourne, Australia: Centre for the Study of Higher Education, University of Melbourne.

Horn, S. (2016, November 7). Is neuroeducation the key to online retention? *eCampus News: Technology News & Innovation in Higher Education.* Retrieved from http:// www.ecampusnews.com/online-learning/neuroeducation-online-retention/?all

Hunter, M. S., Keup, J. R., Kinzie, J., & Maietta, H. (2012). *The senior year: Culminating experiences and transitions.* Columbia, SC: National Resource Center for the First-Year Experience and Students in Transition.

Jaggars, S. S. (2011). *Online learning: Does it help low-income and underprepared students?* CCRC Working Paper No. 26. Assessment of Evidence Series. New York, NY: Community College Research Center, Columbia University.

Jantz, C. (2010). Self-regulation and online developmental student success. *Journal of Online Learning and Teaching, 6*(4), 852.

Kerrigan, S. (2015). Sustaining change: Successes, challenges and lessons learned from twenty years of empowering students through community based learning capstones. *Metropolitan Universities, 26*(3), 11–31.

Kerrigan, S., & Jhaj, S. (2007). Assessing general education capstone courses: An in-depth look at a nationally recognized capstone assessment model. *Peer Review, 9*(2), 13–16.

Khan, R., & Hill, J. (2014). A conceptual framework for integrating industry/client-sponsored projects into online capstone courses. *Journal of Asynchronous Learning Networks, 17*(4), 113.

Kidder, L. C. (2015). The multifaceted endeavor of online teaching: The need for a new lens. In B. Hokanson, G. Clinton, & M. Tracey (Eds.), *The design of learning experience* (pp. 77–91). Gewerbestrasse, Switzerland: Springer International Publishing.

Kilcommins, S. (2015). Capstone courses as a vehicle for integrative learning. *Integrative Learning: International Research and Practice*, pp. 143–156.

Kilcommins, S., & Spain, E. (2016). "Deaths in Prison Custody" capstone course: Engaging final-year law students in service learning and public value. *Journal of Criminal Justice Education, 27*(3), 285–298.

Kinzie, J. (2013). Taking stock of capstones and integrative learning. *Peer Review, 15*(4), 27–30.

Kizilcec, R. F., Saltarelli, A. J., Reich, J., & Cohen, G. L. (2017). Closing global achievement gaps in MOOCs. *Science, 355*(6322), 251–252.

Kuh, G. D. (2008). *Excerpt from high-impact educational practices: What they are, who has access to them, and why they matter.* Washington DC: Association of American Colleges & Universities.

Marzilli, C., Delello, J., Marmion, S., McWhorter, R., Roberts, P., & Marzilli, T. S. (2014). Faculty attitudes towards integrating technology and innovation. *arXiv preprint arXiv:1404.4334.*

McNair, T. B., & Albertine, S. (2012). Seeking high-quality, high-impact learning: The imperative of faculty development and curricular intentionality. *Peer Review, 14*(3), 4.

Okwumabua, T. M., Walker, K. M., Hu, X., & Watson, A. (2010). An exploration of African American students' attitudes toward online learning. *Urban Education, 46*(2), 241–250.

Rhodes, T. L., & Agre-Kippenhan, S. (2004). A multiplicity of learning: Capstones at Portland State University. *Assessment Update, 16*(1), 4–5.

Riggs, S., & Linder, K. (2016, December). Actively engaging students in asynchronous online classes. *IDEA Paper, 64*, 1–10.

Roblyer, M. D., & Ekhaml, D. (2000). How interactive are YOUR distance courses? A rubric for assessing interaction in distance learning. *The Online Journal of Distance Learning Administration, 3*(2).

Schermer, T., & Gray, S. (2012). *The senior capstone: Transformative experiences in the liberal arts* (Final report to The Teagle Foundation). Retrieved from The Teagle Foundation website: http://www.teaglefoundation.org/Library-Resources/Special-Projects/The-Senior-Capstone-Transformative-Experiences-in

Shaffer, P. (2013). Five high-impact practices: Research on learning outcomes, completion, and quality. *Teaching Theology & Religion, 16*(2), 190–191.

Songer, S. (2015). Setting student expectations for distance learning. Handout. Carolina Distance Learning.

Starr-Glass, D. (2010). Reconsidering the international business capstone: Capping, bridging, or both? *Journal of Teaching in International Business, 21*(4), 329–345.

Swain, J., French, S., Barnes, C., & Thomas, C. (Eds.). (2004). *Disabling barriers enabling environments* (2nd ed.). London: SAGE.

Tappert, C. C., & Stix, A. (2010). The trend toward online project-oriented capstone courses. *Computers in the Schools, 27*(3–4), 200–220.

Thomas, K., Wong, K. C., & Li, Y. C. (2014). The capstone experience: student and academic perspectives. *Higher Education Research & Development, 33*(3), 580–594.

Todd, R. H., & Magleby, S. P. (2005). Elements of a successful capstone course considering the needs of stakeholders. *European Journal of Engineering Education, 30*(2), 203–214.

Uijl, S., Filius, R., & Ten Cate, O. (2017). Student interaction in small private online courses. *Medical Science Educator,* pp. 1–6.

van Acker, L., & Bailey, J. M. (2011). Embedding graduate skills in capstone courses. *Asian Social Science, 7*(4), 69.

Verene, D. P. (2013). Does online education rest on a mistake? *Academic Questions, 26*(3), 296–307.

Wakefield, M. A. (2011). *Universal design for learning guidelines version 2.0.* Wakefield, MA: Center for Applied Special Technology (CAST).

Xu, D., & Jaggars, S. S. (2013). *Examining the effectiveness of online learning within a community college system: An instrumental variable approach* (CCRC Working Paper No. 56). New York, NY: Community College Research Center, Columbia University.

ePORTFOLIOS

Jennifer Sparrow and Judit Török

Electronic portfolios, referred to as ePortfolios, are electronic representations of what students know and can do (Watson, Kuh, Rhodes, Light, & Chen, 2016). As this volume was in its planning stages, George Kuh and the Association of American Colleges & Universities designated ePortfolios as the 11th high-impact practice (HIP). ePortfolios differ in appearance and content depending on the ePortfolio platform and purpose; however, what they have in common is that they are digital, are owned and managed by the user, and include a collection of electronic evidence of, and reflection on, learning. Generally, ePortfolios are grouped into three categories: learning or developmental portfolios, which are more tentative works-in-progress; assessment portfolios, which encourage organizing the evidence of learning around certain outcomes or competencies; and showcase or career portfolios, which highlight the most polished work. Regardless of the diversity in style and function, the use of ePortfolios as an educational practice engages learners and improves their performance.

Kuh and others argue that HIPs have "a cumulative effect" (Finley & McNair, 2013), meaning that the power of a HIP strengthens when it is deployed in concert with other HIPs (Watson et al., 2016). In *Ensuring Quality & Taking High-Impact Practices to Scale*, Kuh and O'Donnell (2013) identify eight "Key Elements" of HIPs, such as, "opportunities to discover the relevance of learning through real world applications" and "periodic, structured opportunities to reflect on and integrate learning" (p. 10). Considering ePortfolios in this light reveals how they function not only as a HIP in themselves but also as a nexus for other HIPs, providing a space for connection and reflection on learning experiences. Indeed, in their editorial, "ePortfolios: The Eleventh High Impact Practice," Watson and colleagues (2016) argue that "ePortfolios may be the most impactful when thought of and employed as a meta-HIP" (p. 67), connecting and amplifying the power of other HIPs.

Put differently, as with the other 10 HIPs, "when done well and with considered thought and implementation, ePortfolios lead to deeper student learning, especially for traditionally under-served populations of learners" (Watson et al., 2016, p. 66). Well-crafted ePortfolios provide students with a longitudinal and portable online space in which they can store artifacts of their learning and share their reflections with teachers, advisers, peers, and prospective employers. ePortfolios, as authentic representations of learning, serve as more than just an enhancement to an academic transcript; they encourage ongoing processes of reflection, integration, and collaboration. In this way, we see the expansion of ePortfolios being especially relevant for the online learning community (LC).

The application of ePortfolios in the online space holds particular significance for the growing number of nontraditional learners. Fitting HIPs into the already crowded lives of online adult learners poses a challenge as they juggle a host of other nonacademic responsibilities such as children, partners, extended family, and full-time employment. As a virtual space that exists outside of the temporal constraints of traditional classrooms, ePortfolios are ideally positioned to fulfill what Scobey (2016) called the "design imperative" to seek new ways to provide inclusive excellence for this "marginalized majority." Project-based "signature work," such as an ePortfolio, prompts learners to make connections and articulate their learning while also providing opportunities to showcase and integrate the lessons from their school work and lived experiences (Scobey, 2016).

Done well, ePortfolios in fully online programs can help bring together the disparate learning experiences that online adult degree completers who have already "swirled" (Adelman, 1992) through multiple institutions bring with them. Done poorly, the ePortfolio can become just another tool, another online space, resented as busywork. Sophisticated integrative ePortfolio practice has been shown to have significant success for student learning (Eynon, Gambino, & Török, 2014). Data collected from the Connect to Learning (C2L)[1] research project suggests that ePortfolio pedagogies informed by reflection help students link different parts of their learning and connect their own learning to others. They are also more likely to engage in higher order thinking, integrative thinking, and other high-impact behaviors (Eynon et al., 2014). However, the many ways that a "sophisticated ePortfolio" design manifests itself in various learning environments and modalities is a question that continues to puzzle many educators, even more so in the online environment, where ePortfolio design intersects with instructional design of the learning management system (LMS).

In this chapter, we discuss the challenges and benefits of ePortfolios in fully online learning environments and pose recommendations for implementation and support, using examples drawn from our ePortfolio practice at the City University of New York School of Professional Studies (CUNY SPS) where ePortfolios have been used in fully online undergraduate and graduate programs since 2008.

ePortfolios as a Remedy to Learning Management System Fragmentation

The special challenges that online learning environments present are well documented. The two most pressing issues are connectedness and communication. Because learning is a social process, online students often feel isolated and disconnected (Bollinger & Shepherd, 2010). Despite its promise of agility and 24/7 connectivity, online learning can be inflexible and isolating, largely due to the structure of LMSs that fragment the learning into course-based silos. Student work cannot easily be exported or shared beyond the course; indeed, in many online programs, students are not even allowed to access old course sites after the semester ends.

ePortfolios, as part of online course or program design, span learning across courses and semesters. Students develop their metacognitive skills through reflection and connect their learning experiences with extra and co-curricular learning. As one student wrote about putting the finishing touches on her Nursing Program ePortfolio, "It was interesting to revisit my work from past semesters because you do see your growth . . . it's kind of fascinating and kind of cool" (Kathleen Heck, SPS Nursing graduate). By making learning visible outside of the LMS, ePortfolios also speak to an authentic audience beyond the instructor and create opportunities for social connections that break out of the "formal curriculum" (Bass, 2012). One example of how ePortfolios foster the development of social connections is through the "Conversations" feature in the Digication ePortfolio platform, which allows students to participate in an online conversation with classmates and the professor via a live stream, similar to a social media activity feed. Deployed in an online history course, "Conversations" facilitates deep textual analysis of digitized primary source documents in a way that is not possible in a traditional online discussion forum because of the discussion forum's focus on individual posts, rather than on the document and the larger conversation (Getman-Eraso & Culkin, 2017).

As mentioned previously, a connected ePortfolio practice particularly benefits adult learners who occupy a growing proportion of the virtual seats in online classrooms. Adult and nontraditional learners tend to gravitate to online programs for many reasons, but they are not necessarily interested in replicating the traditional undergraduate classroom-based experience in a virtual environment. Adult learners actively seek flexible degree programs that allow them to aggregate and credential prior college-level learning acquired both within and outside of the classroom in a way that results in a coherent presentation of skills and knowledge. However, without an overarching structure or container in which to curate and document disparate learning experiences, they find themselves, instead, with an inchoate grab-bag of college credit courses, self-paced massive open online courses (MOOCs), workplace online training modules, and earned badges or credentials that do not advance degree completion. ePortfolios seem to be ideally designed, if not a natural fit, to provide adult learners with the freedom and flexibility to make connections with and across experiences that may fall outside the rigid traditional undergraduate learning pathways. Using an ePortfolio, adult learners are able to document their learning and represent their growth in new competencies or fields of study in an authentic way. By allowing for individualized expression of learning and an inclusive, personalized means of assessing nontraditional learning, ePortfolios can help address some of the social justice challenges that online learners and educators face.

ePortfolios as Student-Owned Spaces

LMS courses and learning spaces are often designed by faculty or instructional designers. Without careful oversight and curation, online course sites tend to become calcified because, despite good intentions, it is easier for an instructor to roll over a course from one semester to the next than to invest time and effort in updating it. Updating a course might require developing sophisticated technical and instructional design expertise: coding, video production and editing, and knowledge of discipline-specific online technologies. Students take these online courses but—understandably—may not feel invested in or connected to these learning spaces.

ePortfolios, in contrast, are student-owned online spaces. They foster students' creativity and self-representation without the limitations of LMS technology. By extending the "walls" of virtual classroom space beyond the LMS, integrating ePortfolios into online courses involves students in the course design process. Through building ePortfolios, students practice sharing what they know and what they can do while contributing to course learning materials. They might create or curate multimedia content, contribute to resources and references for the course, find connections to real-life situations, and use modes of learning that are most appropriate and interesting for them. For example, in the CUNY SPS course "American History and Culture," students produce short screencasts that explain how a concept in U.S. culture has changed over time. Using the previously mentioned Conversations feature, students are easily able to view and discuss their classmates' work. These kinds of collaborative multimedia assignments move away from the dominance of text-based online course content and are in synch with current digital media trends.

While building their ePortfolios, students also learn important digital literacy skills, including attributing their sources properly and self-censoring text and images for appropriate audiences. With proper permission and attribution, instructors are able to utilize this student-created content in future iterations of the course. In this sense, ePortfolio pedagogy helps online students find their own role and voice in our increasingly participatory online culture while contributing to online course design.

Creating Online Communities

Another challenge of fully online learning environments is that they often lack truly engaging communities. Whether on the ground or online, social networks foster stability and positive affect for students (Tinto, 1999). Students in fully online courses have few opportunities to get to know their peers and classmates well; they are "attending class" with classmates whom they may never see or hear. Limited by time, space, and technology, online program administrators strive to create thriving online student communities, where friendships are formed and networking is valued, but it is not easy. What is the best way to create meaningful online LCs in a digital ecosystem teeming with competing claims to online time made from social networking sites? Online courses locked into rigid LMS templates and lacking the immediacy and fun of social media apps can indeed be limiting.

In contrast, the ePortfolio, as a more nimble learning platform, allows for dynamic social interactions and offers the possibility of inclusive learning design by bringing learners and experts together on local and global levels. The ability to set several levels of sharing permissions (private, shared with classmates, shared with the college community, or shared with everyone) makes the ePortfolio a useful platform for creative teamwork and collaborative projects. With flexible platforms, learners can invite other students from the school, from other schools, or even "experts from the field" to review, comment on, or contribute to their collaborations. With an ePortfolio-based online community, the focus of connection is around learning itself.

Peer feedback, team-based work, and LCs are examples of social pedagogies that are particularly important for improving student engagement and success. Evaluation of our ePortfolio practice in online programs at CUNY SPS aligns with findings from our colleagues teaching in-person programs, and demonstrates that effective ePortfolio practice does indeed "make a difference" by advancing student success through "reflection, social pedagogy, and deep learning" (Eynon et al., 2014, p. 98). As participants of the C2L research project, our campus ePortfolio team administered the C2L Core Survey to students in ePortfolio sections over four semesters, from fall 2013 through fall 2015. Using questions specifically about ePortfolios, as well as questions adapted with permission from the Core Survey, we sought to capture evidence of how ePortfolio practice influenced student learning. With other questions adapted with permission from the National Survey of Student Engagement, the C2L Core Survey also sought to measure the extent to which ePortfolio helped students think about their learning in new ways, especially in terms of connecting learning across courses and sharing their ideas with peers.

Figure 12.1 shows the aggregated survey results indicating the percentage of respondents who answered either "agreed" or "strongly agreed" in response to questions about integrative learning experiences in course sections using ePortfolios. Of particular importance for our adult, transfer student online population, is the high percentage of responses indicating that ePortfolios helped with making connections between coursework and prior experiences and knowledge and the extent to which ePortfolios fostered social learning and the exchange of ideas with classmates. The results from our relatively small sample size ($n = 132$) are born out in data from the aggregated results from the C2L Core Survey ($N = 9,542$), which suggest that "reflective ePortfolio pedagogy helps students make meaning from specific learning experiences and connections to other experiences, within and beyond the course" (Eynon et al., 2014, p. 101).

Figure 12.1. ePortfolio survey responses.

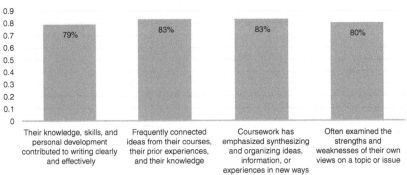

Student ePortfolio survey responses

Peer Engagement and Feedback

Allowing students to see and comment on each other's work poses another challenge for online educators. Kuh and O'Donnell (2013) specified "public demonstration of competence" (p. 10) as one of the behaviors associated with HIPs. However, paradoxically, despite the visual nature of the Web, making learning visible, or "public," proves to be difficult in the password-protected environment of online education. Along with helping students make connections across their own learning experiences, ePortfolios also connect students to their professors and each other. An annual ePortfolio showcase is an especially effective way to make this happen. Each semester at our institution, student ePortfolio creators and faculty teaching ePortfolio sections receive an invitation to nominate entries for the ePortfolio showcase. Using a rubric created by the CUNY SPS ePortfolio support team, 12 winners are selected and featured in our online showcase as well as on the school website and in social media feeds. The showcase has become a program recruitment tool and a way for faculty and students who are often separated by time and space to interact with and get to know each other.

ePortfolios as Authentic Assessment

Working with geographically dispersed, part-time faculty makes convening face-to-face assessment meetings a challenge for online program administrators. However, our accreditors seek evidence that we have indeed engaged in faculty-led authentic assessment of student learning. Because ePortfolios digitally capture the evidence of student learning in a way that can be viewed and scored online, assessments can be organized remotely.

At CUNY SPS, ePortfolios are used by a number of programs for learning outcomes assessment. Through the Assessment Management System feature of the school's ePortfolio platform, Digication, any faculty can remotely read and score artifacts, using a collaboratively developed and normed rubric for outcomes assessment. We collaboratively develop a rubric using online document sharing tools. A norming process takes place using web-conferencing software. Once the evaluators have agreed on a rubric and benchmarked levels of attainment via the norming process, the rest of the assessment takes place individually, online, over a period of a few days. To ensure interrater reliability, two readers score each artifact, and scores that are misaligned by more than a point are reviewed and discussed.

Another aspect of the assessment process is the collaborative development of Signature Assignments, described by Association of American Colleges & Universities as assignments that require students to demonstrate and apply their proficiency in one or more key learning outcomes: "synthesizing, analyzing, and applying cumulative knowledge and skills through problem or inquiry-based assignments or projects" (Association of American Colleges & Universities, n.d.). Programs at CUNY SPS that have fully integrated ePortfolios include a Signature Assignment for each course that learners deposit into their program ePortfolios as evidence of learning and for reflection on growth.

The online assessment of authentic student artifacts, directly pulled from student ePortfolios, also serves as a catalyst for evidence-based faculty development and curricular change. A key step in the assessment cycle, the collection and scoring of student artifacts provide the basis for further conversations about what is working well and what needs to change. Professional development, discussed more in the following section, supports course-based and curricular changes, which in fully online programs also take place online.

Tips for Implementation

In this section, we will share recommendations for operationalizing and implementing ePortfolios in online environments. The questions and suggestions stem from our own experiences as portfolio practitioners and researchers, but they are in no way conclusive or definitive. Rather, we hope to open further challenges that might lead to conversations around ePortfolio pedagogy, practice, and implementation in online environments.

As discussed previously, ePortfolios tackle several great challenges of online learning. The fragmentation of learning is lessened when ePortfolios create a connected learning space that integrates learning from a variety of sources and across time. Shared ePortfolios and collaborative projects that extend beyond the classroom foster a sense of belongingness. Student-owned, created, and curated online materials reinforce digital literacy skills that—at the same time—open a more contributive and "connectivist" digital learning spaces (Siemens, 2005). Additionally, artifacts from student ePortfolios (or the entire ePortfolios themselves) can be easily utilized for authentic outcomes assessments.

An important question to consider when starting an ePortfolio project is whether to start at the course level—seeking individual instructor buy-in—or at the program level, which requires a commitment from all faculty teaching in a program. Course-level implementation means that each course has its own ePortfolio, in which students post their own assignments and also view and respond to classmates' work. Course-based implementation draws faculty interest and affords opportunities for pedagogical innovation and creativity on the course level; however, it rarely leaves students with a single, coherent showcase ePortfolio that contains samples and reflections on their coursework across the entire academic experience. In contrast, a program ePortfolio stays with the student from the first semester through graduation, capturing evidence of learning and metacognitive reflections across an academic career. Another type of program ePortfolio is the capstone ePortfolio. Rather than being built piece by piece from the beginning of the academic journey, capstone ePortfolios are created in a student's final semester and house a curated presentation of key coursework. Some programs use capstone ePortfolios as an alternative to the senior thesis; others may utilize the capstone ePortfolio as an electronic résumé or extended educational transcript, demonstrating what courses a graduate has taken as well as what the graduate knows and can do.

To ensure that students receive the most benefit from ePortfolio pedagogy, we suggest embedding the creation of a program ePortfolio into a required first-year course. For example, the fully online nursing program at CUNY SPS requires the creation of a program ePortfolio in its entry-level course, "Transition to Professional Nursing." Assignments include setting up the ePortfolio, adding a Personal Philosophy of Nursing to the ePortfolio, and a Signature Assignment exploring ethical issues in nursing.

We recommend starting with program-based implementation of ePortfolios because it is cleaner: a student builds a single ePortfolio with artifacts collected from different courses rather than wrangling multiple ePortfolios. However, without strong institutional support, it is difficult to begin with a program-based ePortfolio. Questions for consideration for a program-level ePortfolio implementation include the following:

- Who is paying for the platform?
- Is there a dedicated administrator?
- Will a department or school adopt ePortfolios?
- Who will support students and faculty?

We suggest beginning with a small-scale project that leverages a few early adopters and uses an open-source platform before securing a department- or institution-wide commitment to the technology and its support.

Professional Development for ePortfolios

Intentional and well-designed faculty development for online faculty will support the success of ePortfolio implementation. Online or blended professional development encourages faculty participants to begin formulating a problem that they wish to address, such as a threshold concept that challenges their students or an assignment that yields disappointing results. The next step is to reenvision the selected course components or assignments through the lens of ePortfolios, focusing on the benefits that ePortfolios provide for the learners. With assistance and through collegial collaboration, faculty then propose solutions to their problem areas by revising and testing their ePortfolio-based assignments. As part of the professional development process, faculty are encouraged to collect and review learning data and feedback from students and to incorporate their findings into new iterations of the assignment.

The structure of professional programs for ePortfolio pedagogy might include small-group faculty discussions for clarifying problem areas and brainstorming solutions. These programs also enable cross-institutional seminars, such as those that review data or collaborate on cross-disciplinary improvements, and focus groups on themes such as assessment, advisement, and the cocurricular revision and testing of new learning structures and assignments. Regardless of the format, however, professional development programs should, in some way, address the following key issues: considerations for quality course and portfolio design, the use of ePortfolios for learning outcomes assessment, online pedagogy and teaching strategies with ePortfolios, and technology usage and its implications for teaching and learning online. We discuss the details for these four key considerations in the remainder of this chapter.

Quality Course and ePortfolio Design

Faculty development programs should encourage discussion of the ways in which each online course, given the learning objectives and course-level assessments, contributes to program or college-wide learning outcomes. This curricular mapping exercise helps with ePortfolio design on the course level as it reveals how individual course ePortfolios or portfolio assignments will contribute to learning at the program level. Online faculty who create portfolio assignments on the course level should also be mindful of how their course content and competencies contribute to supporting students' learning and motivation regardless of what their major or program might be. Best practices and guiding principles in online course design (e.g., Quality Matters[2] or recommended U.S. Distance Learning Association[3] Standards for online course design) should also guide the faculty development process for creating and utilizing ePortfolio assignments and assessments.

ePortfolios and Learning Assessment

As mentioned previously, many programs use ePortfolios for scaffolded, "signature" assignments that develop and display mastery of critical course or program competencies. Assessment of signature assignments can reveal areas of weakness, which might be due to a lack of engaging online materials, lack of sufficient time for practice, content misalignment, or other concerns. In those cases, professional development programs should create opportunities for revising assignments or making significant curricular changes.

ePortfolios and Online Pedagogy

Online faculty who use ePortfolios need to be aware of instructional strategies that best support integrating ePortfolios into their practice. Some of the considerations include how the faculty will manage reviewing, commenting on, and grading student ePortfolios; the support structures for helping students build their ePortfolios; and the consequences for not following the ePortfolio requirements in a given course. In addition, asking faculty members to build and share their own professional ePortfolios with colleagues is a key ingredient for faculty development programs on ePortfolio pedagogy. Conversations that stem from these individual hands-on experiences greatly support the professors' abilities to understand and teach with ePortfolios online.

ePortfolios and the Use of Technology

Faculty members' and students' learning curves for new technologies vary greatly. Technology should not be a hurdle to either students or faculty members during the ePortfolio implementation process. All stakeholders need to be keenly aware of the possibility of technology overload, technology failure, and the rapidly changing features and capacities of new technologies. These considerations are all the more important in a fully online environment, where ePortfolios often necessitate changes to course design and structures of the LMS to avoid duplication of work. Additionally, continuous conversations on the risk of technology overload and students' perception of an ePortfolio experience as nothing more than busywork should be taken seriously. Any data collected throughout ePortfolio implementation, including student technology feedback surveys, need to inform the direction and topics addressed at professional development programs.

Conclusion

In this chapter, we reviewed some of the challenges and opportunities that ePortfolios afford fully online learners and programs. Although it might seem redundant to incorporate another virtual space into the online degree eco-system, successful ePortfolios can ameliorate the sense of isolation or compartmentalization that may come with online learning. For adult students who bring years of work and other experiences with them, ePortfolios can connect learning acquired in formal academic settings with cocurricular and out-of-class learning experiences in a powerful, visual way. For online program faculty and administrators, ePortfolios can increase student and faculty engagement in an authentic learning process, showcase student achievements, and provide a holistic view of learning for collaborative assessment practices, making the ePortfolio well deserving of its designation as the 11th HIP.

Key Takeaways

- Application of ePortfolios in the online space may be particularly significant to the growing number of nontraditional learners.
- ePortfolio pedagogy contributes to online course design by helping students find their own role and voice in a participatory online culture.
- ePortfolios can provide a powerful, visual way to connect the learning acquired in formal academic settings and out-of-class learning experiences.
- Successful ePortfolio implementation can be supported by intentional and well-designed faculty development for online faculty.

Notes

1. As a multicampus collaborative project between 2011 and 2014, the Connect to Learning (C2L) project brought together a diverse collection of 24 campuses, including community colleges, private liberal arts colleges, and research universities, in an effort to share ePortfolio implementation strategies and practices.

2. Quality Matters is a nonprofit organization with a clear mission of defining and maintaining quality assurance in online learning. (See www.qualitymatters.org for more information.)

3. The U.S. Distance Learning Association supports research, development, education, and training for distance LCs. (See www.usdla.org for more information.)

References

Adelman, C. (1992). *The way we are: The community college as American thermometer.* Washington DC: U.S. Department of Education.

Association of American Colleges & Universities. (n.d.). *Integrating signature assignments into the curriculum and inspiring design.* Retrieved from https://www .aacu.org/sites/default/files/Signature-Assignment-Tool.pdf

Bass, R. (2012, March/April). Disrupting ourselves: The problem of learning in higher education. *EDUCAUSE Review*, pp. 23–33.

Bollinger, D. U., & Shepherd, C. E. (2010). Student perceptions of ePortfolio integration in online courses. *Distance Education, 31*(3), 295–314.

Eynon, B., Gambino, L., & Török, J. (2014). What difference can ePortfolio make? A field report from the Connect to Learning Project. *International Journal of ePortfolio, 4*(1) 95–114.

Finley, A., & McNair, T. (2013). *Assessing underserved students' engagement in high-impact practices.* Washington DC: Association of American Colleges & Universities.

Getman-Eraso, J., & Culkin, K. (2017). Close reading: Engaging and empowering history students through document analysis on ePortfolio. *International Journal of ePortfolio, 7*(1), 29–42.

Kuh, G., & O'Donnell, K. (2013). *Ensuring quality and taking high-impact practices to scale.* Washington DC: Association of American Colleges & Universities.

Scobey, D. (2016). Marginalized majority: Non-traditional students and the equity imperative. *Diversity and Democracy, 19*(1). Retrieved from https://www.aacu .org/diversitydemocracy/2016/winter/scobey

Siemens, G. (2005, January). Connectivism: A learning theory for the digital age. *International Journal of Instructional Technology & Distance Learning.* Retrieved from http://www.itdl.org/Journal/Jan_05/article01.htmv

Tinto, V. (1999). Taking retention seriously: Rethinking the first year. *NACADA Journal, 19*(2), 5–9.

Watson, C., Kuh, G., Rhodes, T., Light, T. P., & Chen, H. (2016). Editorial: ePortfolios: The eleventh high impact practice. *International Journal of ePortfolio, 6*(2), 65–69.

13

HIGH-IMPACT PRACTICES AND LIBRARY AND INFORMATION RESOURCES

Stefanie Buck

Libraries are frequently called "the heart of the university," referring not only to their often central physical location on campus but also to their pivotal role in serving all students, faculty, and staff, regardless of discipline or unit, and creating an environment that stimulates learning and academic success (Clink, 2016; Lynch et al., 2007). The role of the library in supporting student learning is often traditionally described as providing access to resources (collections of books, journal, documents), archiving materials (special collections, archives), and offering students assistance in using these effectively (reference services, instruction). More recently, libraries have looked beyond this more traditional role of "support" to being an "academic partner" that works with the faculty and university to promote practices that support student academic engagement and success (Sanabria, 2013).

In his study of academic libraries and high-impact practices (HIPs), Murray (2015) notes, "Academic libraries, with the shifting focus on providing an atmosphere accommodating different academic needs, can provide an informal academic environment that may foster student engagement in high-impact practices" (p. 472). Murray (2015) also notes that librarians "lack a significant body of literature" (p. 472) for conducting research on how libraries support student retention, engagement, and learning. This does not mean that libraries do not have a role to play in supporting HIPs—just the opposite; it has simply been challenging to document the direct impact that libraries have on these practices. The ultimate goal of HIPs is to provide the best learning environment and opportunities possible, and the success of HIPs is often measured in retention and gradua-tion rates. Although the literature directly tying libraries and HIPs together is limited and not always conclusive, it is also clear that libraries can and do have an impact in these areas.

This chapter will provide an overview of the kinds of information resources and pedagogical support services that libraries provide to faculty and instructors in support of HIPs. It will review the current literature on HIPs and libraries and provide examples of successful library integration into activities and programs that support these practices. In addition, it will dis-cuss how improving student information literacy skills can increase the suc-cess of HIPs in the online learning environment.

Traditional Library Services and Student Success

Actions taken by libraries that have been highlighted as having the poten-tial to increase student success and retention include early and frequent use of library resources and early introduction to the library and its ser-vices. Several studies have examined the use of library resources in con-nection with retention and success, including the physical borrowing of materials and the logging into online resources such as e-books and e-journals, and have found some positive impacts on retention and grade point average (GPA) (Allison, 2015; Goodall & Pattern, 2011; Haddow, 2013; Haddow & Joseph, 2010; Jantti & Cox, 2013; Soria, Fransen, & Nackerud, 2014; Wong & Webb, 2010). Stone and Ramsden's (2012) "Library Impact Data Project" explores student library usage, with the authors finding a "statistically significant relation between student attain-ment and e-resources use and book borrowing statistics" (p. 546). Early use of library resources may also improve retention as well as student GPA (Emmons & Wilkinson, 2010; Haddow & Joseph, 2010; Soria, Fransen, & Nackerud, 2013).

Another "traditional" service offered by librarians is an orientation or instruction session on using the library. These sessions appear to be particu-larly beneficial in the early stages of a student's academic career (Crawford, 2015; Stemmer & Mahan, 2015). In some cases, the orientations are part of another course; one example of this is a librarian who participates in first-year experience seminar course (for more on first-year seminars as HIPs, see chapter 1, this volume). Although here too the research is still recent and not entirely conclusive, Sanabria (2013) found that the "data demonstrates encouraging retention numbers and solid increases in aver-age GPAs of freshman students participating in the FYS" (p. 98). In 2015, the Association of College & Research Libraries released "Academic Library Contributions to Student Success," which reports on a study of first-year campus assessment teams at more than 70 North American institutions of higher education. This study used a variety of techniques to determine that library instruction builds student confidence with the research process, contributes to retention and persistence, and can lead to improved grades and better information literacy competencies (Brown & Malenfant, 2015). O'Kelly (2015) also found a "statistically significant difference in retention between students who have seen a librarian in class and those who have not" (n.p.).

However, these studies are not conclusive. For example, Crawford (2015) found that the "relationship between library expenses per FTE and retention and graduation rates is heartening. In contrast, the relationship between library use and graduation and retention rates is less than expected" (p. 55). Kuh and Gonyea (2003) did not find that library experiences increased student engagement. Moreover, no studies have dealt specifically with the issue of retention and graduation and library services from an online perspective. Needham, Nurse, Parker, Scantlebury, and Dick (2013) have a proposal on how we might gather this information, but this research has not yet been published. However, as Kuh and Gonyea (2003) conclude, "library experiences of undergraduates positively relate to select purposeful activities," and "those students who more frequently use the library reflect a studious work ethic and engage in academically challenging tasks that require higher-order thinking" (p. 207).

Services Related to Information Literacy

The term *information literacy* is referenced or implied in several of Kuh's (2008) HIPs, such as first-year seminars and experiences as well as writing-intensive courses. Undergraduate research and capstone courses and projects are another set of HIPs where student achievement is also strongly tied to information literacy skills. In brief, *information literacy* is defined by the Association of College & Research Libraries (2016a) as "the set of integrated abilities encompassing the reflective discovery of information, the understanding of how information is produced and valued, and the use of information in creating new knowledge and participating ethically in communities of learning" ("Introduction," para. 7). Information literacy skills are identified in Liberal Education and America's Promise among the essential learning outcomes (Kuh, 2008). Other HIPs, such as LCs and common intellectual experiences, although not specifically calling out information literacy or research skills, are clearly tied to the ability of students to exercise their critical thinking skills (for more on common intellectual experiences and LCs as HIPs, see chapters 2 and 3, this volume).

Many university libraries offer courses to help students acquire these information literacy skills. Librarians often go into classes to teach a brief session (often referred to by librarians as a "one shot") to give the students a basic understanding of how to use library resources. However, information literacy skills are not necessarily gained in a single class or at a specific time in a student's academic career (Kuh & Gonyea, 2003). These skills come at different points and are most effectively learned in conjunction with an activity or assignment. Librarians have addressed information literacy skills with a variety of offerings of credit courses, noncredit workshops, tutorials, guides, one-on-one consultations, and traditional reference desk services, but students also learn these skills in the classroom, in service-learning opportunities, when doing independent research, when seeking out the news, or even when doing research on subjects of personal interest. For online learners, information literacy skills are particularly important because many of these students do not come to campus to use the library and get assistance (Bourdeau & Bates, 1996).

Library Services for Online Learners

Academic libraries consider seriously the needs of their online user populations. As early as the late nineteenth century, librarians have understood that off-campus users need support as much as on-campus users. In 1966, the Association of College and Research Libraries Distance Learning Section wrote *The Guidelines for Library Services to Extension Students* on how academic libraries should support students taking, at that time, mainly correspondence courses (Casey, 2009). Time and technology have improved access and services to online learners, and the guidelines have since become the *Standards for Distance Learning Library Services* (Association of College & Research Libraries Distance Learning, 2016b). This document was revised in 2016 to reflect the changes in the technological and online learning environment, the growing and diverse nature of students taking online courses, and the rapid growth of online programs. The *Standards* are guidelines, not enforceable rules or regulations, but they demonstrate the commitment that librarians feel to all their users regardless of location. In fact, they predate any accreditation requirements that students taking courses of campus receive some kind of library support services (Casey, 2009).

In addition to making more resources available online, (e.g., e-journals, e-books, streaming media, online databases, digital collection) many academic libraries mail books or other print materials to their remote users. They also offer online workshops, classes, webinars, tutorials, and other resources to help students learn to navigate the library resources and locate appropriate materials. In addition, numerous university libraries offer optional or required lower division courses on information literacy skills to help students develop the necessary information literacy skills. In addition, online library orientations are often offered asynchronously so online learners can watch at their convenience (Cannady, Fagerheim, Williams, & Steiner, 2013). Some universities have a librarian or library staff dedicated to serving their online population; others do not have a designated individual but have dispersed the responsibilities among the existing staff.

Although offering these options represents the ideals as outlined in the *Standards*, the reality is that budgetary constraints may mean that some libraries cannot mail books to students or staff size prohibits having a single individual dedicated to online learning (Huwiler, 2015; Shell et al., 2010). Nevertheless, academic librarians clearly understand the need for such services. It is also important to note that the *Standards* call for equivalent services not replicated services (Casey, 2009). The wording here is deliberate; not everything translates well into an online setting. The job of the online-learning librarian is to create resources or services that provide the same learning opportunities. Anyone who has moved a course from a face-to-face to an online modality knows this is not simply a task of cutting and pasting content into the content management system; the same holds true for library services. Online-learning librarians are faced with the challenge of making online students aware of the many resources available to them. After all, we cannot expect students to use library resources to support their writing intensive coursework or internships or any other HIP if they do not even know those resources exist.

The research on online learners provides us with a profile of users who are as diverse as any campus community; however, they do have some characteristics that make them a little different from their on-campus counterparts regarding their library and research support needs. For example, we know online learners want immediate access to resources. They prefer online materials and often will choose a resource based on its availability (Mussell & Croft, 2013; Tang & Tseng, 2013). Online students tend to be self-reliant, so there is a need for libraries to actively promote their services to students (Huwiler, 2015). Online learners are also hesitant to ask questions, which means that help needs to be easy to locate and online resources easy to navigate (Lee, Hayden, & MacMillan, 2004). They often require additional asynchronous support, in addition to the synchronous support many libraries offer, because they are not always in the same time zone as the librarian or the open hours of the library when they could ask for assistance. Online learners also want their help in bite-sized chunks that answer the immediate questions of how to find and use resources (Cannady et al., 2013). In the following sections, I look beyond the basics of access to collections and general research assistance to other ways libraries can and have supported HIPs specifically through embedded librarianship, support of undergraduate research practices, and the library as a place that supports community and collaboration.

Embedded Librarianship

Embedded librarianship can be defined in a variety of ways, but all definitions focus on the more intense, personalized, and targeted participation of a librarian in a course (Edwards & Black, 2012). The concept of an embedded librarian reflects a fundamental shift in how librarians envision their role in the academic community. It reflects a more proactive outlook, encouraging librarians to become more integrally involved in course design, instruction, and assessment. Embedded librarians are flexible—they tailor their instruction to the needs of the course and discipline. They form part of the instructional team of a class. In on-campus communities, librarians are sometimes "embedded" in a college—they have an office or hold consultation hours in the college rather than expecting students to come to the library (Summey & Kane, 2016). This practice of being embedded is also a way for librarians to translate what they do face-to-face in the library into the online learning environment by being a presence in a course management system. Shumaker (2014) notes that

> to date, there is no evidence that virtual embedding is any less successful than an embedded relationship that involves physical co-location. While it can be easier to develop a strong working relationship face-to-face, experience indicates that it can also be done successfully via digital technologies. (p. 7)

HIPs such as online first-year experience (see chapter 1, this volume) and writing-intensive courses (see chapter 4, this volume) can benefit from having an embedded librarian who can provide instruction on how to use the library. First-year seminars and writing-intensive courses are an ideal place for the library to collaborate with the classroom instructor. Indeed, both of these HIPs have information literacy specifically called out as a competency students should master (Kuh, 2009). Students entering college are often underprepared when it comes to their ability to locate and use information sources, particularly scholarly sources. Therefore, many universities have integrated the library into courses that are designed to not only create community but also orient students to the academic and scholarly culture of an institution. There are many examples of libraries partnering with first-year experience course instructors or otherwise being active participants in the planning and execution of such a course (O'Kelly, 2015). In on-campus courses, librarians come into the classroom to do instruction on information literacy-related topics. This instruction is not easily replicated in an online course, but a similar model can be achieved via asynchronous online tutorials or webinars. Librarians may participate in the course in a variety of ways: participating in discussion boards to respond to questions at the time of need, designing course and Web guides with resources and guidance on the research process, teaching an information literacy session or sessions via a webinar, and assessing the artifacts produced in the course. Librarians may also teach these courses either alone or in partnership with another instructor from a different discipline (Edwards & Black, 2012).

Over time librarians have developed "best practices" about what makes embedded librarianship successful. Several recently published books on the practice of embedded librarianship with case studies and best practices can provide useful guidance (Daugherty & Russo, 2013; Reale, 2015; Shumaker, 2014). Although these recommendations are generally intended for librarians, instructors who want to have an embedded librarian in the course may also benefit from an overview of these best practices and what makes a successful embedded librarian experience for the students, instructors, and the librarian.

It is important to note that there is no one-size-fits-all model of embedded librarianship; the activities or services offered will be largely dependent on the course content, audience level and research experience, as well as learning outcomes of the course (Markgraf, 2002). In addition, a librarian may want to start with a survey of what skills the students already possess and what they need to learn, based on the curriculum, to be successful as a tool for designing effective research interventions (Tumbleson & Burke, 2010). This information will help the librarian design appropriate scaffolded activities and learning opportunities. However, the key to any successful embedded librarianship program in support of HIPs is collaboration with faculty and the integration of the librarian into the curriculum (Edwards & Black, 2012). Librarians should be incorporated early on into the course design so that the library or information literacy concepts in the course can be identified early on and the activities that reinforce these concepts can be fully integrated into the course content. To make this possible, the librarian needs to have access to the learning management system, which allows him or her to integrate materials and activities at the appropriate time in the course and is not always granted to him or her by the instructor (Shell, Crawford, & Harris, 2013).

Although noting that librarian presence in and of itself can be positive (Heathcock, 2015), it is not generally enough to benefit the students (Matthew & Schroeder, 2006). An embedded librarian needs to offer a variety of ways to provide assistance and be proactive in sending out ideas, reminders, and suggestions on improving research strategies or recommending resources. Edwards and Black (2012) note that successfully embedded librarians use a variety of methods to provide this information, including chat, asynchronous and synchronous tutorials and webinars, announcement, and blog postings. Some courses include a separate discussion board where students can post research questions or the librarians may be part of a discussion board where students are discussing their research activities and can offer suggestions and guidance.

One of the challenges faced by librarians in the embedded librarian model is that it is not easily scalable. Truly embedded librarianship is high touch but difficult to sustain. Hawes (2011) notes that in her efforts to succesfully embed herself in online courses, she needs to limit the number of courses in which she engages. A study by Heathcock (2015), however, shows that librarians do not need to be active in the entire course, just those weeks where it is most relevant to have a positive impact. Here again close faculty-librarian collaboration is important in determining when and where the librarian should be embedded in the course.

Finally, assessment is an essential component of a successful library-instructor partnership (Tumbleson & Burke, 2010). On the most basic level, just knowing that a librarian is there to assist them if they have questions provides stress relief to students who may be experiencing anxiety about doing research. However, allowing the librarian to assess student work products can also be beneficial. Feedback from the instructor and librarian on this work provides students the most benefit and learning opportunities.

Supporting Undergraduate Research

In addition to the aforementioned obvious access to scholarly resources, libraries can provide a variety of support services for undergraduate research. The mainstay activity for a lower division course that includes the use of library resources has traditionally been the research paper. Riehle and Weiner (2013) recommend considering a critical reflection paper or guided reflection exercises and potentially moving away from the traditional research paper to a more inquiry-based project that requires the student to locate supporting materials. The following are additional ways of supporting undergraduate research that can translate easily into the online learning environment: (a) making student research available via an institutional repository (IR), and (b) providing undergraduate research awards.

IRs are dedicated to preserving the academic record of the institution. Usually, the guidelines of such repositories focus on faculty submitting their publications in an effort to make this research available to a wider audience. IRs are generally administered and supported by the library in its role as both archive and sharer of information. However, some universities use the IR for a wider purpose. For example, it has long been a tradition for libraries to collect and store theses and dissertations conducted at a university, and these are now being digitized and made available electronically, often through the institution's IR. But some IRs are not stopping with only graduate student-level work or faculty publications. Passehl-Stoddart and Monge (2014) document how their institution developed a student-centric IR, designed to include undergraduate research. Murray's (2015) research with deans and administration noted a strong theme in the comments of support for undergraduate research:

> A theme prevalent for this HIP, and seen again only in data for HIP 10 (capstone courses and projects), centered on the archival and publication responsibilities of the academic library with regard to undergraduate research, particularly among the highly aligned libraries. Within this theme, comments ranged from the publication of student research journals to hosting student research in digital repositories. Additionally, the provision of personalized assistance for students with regard to preparation of presentations or posters appeared across alignment categories. (p. 480)

Another support mechanism is the undergraduate research award that many libraries offer students (Stamatoplos, 2009; Tchangalova & Cossard, 2015). Research awards can be a positive factor in encouraging undergraduate research practices, and numerous libraries offer research awards or support other college research awards (Healey & Jenkins, 2009; Hunter, Laursen, & Seymour, 2007). There is no reason that online learners cannot be included in this program, and it could even be expanded to create an award just for online learners.

Promoting Student Engagement in High-Impact Practices

Kuh and Gonyea's (2003) study on academic libraries and their role in promoting student engagement notes that HIPs often take place in informal academic environments. These informal environments can and should include the library—a place where students can gather, evaluate information, discuss, research, create, and write (Murray, 2015). A discrete body of library literature focuses on the *library as space*, defining and describing the role a library can play as a physical location that supports academic success (Aabø & Audunson, 2012; Kim, 2016; Mandel, 2016; Ward, 2013; Yates, 2014). Many libraries have dedicated space to *learning commons*, where students can gather, collaborate, consult, research, and write. In addition, the integration of libraries with other units, such as writing centers or tutorial centers, helps to foster a supportive learning environment. Other services a library may supply that go beyond the "traditional" are the lending of computing or other technology; advanced spaces such as a visualizations lab; and, most recently, "maker spaces" (Barrett et al., 2015). All of these activities and services have been created to support those practices that improve student learning.

A sense of space is probably the most challenging environment to re-create online and one with which libraries serving distance populations have struggled. Coonin, Williams, and Steiner (2011) have developed some best practices that can help online learners feel more of a sense of place and foster library-student relationships. These best practices include creating an online environment that caters to online students' needs, creating personal connections to create a sense of community and belonging ("being real"), and being available at the point of need, in addition to the more traditional activities of access and instruction.

Librarians can make ideal partners in the effort to bring HIPs into the online classroom, and there are many examples in the literature of those partnerships yielding positive results. In an online course, librarians can help faculty to develop research and learning activities that support the faculty member's HIPs. It is, however, only through a collaborative effort on both sides that this partnership can work.

Key Takeaways

- Having an embedded librarian who can provide instruction on how to use the library may prove beneficial to other HIPs such as online first-year experiences and writing-intensive courses.
- Although libraries clearly can and do have an impact on the areas of HIPs, the literature directly tying libraries to HIPs is currently limited.
- Through a collaborative effort on both sides, librarians can assist faculty to develop research and learning activities that support the faculty member's HIPs in an online course.

References

Aabø, S., & Audunson, R. (2012). Use of library space and the library as place. *Library & Information Science Research, 34*(2), 138–149.

Association of College and Research Libraries (2016a, January 11). *Framework for information literacy for higher education*. Retrieved from http://www.ala.org/acrl/sites/ala.org.acrl/files/content/issues/infolit/Framework_ILHE.pdf

Association of College and Research Libraries. (2016b, June). *Standards for distance learning library services*. Retrieved from http://www.ala.org/acrl/standards/guidelinesdistancelearning

Allison, D. (2015). Measuring the academic impact of libraries. *Portal: Libraries and the Academy, 15*(1), 29–40.

Barrett, T., Pizzico, M., Levy, B. D., Nagel, R. L., Linsey, J. S., Talley, K. G., Forest, C. R., Newstetter, W. C. (2015, June 14–17). *A review of university maker spaces*. Paper presented at the 122nd ASEE Annual Conference and Exposition. Seattle, WA. Retrieved from https://smartech.gatech.edu/handle/1853/53813

Bourdeau, J., & Bates, A. (1996). Instructional design for distance learning. *Journal of Science Education and Technology, 5*(4), 267–283.

Brown, K., & Malenfant, K. J. (2015). *Academic library contributions to student success: Documented practices from the field*. Chicago, IL: Association of College and Research Libraries. Retrieved from http://www. ala.org/acrl/files/content/issues/Value/Contributions_report.pdf

Cannady, R. E., Fagerheim, B., Williams, B. F., & Steiner, H. (2013). Diving into distance learning librarianship: Tips and advice for new and seasoned professionals. *College & Research Libraries News, 74*(5), 254–261. Retrieved from http://crln.acrl.org/index.php/crlnews/article/view/8948/9684

Casey, A. M. (2009). Distance learning librarians: Their shared vision. *Journal of Library & Information Services in Distance Learning, 3*(1), 3–22.

Clink, K. D. (2016). The academic library's role in student retention. *PNLA Quarterly, 80*(1), 20–24. Retrieved from https://arc.lib.montana.edu/ojs/index.php/pnla/article/view/296

Coonin, B., Williams, B. F., & Steiner, H. (2011). Fostering library as a place for distance students: Best practices from two universities. *Internet Reference Services Quarterly, 16*(4), 149–158.

Crawford, G. A. (2015). The academic library and student retention and graduation: An exploratory study. *Portal: Libraries and the Academy, 15*(1), 41–57.

Daugherty, A. L., & Russo, M. F. (2013). *Embedded librarianship: What every academic librarian should know*. Santa Barbara, CA: Libraries Unlimited.

Edwards, M. E., & Black, E. W. (2012). Contemporary instructor-librarian collaboration: A case study of an online embedded librarian implementation. *Journal of Library & Information Services in Distance Learning, 6*(3–4), 284–311.

Emmons, M., & Wilkinson, F. C. (2010). The academic library impact on student persistence. *College & Research Libraries, 72*(2), 128–149.

Goodall, D., & Pattern, D. (2011). Academic library non/low use and undergraduate student achievement: A preliminary report of research in progress. *Library Management, 32*(3), 159–170.

Haddow, G. (2013). Academic library use and student retention: A quantitative analysis. *Library & Information Science Research, 35*(2), 127–136.

Haddow, G., & Joseph, J. (2010). Loans, logins, and lasting the course: Academic library use and student retention. *Australian Academic & Research Libraries, 41*(4), 233–244.

Hawes, S. L. (2011). Playing to win: Embedded librarians in online classrooms. *Journal of Library & Information Services in Distance Learning, 5*(1–2), 56–66.

Healey, M., & Jenkins, A. (2009). Developing undergraduate research and inquiry. *Innovations in Education and Teaching International, 47*, 247–248.

Heathcock, K. (2015). Embedded librarians: Just-in-time or just-in-case? A research study. *Journal of Library & Information Services in Distance Learning, 9*(1–2), 1–16.

Hunter, A.-B., Laursen, S. L., & Seymour, E. (2007). Becoming a scientist: The role of undergraduate research in students' cognitive, personal, and professional development. *Science Education, 91*(1), 36–74.

Huwiler, A. G. (2015). Library services for distance students: Opportunities and challenges. *Journal of Library & Information Services in Distance Learning, 9*(4), 275–288.

Jantti, M., & Cox, B. (2013). Measuring the value of library resources and student academic performance through relational datasets. *Evidence Based Library and Information Practice, 8*(2), 163–171.

Kim, J.-A. (2016). Dimensions of user perception of academic library as place. *The Journal of Academic Librarianship, 42*(5), 509–514.

Kuh, G. D. (2008). Why integration and engagement are essential to effective educational practice in the twenty-first century. *Peer Review, 10*(4), 27.

Kuh, G. D. (2009). What student affairs professionals need to know about student engagement. *Journal of College Student Development, 50*(6), 683–706.

Kuh, G. D., & Gonyea, R. M. (2003). Role of the academic library in promoting student engagement in learning. *College & Research Libraries, 64*(4), 256–282.

Lee, J., Hayden, K. A., & MacMillan, D. (2004). "I wouldn't have asked for help if I had to go to the library": Reference services on site. *Issues in Science and Technology Librarianship, 41*. Retrieved from http://prism.ucalgary.ca/handle/1880/44205

Lynch, B. P., Murray-Rust, C., Parker, S. E., Turner, D., Walker, D. P., Wilkinson, F. C., & Zimmerman, J. (2007). Attitudes of presidents and provosts on the university library. *College & Research Libraries, 68*(3), 213–228.

Mandel, L. H. (2016). Visualizing the library as place. *Performance Measurements and Metrics, 17*, 165–174.

Markgraf, J. S. (2002). Collaboration between distance education faculty and the library: One size does not fit all. *Journal of Library Administration, 37*(3–4), 451–464.

Matthew, V., & Schroeder, A. (2006). The embedded librarian program. *Educause Quarterly, 29*(4), 61.

Murray, A. (2015). Academic libraries and high-impact practices for student retention: Library deans' perspectives. *Portal: Libraries and the Academy, 15*(3), 471–487.

Mussell, J., & Croft, R. (2013). Discovery layers and the distance student: Online search habits of students. *Journal of Library & Information Services in Distance Learning, 7*(1–2), 18–39.

Needham, G., Nurse, R., Parker, J., Scantlebury, N., & Dick, S. (2013). Can an excellent distance learning library service support student retention and how can we find out? *Open Learning: The Journal of Open, Distance and E-Learning, 28*(2), 135–140.

O'Kelly, M. (2015). Correlation between library instruction and student retention. Presentations. 55. Retrieved from https://works.bepress.com/maryokelly/4/

Passehl-Stoddart, E., & Monge, R. (2014). From freshman to graduate: Making the case for student-centric institutional repositories. *Journal of Librarianship and Scholarly Communication, 2*(3), p.eP1130.

Reale, M. (2015). *Becoming an embedded librarian: Making connections in the classroom.* Chicago; IL: American Library Association.

Riehle, C. F., & Weiner, S. A. (2013). High-impact educational practices: An exploration of the role of information literacy. *College & Undergraduate Libraries, 20*(2), 127–143.

Sanabria, J. E. (2013). Library as an academic partner in student retention and graduation: The library's collaboration with the Freshman Year Seminar initiative at the Bronx Community College. *Collaborative Librarianship, 5*(2), 94–100. Retrieved from https://digitalcommons.du.edu/collaborativelibrarianship/vol5/iss2/4

Shell, L., Crawford, S., & Harris, P. (2013). Aided and embedded: The team approach to instructional design. *Journal of Library & Information Services in Distance Learning, 7*(1–2), 143–155.

Shell, L., Duvernay, J., Ewbank, A. D., Konomos, P., Leaming, A., & Sylvester, G. (2010). A comprehensive plan for library support of online and extended education. *Journal of Library Administration, 50*(7–8), 951–971.

Shumaker, D. (2014). *Embedded librarian innovative strategies for taking knowledge where it's needed.* Medford, OR: Information Today, Inc.

Soria, K. M., Fransen, J., & Nackerud, S. (2013). Library use and undergraduate student outcomes: New evidence for students' retention and academic success. *Portal: Libraries and the Academy, 13*(2), 147–164.

Soria, K. M., Fransen, J., & Nackerud, S. (2014). Stacks, serials, search engines, and students' success: First-year undergraduate students' library use, academic achievement, and retention. *The Journal of Academic Librarianship, 40*(1), 84–91.

Stamatoplos, A. (2009). The role of academic libraries in mentored undergraduate research: A model of engagement in the academic community. *College & Research Libraries, 70*(3), 235–249.

Stemmer, J. K., & Mahan, D. M. (2015). Investigating the relationship of library usage to student outcomes. *College & Research Libraries, 77*(3), 359–375.

Stone, G., & Ramsden, B. (2012). Library Impact Data Project: Looking for the link between library usage and student attainment. *College & Research Libraries, 74*(6), 546–559.

Summey, T. P., & Kane, C. A. (2016). Going where they are: Intentionally embedding librarians in courses and measuring the impact on student learning. *Journal of Library & Information Services in Distance Learning, 11,* 1–17.

Tang, Y., & Tseng, H. W. (2013). Distance learners' self-efficacy and information literacy skills. *The Journal of Academic Librarianship, 39*(6), 517–521. Retrieved from https://doi.org/10.1016/j.acalib.2013.08.008

Tchangalova, N., & Cossard, P. (2015). Library award for undergraduate research: Increasing the library profile. *Practical Academic Librarianship: The International Journal of the SLA Academic Division, 4*(2), 1–27.

Tumbleson, B. E., & Burke, J. J. (2010). When life hands you lemons: Overcoming obstacles to expand services in an embedded librarian program. *Journal of Library Administration, 50*(7/8), 972–988.

Ward, P. L. (2013). The library as place: History, community, and culture. *Library Review, 56*(9), 834–836.

Wong, S. H. R., & Webb, T. D. (2010). Uncovering meaningful correlation between student academic performance and library material usage. *College & Research Libraries, 72,* 361–370.

Yates, F. (2014). Beyond library space and place: Creating a culture of community engagement through library partnerships. *Indiana Libraries, 33*(2), 53–57.

CONCLUSION

Future Directions For High-Impact Practices Online

Kathryn E. Linder and Chrysanthemum Mattison Hayes

This is an exciting time for higher education pedagogy as technology, instructional design, and curricular innovation provide many new resources and tools to help our students succeed. Findings from the recent Distance Education Enrollment Report reveal that 29.7% of postsecondary students now take at least one course online (Allen & Seaman, 2017). Additionally, there is a steady increase of more than 225,000 students annually added to the distance learner population, with most of this growth occurring at public institutions. More than six million online postsecondary learners (Allen & Seaman, 2017) now engaged in online learning are seeking courses and degrees with richer online educational experiences and clear pathways to success (Mosteller, 2017). The agility to provide high-quality learning and degree experiences, regardless of modality, is quickly becoming a target for institutions seeking to lead the future of higher education.

Amid this growth and change, it is not surprising that institutions, administrators, and faculty may also feel overwhelmed as online education has created a shifting sand of new pedagogies, tools, and strategies to engage more and different students in a range of ways. In their discussions of how online high-impact practices (HIPs) may look different from the traditional classroom, each contributor to this volume demonstrates how much we have to learn from online pedagogy. Usually, we look to the traditional environment to inform our online practices—indeed, traditional teaching has decades of research from which to draw—but this volume also illustrates how we can use what we know about effective online engagement to also inform our face-to-face teaching efforts. Just as we can ask ourselves how best to transition face-to-face activities, strategies, and methods to the online modality, we can also ask: What do we gain from online that can benefit the face-to-face environment?

Benefits From High-Impact Practices in Online Learning

It is not hard to identify the extensive benefits of HIPs in online learning spaces. Throughout this volume, we see examples of how HIPs in distance education provide instructors and students with the tools and frameworks to engage more deeply with the course content and each other. Additionally, online HIPs are often structured like a collaborative sandbox that can spur deeper learning, connection, and increased opportunities for innovation, creativity, and meaning-making. Across the chapters, the authors point out several advantages that accompany successfully incorporating HIPs into distance-education courses. To begin this conclusion, we elaborate on several benefits that we identified across multiple HIPs.

Democratization of access. Online education not only expands participation in postsecondary education but also serves to broaden and equalize access for diverse groups of learners who, in the past, may not have had a clear entry point to continuing their education (Clancy & Goastellec, 2007). As Keup (chapter 1) and Robertson and Riggs (chapter 5) mention, implementation of online HIPs means that these new groups of learners also have access to and receive the subsequent benefits from the high-impact educational practices and opportunities. Additionally, Holmes Pearson and McClurken (chapter 6) and Nelson and Soto (chapter 8) write about how the democratization of access to these experiences means that a wider range of learners are able to contribute to the classroom dialogue and learn along with peers who are different from themselves. These collaborations of perspectives and worldviews enhance the learning environments and also help institutions move closer to a vision of providing access and education in accessible and progressive ways.

Community building/engagement. HIPs online help transcend many of the community-building challenges through the creation of a variety of structured and/or intentional spaces for interaction, collaboration, and sharing. The variety of dialogue and discussion pathways also allows for the incorporation of multiple communication methods by removing barriers that may exist for in-person classes—for example, students who would be uncomfortable speaking in class may engage more fully in a discussion post (Vonderwell, 2003). Baker and Pregitzer (chapter 2) argue for the expansion of the shared learning experiences that are campus-independent. In their discussion of the Engagement portion of the Narrative, Engagement, Transformation (NET) framework, they discuss the types of interactions that need to be considered and addressed to have a truly engaged classroom. In chapters 3 and 5, the authors describe the benefits of well-designed structured group work as a means to help build community and enhance learning.

Scaffolded HIPs for a transformative experience. A persistent challenge in online learning modalities is the cohesiveness of the student experience. This is due in part to a perceived disjointedness of classroom work and discussions (Shank & Doughty, 2002). Additionally, today's online learners often have competing schedules as well as a wide range of goals that could interfere with curricular continuity as they pursue a postsecondary degree (Soares, 2013). Online HIPs, especially when offered in a scaffolded way or as a progressive set of experiences, can foster or create the continuity and deep learning often assumed to only be part of the traditional, four-year, on-campus student experience. Thus, several of the chapters mention the potential benefits of partnering HIPs together. First-year seminars (chapter 1) partner nicely with common intellectual experiences (chapter 2) and learning communities (LCs) (chapter 3). Students may also experience increased agency in writing-intensive courses (chapter 4), collaborative assignments (chapter 5), and eService-Learning (chapter 9). These HIPs, in turn, sharpen the skills that students will need when they pursue internships (chapter 10), undergraduate research (chapters 6 and 7), and capstone projects (chapter 11). As a consistent thread throughout a student's entire experience, ePortfolios (chapter 12) provide clear bookends to students' growth and evolution in terms of their skills and ability to synthesize information and demonstrate the critical skills needed to move beyond the classroom to the real-world applications.

Enhanced learning environment. Strategic and relevant use of technology can yield more dynamic learning environments and better experiences for both instructors and students. In chapter 4, Griffin describes how utilizing screencasts to provide feedback on writing assignments can provide a more personalized experience for distance learners. In chapters 6 and 7 on undergraduate research, the authors share creative ways of thinking about how to engage technology to help their students create new knowledge. Strait and Nordyke in their chapter on eService-learning (chapter 9) provide examples of essential technology not only in the online classroom environment but also what serves as aids for data collection and reflection. Additionally, in chapter 13 on HIPs and library and information resources, Buck introduces readers to how embedded librarians in a variety of online HIPs can stimulate learning and success for distance learners and instructors.

Outward-facing knowledge sharing. An especially exciting part of online HIPs is that, in many instances, students engage in meaning-making and contributions to the greater body of knowledge. As highlighted by Holmes Pearson and McClurken (chapter 6) and Downing and Holtz (chapter 7), institutions of higher education have an obligation to prepare and produce future scholars. More and more, the student experience is being shared between the online and face-to-face environments, and so we need to adapt our most impactful experiences for all modalities and learners. Given the rapid increase and changing profile of the student body in the online sphere, it is important that the education, training, and mentoring required to gain the skills to tackle problems or generate new knowledge is not limited to the students who are situated in the traditional campus-based four-year programs. Additionally, it is also important that students have opportunities to make meaning in their own experiences and education in a way that will be valuable to them regardless of whether they continue on an academic trajectory. In chapter 12, Sparrow and Török describe how ePortfolios empower students to synthesize and share their learning in ways that communicate easily to future employers or to apply in a variety of settings.

Challenges of High-Impact Practices in Online Learning

Along with the benefits that accompany HIPs in the online classroom, the chapters in this book also call attention to thematic challenges. It should be noted that many of the common challenges observed in this volume are not unlike those experienced in face-to-face environments. In many cases, the authors' recommendations and considerations when responding to these challenges may be simultaneously beneficial in face-to-face courses.

Complexity. In the online classroom, it is especially important that the content and format be fully formed from the beginning of the course and that the structure and content work well with the online format (Li & Irby, 2008). The type and level of engagement required of a HIP-infused classroom elevates that complexity in at least two key areas. First, communication is key. The communication that occurs between students and instructor, students with each other, and, in some cases, the external communication with external sites or other related entities poses unique challenges in the online environment. Almost universally, the authors in this volume cited both verbal and written communication challenges as potential stumbling blocks in online HIPs. As Keup (chapter 1), Baker and Pregitzer (chapter 2), and Johnson, Powell, and Baker (chapter 3) all point out, these courses require the intentional design and application of strategies, expectations, and active monitoring and facilitation from the instructor.

Course organization and structure is foundational. In addition to communication challenges, the course design and structure can also pose unique challenges to the instructor and students in an online HIP course. Robertson and Riggs (chapter 5), Nelson and Soto (chapter 8), Newton-Calvert and Smith Arthur (chapter 11), and Buck (chapter 13) all consider the variable challenges posed by the synchronous versus asynchronous or fully online versus hybrid classroom models.

Faculty skepticism. Faculty may feel skeptical of or resist the online learning environment as a suitable or an equivocal quality alternative to the face-to-face classroom. As noted in *Inside Higher Ed's* 2014 Survey of Faculty Attitudes on Technology, although more faculty are teaching online, the perception that online education is less effective than traditional classrooms persists, with only 26% of the faculty respondents agreeing that they believe online courses provide equal results for students (Jaschik & Lederman, 2014). Keup (chapter 1) and Newton-Calvert and Smith Arthur (chapter 11) both suggest entry points to work with faculty and institutions on ways to address these underlying beliefs and work toward improving the teaching and learning environments by infusing technology into faculty development and engaging faculty creativity in ways that enhance student learning.

Time-consuming redesigns. Adopting a HIP in an online course is no small undertaking. It requires the course to be translated to or created with a structure that works in the online modality, and the design of the HIP elements must be well planned and integrated into the curriculum. Whether the course is being modified or created from scratch poses slightly different challenges for instructors, but this category of challenges largely stems from the additional time (in both preparing and delivering the course) and deliberate planning needed to implement and run effective online HIP courses.

Griffin (chapter 4) emphasizes the need to edit and be intentional about the function and design of the curriculum. As Robertson and Riggs (chapter 5) point out, group assignments and other active learning that go hand in hand with high-impact learning experiences take additional planning and also increase the time on task that students need to get the most from these learning experiences. Additionally, as discussed by Strait and Nordyke (chapter 9), if the course is being reimagined as an online course, there is most often not a one-to-one translation that occurs between face-to-face and online formats. It is important for administrators and faculty to understand that the translation may require a full course redesign. Moreover, several authors suggest it is the responsibility of the institution to provide the course development support and virtual infrastructure needed to help make the instructor and students successful.

Faculty development. Without exception, every chapter in this volume raised the matter of faculty development being essential to the design and delivery of HIPs online. Two big themes that emerged within the category of faculty development include helping faculty gain a solid understanding of HIPs generally, as well as developing the pedagogical skills and knowledge that accompany teaching in the online modality. Skills emphasized in this volume include: effective technology use (what tools to use and when), relevant and embedded direct assessment, effective communication and engagement strategies, integration of effective pedagogical approaches, and consistent and clear course structure.

Broader support and integration. Several of the chapters highlighted the compound benefit of scaffolding HIPs and integrating them into broader curricular pathways (chapters 1, 2, 3, 11, and 12). That benefit, however, comes along with a significant lift and, in many cases, a deep cultural shift by faculty, degree programs, and the institutional leadership. Alignment across the curriculum or to other similar courses takes coordination and also a willingness to let go of what was and to reimagine the structure of a degree in a student-centered way. Rather than stand-alone courses, HIPs and well-designed online courses are stronger when they are an intentional part of a bigger vision and progressive curriculum. Buy-in, support, and expectations from leadership are required for this strategic investment. Although academic leaders' attitudes toward online education are becoming more positive (Allen & Seaman, 2013), there remains a need to consider all curriculum, not just that online, from a more holistic and comprehensive student experience perspective. To that end, there needs to be both a grassroots and top-down support for expansion and integration of HIPs in strategic and meaningful ways.

Principles That Cross Modalities

Reading the chapters in this book and considering the benefits and challenges made one thing clear to us: there are several underlying pedagogical principles in these HIPs for teaching and learning that cross modalities. Whether students are learning in face-to-face, blended, or fully online environments, there are some best practices that, although they may look different, are frequently present across these modalities and that impact how students learn. These principles of effective teaching and learning are many.

Aligned course design. Students need to understand the "why" of a course or opportunity to be motivated and engaged in their learning (Jones & Hill, 2003; Pintrich & Zusho, 2007). It is important that we help students to see the connections among what they are expected to know, understand, and be able to do by the end of a course or program. Additionally, these learning goals should also be connected to the assignments and activities that students are completing throughout a course or program. The need for alignment is critical no matter what modality you are teaching in.

We found this to be especially true with the HIPs of first-year engagement (chapter 1), common intellectual experiences (chapter 2), capstone courses (chapter 11), and ePortfolios (chapter 12) but the concept of aligned course design certainly extends much further in the individual practices of instructors across modalities. In blended and online environments, where an entire course may be designed before the term even begins, students can reap the benefits of seeing the connections among all aspects of their course and the expectations for their learning.

Intentional social presence and community-building. Across modalities, students learn in community. Although that community may look different based on the environment, students' engagement with the instructor and their peers is a factor that can serve to enhance their motivation and engagement for learning. An important component of offering students different learning environments is that they get to choose the kind of community that is most impactful and comfortable for them. Moreover, as online communication continues to grow in a range of fields and industries, exposing our students to more opportunities where they can practice social presence online and relate to peers in a range of technology-enhanced modalities ensures that they will be better prepared for what they will encounter in the workplace.

Examples of this principle were most clear to us in the HIPs on first-year experience (chapter 1), LCs (chapter 3), collaboration (chapter 5), and diversity and global learning (chapter 8). In each of these HIPs, community-building and social presence are emphasized, particularly through the exposure of students to multiple and diverse viewpoints that model what they find once they leave our campuses. Although it may take more intentionality on behalf of instructors to help students learn how to best engage in these communities, especially if they are being built in unfamiliar online spaces, the benefits that students will gain make our efforts worth it.

Active learning. Research has demonstrated the efficacy of active learning (Michael, 2006; Prince, 2004). However, active learning can look different online, especially in courses that are primarily asynchronous. With each passing year, we are coming to a better understanding of what active learning "looks like" online. This is especially impacted by adaptive and personalized technologies and tools (a topic we will turn to a little later in this chapter), which allow students to receive individualized pathways for their learning based on their prior experience in the classroom and their current performance. The possibilities for active learning across modalities grow as educational technologies become more advanced.

HIPs such as collaborative projects (chapter 5), undergraduate research in a range of disciplines (chapters 6 and 7), and diversity and global learning (chapter 8) help our students to engage in active learning across time and space. Several chapters in this volume provide evidence that students can engage with peers from across the world or contribute to long and complex projects over a significant period of time, and that both experiences are made easier with current technologies. Additionally, what we are learning about what is possible online is impacting our face-to-face and blended environments as we "flip" our classrooms to create more space for face-to-face active learning.

Frequent assessment. Helping our students to understand and be aware of their own progress in learning is another core principle that crosses modalities. Assessing students' learning early and often through both formative and summative measures can help students to see their strengths and areas where they need to invest more of their time and energy.

HIPs such as common intellectual experiences (chapter 2) and writing-intensive courses (chapter 4) serve as exemplars for aligning assessment across courses in ways that encourage students to keep developing a skillset over the course of their academic careers. Assessment is not something that we do only in individual courses; rather, it is paramount to our students' success across programs of study, their persistence through a degree, and their successful graduation. Further, these frequent assessments can help us to know better what is working (or not) in particular courses, programs, or modalities where students struggle to succeed.

Metacognition and reflection. Identified by Ambrose and colleagues (2010) as one of the seven principles of student learning, metacognition and reflection can be a useful practice to model for students in any modality. The more students know and understand about how they learn best, the better they will be prepared to engage in lifelong learning once they leave our institutions.

HIPs such as service- and community-based learning (chapter 8), internships (chapter 10), capstone courses (chapter 11), and ePortfolios (chapter 12) are all examples of pedagogical strategies that have reflective components built in to their structures for the benefit of student learning. When students are asked to process their experiences, and especially how they have changed and grown over time as learners, they are given the opportunity to synthesize their learning and make connections that they might not otherwise see.

Universal design for learning. In 2015, EDUCAUSE named accessibility and universal design as a "core functional dimension" of the Next Generation Digital Learning Environment (Brown, Dehoney, & Millichap, 2015). Although this dimension continues to be an area of growing interest and research, it is clear that universal design can impact students across modalities (Scott, Mcguire, & Foley, 2003).

In this volume, we saw this most clearly in writing-intensive courses (chapter 4), capstone courses (chapter 11), and ePortfolios (chapter 12), where each of the authors described how attention to universal design principles—including how information is represented and how students provide evidence of their learning—can be adapted to best showcase students as unique individuals. Offering students a range of options that they can choose from to accomplish their learning goals and demonstrate their learning is one of the important affordances we gain from the increase in options offered by different learning modalities.

Future Directions and Emerging High-Impact Practices

As technology use in all classrooms increases, and as instructors teach through multiple modalities across their course loads, it may be time to shift our faculty development models so that they focus on best practice principles first and modality second. In practice, this might look like

- more online faculty development programming that allows instructors who teach across modalities to connect with one another, share practices, and learn together;
- LCs for instructors that focus on best practice principles first and modality second;
- resource guides, group workshops, and one-on-one support to help instructors translate best practices across modalities;
- on-demand faculty development programming on best practices that cross modalities that instructors can access when and where is convenient to their schedules; and
- encouraging additional collaborations between subject matter experts and instructional designers, specifically to achieve better integration of HIPs in online learning environments.

It will also be important for HIP scholars to consider HIPs through the lens of emerging online and blended learning research. We must ask ourselves whether additional HIPs need to be added to the current list that may be rooted in online pedagogies. For example, adaptive and personalized learning and the rising use of learning analytics across the university landscape are already impacting how instructors teach and how students learn in a range of disciplines. These new technologies are creating important new areas of study related to student retention, engagement, and motivation. As we gain more experience with these technologies in our classrooms in all modalities, it is imperative that we undertake comparative and cross-disciplinary research projects so that we can better understand the ways in which these new tools can help our students learn and be successful in higher education.

This productive back-and-forth dialogue between the modalities demonstrates that *High-Impact Practices in Online Education: Research and Best Practices* can be relevant and useful for instructors who teach in a range of environments. Moreover, as increasing numbers of higher education instructors are dipping their toes into online and blended teaching environments, conversations about pedagogical principles that cross modalities will be foundational to helping our students succeed as they cross modalities as well. Whether teaching online, blended, or face-to-face, this volume demonstrates that instructors can use the resources, strategies, and methods from one modality to also inform their choices in another. Perhaps most important, this leads to a better understanding of how best to help students learn no matter which environment they choose.

References

Allen, E., & Seaman, J. (2013). *Grade change: Tracking online education in the United States.* Retrieved from http://www.onlinelearningsurvey.com/reports/gradechange.pdf

Allen, E., & Seaman, J. (2017). *Digital learning compass: Digital Education Enrollment Report 2017.* Retrieved from https://onlinelearningsurvey.com/reports/digtiallearningcompassenrollment2017.pdf

Ambrose, S. A., Bridges, M. W., DiPietro, M., Lovett, M. C., Norman, M. K., & Mayer, R. E. (2010). *How learning works: 7 research-based principles for smart teaching.* San Francisco, CA: Jossey-Bass.

Brown, M., Dehoney, J., & Millichap, N. (2015). *The next generation digital learning environment.* Educause Learning Initiative. Retrieved from https://library.educause.edu/~/media/files/library/ 2015/4/eli3035-pdf

Clancy, P., & Goastellec, G. (2007). Exploring access and equity in higher education: Policy and performance in a comparative perspective. *Higher Education Quarterly, 61*(2), 136–154.

Jaschik, S., & Lederman, D. (Eds.). (2014). *Survey of faculty attitudes on technology.* Washington DC: Gallup and Inside Higher Ed. Retrieved from https://www.insidehighered.com/system/files/media/IHE-FacTechSurvey2014%20final.pdf

Jones, S. R., & Hill, K. E. (2003). Understanding patterns of commitment: Student motivation for community service involvement. *The Journal of Higher Education, 74*(5), 516–539.

Li, C., & Irby, B. (2008). An overview of online education: Attractiveness, benefits, challenges, concerns and recommendations. *College Student Journal, 42*(2), 449–458.

Michael, J. (2006). Where's the evidence that active learning works? *Advances in Physiology Education, 30*(4), 159–167.

Mosteller, K. (2017). *Study shows: The perception of online education is changing.* Retrieved from https://fosteredu.pennfoster.edu/the-perception-of-online-education

Pintrich, P. R., & Zusho, A. (2007). Student motivation and self-regulated learning in the college classroom. In R. P. Perry & J. C. Smart (Eds.), *The Scholarship of*

Teaching and Learning in Higher Education: An Evidence-Based Perspective, pp. 731–810.

Prince, M. (2004). Does active learning work? A review of the research. *Journal of Engineering Education, 93*(3), 223–231.

Scott, S. S., Mcguire, J. M., & Foley, T. E. (2003). Universal design for instruction: A framework for anticipating and responding to disability and other diverse learning needs in the college classroom. *Equity & Excellence in Education, 36*(1), 40–49.

Shank, P., & Doughty, V. (2002). Learning anew: An exploratory study about new online learners' perceptions of people interaction and learning to learn in an online course. In P. Barker & S. Rebelsky (Eds.), *Proceedings of ED-MEDIA 2002: World Conference on Educational Multimedia, Hypermedia & Telecommunications* (pp. 2167–2171). Denver, CO: Association for the Advancement of Computing in Education.

Soares, L. (2013). *Post-traditional learners and the transformation of postsecondary education: A manifesto for college leaders* (Working paper). Retrieved from American Council on Education website: http://louissoares.com/wp-content/uploads/2013/02/post_traditional_learners.pdf

Vonderwell, S. (2003). An examination of asynchronous communication experiences and perspectives of students in an online course: A case study. *The Internet and Higher Education, 6*(1), 77–90.

EDITORS AND CONTRIBUTORS

Editors

Chrysanthemum Mattison Hayes holds a master's degree in public policy and leads the university-wide efforts to promote data-literacy and engagement with institutional data and analytics for Oregon State University (OSU). Prior to her current role, she worked with nonprofits coordinating service-learning opportunities for students followed by working for over five years as a policy and data analyst for OSU. Hayes's experience in higher education includes working in and across the divisions of academic affairs, student affairs, undergraduate studies, academic programs and learning innovation, and information and technology, as well as designing and teaching first-year experience and academic success courses. Hayes is a frequent speaker and presenter at student success and professional development conferences, meetings, and events. She serves as chair of the board for the Oregon Women in Higher Education professional organization and actively works toward inclusivity and success for both students and colleagues through numerous volunteer roles and professional groups.

Kathryn E. Linder is the research director for eCampus at Oregon State University. She earned her BA in English literature and creative writing from Whitworth University and her MA and PhD in women's studies from The Ohio State University. Linder is the author of *Rampage Violence Narratives* (Lexington Books, 2014) and *The Blended Course Design Workbook: A Practical Guide* (Stylus Publishing, 2016). She is also the editor of the New Directions volume on *Hybrid Teaching and Learning* (Wiley, 2017) and the series editor for *Thrive Online* from Stylus Publishing. As part of her work at Oregon State eCampus, Linder also hosts the weekly "Research in Action" podcast on topics and issues related to research in higher education.

Contributors

Jason D. Baker is associate vice president for teaching and learning and professor of education at Regent University. He has more than 20 years of online learning leadership experience, including undergraduate and graduate program administration, asynchronous and synchronous online course development, technology-enhanced instructional design, assessment, accreditation, data analysis, marketing, lead generation, enrollment, massive open online courses (MOOCs), and learning analytics. He holds a PhD in communication from Regent University, an MA in educational technology leadership from The George Washington University, and a BS in electrical engineering from Bucknell University.

Sarah S. Baker was associate dean of academic affairs for University College at Indiana University–Purdue University Indianapolis (IUPUI) prior to her retirement in 2017. In this role, she oversaw the curriculum and programming for beginning students along with faculty. Within her portfolio was the oversight of high-impact practice programs (Summer Bridge, First-Year Seminars, and Themed Learning Communities). Furthermore, she provided oversight to the Gateway to Graduation Program, Special Programs for Academic Nurturing, University College lecturers/senior lecturers, and University College faculty fellows. Baker was associate professor of Radiologic Sciences, School of Medicine, at IUPUI. In addition to her radiologic technology degree, she has completed an MS in education and a PhD in higher education administration with a minor in curriculum studies. Her interests included facilitation of high-impact practices on campus and assessment.

Stefanie Buck is the eCampus and Instructional Design librarian at Oregon State University (OSU). She works primarily with distance-learning students and instructors supporting their research and teaching needs. Prior to joining OSU, she was the distance-education librarian at Western Washington University. She has an MLS and an MA in history from the University of Hawai'i and an MEd degree from the University of Massachusetts in Boston.

Kevin F. Downing is a professor (Earth sciences and biosciences) at DePaul University, where he has developed and taught online science courses and has mentored online students pursuing their undergraduate research projects for nearly two decades. Downing's ongoing research activities involve the investigation of Miocene age fossil mammals, evaluating Ocean Acidification Events from fossil coral skeletons, and exploring best practices and technological innovation in online science learning environments, including an ongoing study on the efficacy of virtual reality and augmented reality-based components in online bioscience labs. He received BS degrees in astronomy and geology (University of Illinois, Urbana), an MST in Geology

(University of Florida), and a PhD in Geosciences (University of Arizona). Downing has published widely in the fields of paleobiology, geology, and science education.

June Griffin is associate dean for undergraduate education in the College of Arts and Sciences and associate professor of practice in the Department of English at the University of Nebraska-Lincoln. She has published articles on online writing instruction, student revision practices, textual coherence, and electronic portfolios. The former faculty coordinator of the William H. Thompson Scholars Program (a learning community for students receiving need- and merit-based scholarships), she is committed to fostering high-impact practices as a teacher, scholar, and administrator.

Ellen Holmes Pearson is professor of history at the University of North Carolina, Asheville. She received her BA in history from Spring Hill College, her MA in history from the University of New Orleans, and her PhD in early American history from Johns Hopkins University. Pearson is the author of *Remaking Custom: Law and Identity in the Early American Republic* (University of Virginia Press, 2011). She entered the world of digital pedagogy in 2013, when she and her coauthor, Jeffrey McClurken, developed and taught "Century America," a distance mentoring/digital history course. Since then she has helped to develop additional distance mentoring and digital courses within the Council of Public Liberal Arts Colleges through grants from the Teagle Foundation of New York and, most recently, the Mellon Foundation. Recent book chapters and articles include "Digital Liberal Arts at a Distance: A Consortium-Wide Approach," coauthored with Jeffrey W. McClurken and Claire Moseley Bailey, *Change Magazine*, June 2016; "Neither Here nor There: Testing the Boundaries of Place and Pedagogy," in *Roads Taken: The Professorial Life, Scholarship in Place, and the Public Good*, edited by Roger Epp and William Spellman (Truman State University Press, 2014); and "1775–1815," in the *Blackwell Companion to American Legal History*, edited by Sally E. Hadden and Alfred Brophy (Wiley E. Blackwell Publishing, 2013).

Jennifer K. Holtz, PhD, is associate professor and director of the School of Counseling, Human Performance and Rehabilitation at the University of Arkansas at Little Rock, where she also serves as program coordinator for the adult education graduate programs. Holtz's PhD is in adult, continuing, and occupational education, with an emphasis in medical education, from Kansas State University. She holds an MA in gerontology from Wichita State University and a BA in biology, with an emphasis in human biology, from Newman University. Her memberships include the American Association of Adult and Continuing Education, Commission of Professors of Adult Education, American Educational Research Association, and Generalists in Medical Education. Holtz's research interests focus on improving online adult education, particularly in the sciences, with an emphasis on experiential learning.

Kathy E. Johnson serves as executive vice chancellor and chief academic officer of Indiana University–Purdue University Indianapolis (IUPUI), a core campus of Indiana University and the state's urban research and academic health sciences campus. Johnson joined IUPUI in 1993 as an assistant professor of psychology. She has served as chair of the Department of Psychology, dean of University College, and associate vice chancellor for undergraduate education. Johnson is a graduate of Emory University with a PhD in psychology, specializing in cognition and development. She has published extensively in the areas of language development, categorization, symbolic development, expertise acquisition, and science interests, along with current projects focused on undergraduate student learning and success.

Jennifer R. Keup is the director of the National Resource Center for the First-Year Experience and Students in Transition, where she provides leadership for all operational, strategic, and scholarly activities of the center in pursuit of its mission "to support and advance efforts to improve student learning and transitions into and through higher education." Before joining the staff at the National Resource Center, Keup had professional roles in the national dialogue on the first-year experience as a project director for the Cooperative Institutional Research Program at the Higher Education Research Institute. Her research interests focus on two primary areas of scholarship: the first-year experience and students in transition, and high-impact practices and institutional interventions to facilitate student learning, development, and success. Keup has been a frequent contributor in higher education, as both a presenter and an author, including coauthorship of *Developing and Sustaining Successful First-Year Programs* (Jossey-Bass, 2013) and *The First-Year Seminar: Designing, Implementing, and Assessing Courses to Support Student Learning and Success: Volume I: Designing and Administering the Course* (National Resource Center for the First Year Experience, 2011). Keup also serves as an affiliated faculty member in the Department of Educational Leadership and Policies in the College of Education at the University of South Carolina.

Jeffrey W. McClurken is professor of history and special adviser to the president at the University of Mary Washington. He received his BA in history from the University of Mary Washington and his PhD in American History from The Johns Hopkins University. McClurken is the author of "*Take Care of the Living*": *Reconstructing the Confederate Veteran Family in Virginia* (University of Virginia Press, 2009). Recent book chapters and articles include "Digital Literacy and the Undergraduate Curriculum" in *Hack the Academy* (University of Michigan Press, 2011) and "Archives & Teaching Undergraduates in a Digital Age" in *A Different Kind of Web: New Connections between Archives and Our Users*, edited by Kate Theimer (Society of American Archivists, 2011). He was the 2014 Teaching with Technology winner of the Virginia State Council of Higher Education's Outstanding Faculty Award. McClurken has also written essays for the Chronicle of Higher Education's ProfHacker column and articles related to teaching with technology in *Learning Through Digital Media* and the *Journal of the Association of History and Computing*. He sits on the review board for the *Journal of Instructional Technology and Pedagogy* and is the Digital History Reviews editor for the *Journal of American History*. He cochairs the inaugural Digital History Working group for the American Historical Association. His work and teaching can be found at mcclurken.org.

Jesse Nelson, PhD, is associate provost for academic achievement at Oregon State University. Throughout his career, he has focused on student success, with specific emphasis on issues of persistence, equity, inclusivity, experiential learning, systems of support, and assessment. In addition to administrative responsibilities, Nelson regularly teaches online graduate courses in education and undergraduate courses in student success and leadership. Recently, he codirected the development and implementation of student organizations for students identifying with autism spectrum disorder.

Zapoura Newton-Calvert, MA, serves as digital coordinator and capstone faculty member in Portland State University's (PSU's) University Studies Program. Her research and pedagogical foci include removing barriers to educational equity, social justice in online learning, community-based learning online, and universal design for learning. She served as faculty-in-residence for community-based learning (CBL) in PSU's Office of Academic Innovation for three years and also worked as a service-learning coordinator at Portland Community College. Her recent publication (also coauthored with Deborah Smith Arthur), "Online Community-Based Learning as the Practice of Freedom: The Online Capstone Experience at Portland State University," explores instructor presence and community formation in online CBL courses.

Katherine Nordyke serves as the director of citizenship and service-learning, the codirector of the Center for Community Engagement, and adjunct faculty at Missouri State University. She holds an MA in leadership from Fort Hays State University and a PhD in education–instructional leadership from Northcentral University. Nordyke is recognized for her commitment to student success and her distinctive work and accomplishments in support of Missouri State University's mission in public affairs. Over the past six years, she has grown the academic service service-learning program from 2,100 to nearly 5,000 students. She is the coeditor of *eService-Learning: Creating Experiential Learning and Civic Engagement Through Online and Hybrid Courses* (Stylus Publishing, 2015). Her research focuses on understanding what deters faculty from using the teaching pedagogy of service-learning, a high-impact practice, in the development of their curriculum and courses.

Pamela D. Pike is the Aloysia L. Barineau Professor of Piano Pedagogy at Louisiana State University. During the past decade, Pike has presented papers at international conferences throughout Asia, Europe, Scandinavia, the United Kingdom, and North and South America. Nationally, she is regularly invited to present at the Music Teachers National Association, College Music Society, National Conference on Keyboard Pedagogy, and Association for Technology in Music Instruction national conferences. Pike is the author of *Dynamic Group-Piano Teaching: Transforming Group Theory Into Teaching Practice* (Routledge, 2017). She has published more than three dozen scholarly articles in peer-reviewed journals, including the *International Journal of Music Education, American Music Teacher, Journal of Music, Technology & Instruction, Journal of Music Teacher Education, MTNA e-Journal, Symposium,* and *Problems in Music Pedagogy.* She has contributed chapters to pedagogical publications from the Royal Conservatory of Music (Toronto) and Oxford University Press. She has been honored with numerous teaching, research, and service awards, including: MTNA Foundation Fellow (2017), LMTA Outstanding Teacher (2016), *American Music Teacher* Article of the Year (2013), and the LSU Tiger Athletic Foundation Undergraduate Teaching Award (2012). She is President of the Louisiana Music Teachers Association, serves on the editorial boards for the *MTNA e-Journal* and the *Journal of Music, Technology & Education,* is a commissioner for the International Society for Music Education CEPROM committee, and chairs national committees for the College Music Society and the National Conference on Keyboard Pedagogy. Her research interests include cognition, teaching and learning, and distance education.

Amy A. Powell is the director of the Themed Learning Communities program at Indiana University–Purdue University Indianapolis (IUPUI) and teaches a first-year seminar course in a themed learning community. Powell has served as resource faculty at the National Summer Institute on Learning Communities and represents IUPUI in the National Learning Communities Consortium. Prior to joining the Themed Learning Communities program, she was an instructional technology consultant at IUPUI's Center for Teaching and Learning, leading faculty development in online course design, ePortfolio pedagogy, structured reflection, and the integration of pedagogy and technology. She holds a BA in music education from the University of Minnesota and an MS in education in instructional systems technology from Indiana University.

Michael Pregitzer is associate dean of instruction in the College of Arts and Sciences at Regent University, overseeing program, curriculum, course development, and initiatives related to retention, academic rigor, quality, and faculty development. He has worked in several other capacities at the university, including as an instructor in the School of Business and Leadership and an instructional designer for the Center of Teaching and Learning. Prior to coming to Regent, he spent 20 years in the human resources field. Pregitzer earned his BA in English from the University of Rochester and his MS in industrial relations and human resources from Rutgers University. He has published articles related to management, learning technology, and education.

Shannon Riggs serves as executive director for Oregon State University's Extended Campus, in charge of course development and learning innovation. She holds an MA in professional writing and began her career in higher education teaching writing in face-to-face, hybrid, and online modalities. A passion for online education and course design led to opportunities in faculty development and support, then to instructional design, and later to leadership roles in online education. Together with her team, Riggs is the recipient of two awards from the Online Learning Consortium, an Award for Excellence in Faculty Development for Online Teaching and an Effective Practice Award, as well as an Eduventures Innovation Award. Riggs is the author of *Thrive Online: A New Approach for College Educators* (Stylus Publishing, 2018).

Robert John Robertson holds MAs in information and library studies and church history and a certificate in Teaching English to Speakers of Other Languages (TESOL). He has worked in higher education for more than 10 years, beginning in metadata, digital library, and repository projects and subsequently working with open educational resources, ePortfolios, and institutional change initiatives. Before moving to Seattle Pacific University as a digital education librarian, Robertson worked at Oregon State eCampus as an instructional designer. Previously, Robertson worked at the University of Wisconsin Oshkosh as part of the University Studies Program core team. In this role, he was responsible for the technical and pedagogical issues around implementing ePortfolios as part of Oshkosh's Association of American Colleges & Universities–featured reform of their general education program. Robertson tends to be an information omnivore and is interested in the impact of open education, the affordances and limits of technology in learning, digital badges, games in learning, threshold concepts, and disciplinary knowledge.

Deborah Smith Arthur is an associate professor at Portland State University (PSU) and has been teaching capstone courses at PSU since 2003, most often in a hybrid format. She holds a BA in religion from Trinity College in Hartford, Connecticut, an MA in Black studies from The Ohio State University, and a JD from The University of Connecticut School of Law, making the interdisciplinary university studies department at PSU her ideal academic home. Prior to teaching, Smith Arthur practiced juvenile and criminal law for 10 years. Her scholarly agenda and numerous publications are focused on critical community-based learning and engagement opportunities in nontraditional academic settings, including online, and she developed and teaches a fully online capstone, Mobilizing Hope. In addition to the scholarship of teaching and learning, she is passionate about the intersection of juvenile and criminal justice and educational equity issues.

Nelson Soto, PhD, serves as provost and vice president for academic affairs at Union Institute and University. His professional interests focus on access and retention, faculty and organizational development, administration of programs for marginalized student populations, creating and fostering internal and external relationships, and assessment. Soto has served on several boards, including Harvard Business Publishing Advisory Board, Cengage Private Sector Advisory Board, and Pearson Service Learning Board, and was chair of the Harrison College Military Advisory Board.

Jennifer Sparrow is the assistant dean of academic affairs for CUNY School of Professional Studies, where she has oversight for the General Education Program and student success initiatives, including online undergraduate new student orientation, general education outcomes assessment, ePortfolio, and credit for prior learning. Sparrow has run faculty and course development programs for fully online and hybrid course development and course revision, ePortfolio integration, and program assessment. She holds a PhD in English literature from Wayne State University.

Jean Strait is senior faculty of the School of Education at Hamline University where she is also the first female Native American tenured full professor. Strait brings a wealth of first-hand experience in the urban classroom—having taught reading, literacy, and educational psychology in higher education for more than 30 years. Strait has several publications, including her most popular book, *The Future of Service-Learning* (Stylus Publishing, 2009). Her most recent publications include *eService-Learning: Creating Experiential Learning and Civic Engagement Through Online and Hybrid Courses* (with Katherine Nordyke; Stylus Publishing, 2015) and *Service-Learning to Advance Social Justice in a Time of Racial Inequality* (with Tinker, Tinker, and Jagla; Information Age Publishing, 2015) Strait is recognized for her program, Each One, Teach One, a distance service-learning project between high school and college students in Minnesota partnered with struggling middle-school students in New Orleans, Louisiana. Strait is the executive director of the Foundation for the Advancement of Culture and Education (FACE). The mission of FACE is to promote the teaching of cultural competencies, increase parent and family engagement in schools, recruit and retain teachers of color, and support at-risk students in academic success and college readiness.

Judit Török, PhD, is the director of the teaching and learning commons at Berkeley College. In this role, she fosters professional development communities for faculty to collaborate and learn about high-impact pedagogical practices, instructional design, and creative digital technologies, with special emphasis on fostering agency and empowering learners. She also teaches philosophy, ethics, critical, and creative thinking courses. Her research interests include theories of learning, ePortfolios, online and blended course design, massive online open courses, and pedagogies for global citizenship and social change. She engages with Solutions U, a community that connects students and educators to bring solutions to social problems into the classroom. From 2011 to 2014, she worked as the codirector of the Making Connections National Resource Center at CUNY; and co-led the Connect to Learning (C2L) ePortfolio Resources and Research project. Selected publications include "What Difference Can ePortfolio Make" (2014) and "C2L and Using ePortfolio in Hybrid Professional Development" (2013). She is a senior Fellow at the Melton Foundation, promoting global citizenship and empowering change makers across the globe.

INDEX

Timeline JS, 90

time management, 15, 18, 171

TLC. *See* Themed Learning
Community High-Impact Practice
Taxonomy

tools, 211
digital, 85–86, 90
discussion board, 60, 77, 80, 159,
172, 203–4
for online internships, 155–56

transactional, service learning as, 134

transactional nature, of FYS, 18

transformation, 32–33. *See also*
Narrative, Engagement,
Transformation model
of online courses, 119–20, 128

transformational, service learning as,
134

Transforming Remotely Conducted
Research through Ethnography,
Education, and Rapidly Evolving
Technologies (TREET), 107

transparent communication, 80–81

TREET. *See* Transforming Remotely
Conducted Research through
Ethnography, Education, and
Rapidly Evolving Technologies

trust relationships, 126

2012 Digest of Educational Statistics, 2

Twitter, 90

two-year campuses, 16

UDL. *See* Universal Design for
Learning

undergraduate education, online
capstone courses for, 166

undergraduate research (UR), 1, 6–7
award for, 205
support of, 204–5

undergraduate research, in humanities
conclusion to, 96–97
Digital Liberal Arts for, 85–86, 88,
94, 95, 96
digital tools for, 85–86, 90

key takeaways from, 97
in practice, 88–96
scholarly literature review, 86–88

undergraduate research, in sciences
conclusions to, 111–12
as HIP, 101–2
key takeaways from, 112
URES, OURES versus, 105–11

Undergraduate Research Experiences in
Science (URES), 101
ALURES, 103–4, 106
benefits of, 102–3
cognitive and lifelong learning with,
103
CURES, 103–4, 106
GERP, 103–4, 106
for professional scientists, 102
psychological dimension growth
with, 103
SURE, 103–4, 106

underserved and underrepresented
students, 4, 175–76

universal design, for learning, 218

Universal Design for Learning (UDL),
171, 173

University of Adelaide, 107

University of Central Florida's Learning
Environment and Academic
Research Network (LEARN),
106

University of Georgia, 138–39

University of Rhode Island's Inner
Space Center (ISC), 108

University of Richmond, 89

University Studies, 170

UR. *See* undergraduate research

URES. *See* Undergraduate Research
Experiences in Science

URES, OURES versus
assessment, 110–11
communities of practice and
collaboration, 109–10
flexible framework, 106
good dissemination options, 109
implementation, 105–8

collaborative, solutions-oriented, and invested in the greater good."— ***Caryn McTighe Musil***, *Senior Scholar and Director of Civic Learning and Democracy's Initiatives, Association of American Colleges and Universities*

This book provides:

- An overview of language and methods used by professionals engaged in community-based research (CBR)
- A framework for orienting CBR toward concrete community outcomes
- Effective ways to integrate CBR into course content; student-driven projects; and initiatives spanning disciplines, curricula, campuses, and countries
- Lessons learned in working toward positive outcomes for students and in communities

22883 Quicksilver Drive
Sterling, VA 20166-2019   Subscribe to our e-mail alerts: www.Styluspub.com

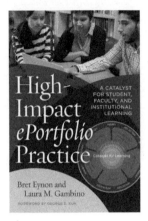

High-Impact ePortfolio Practice

A Catalyst for Student, Faculty, and Institutional Learning

Bret Eynon and Laura M. Gambino

Foreword by George D. Kuh

"Challenging the noisy legion of digital gurus who see job-specific training as the best choice for first-generation learners, Eynon and Gambino provide compelling evidence that ePortfolios can help underserved students achieve those distinctively twenty-first century liberal arts: agency as motivated learners, creativity in connecting myriad kinds of formal and informal learning, and reflective judgment about their own roles in building solutions for the future. An invaluable resource for all." —*Carol Geary-Schneider, Fellow, Lumina Foundation; President Emerita, Association of American Colleges & Universities*

The authors of this book outline how to deploy the ePortfolio as a high-impact practice and describe widely-applicable models of effective ePortfolio pedagogy and implementation that demonstrably improve student learning across multiple settings.

Community Based Research

Teaching for Community Impact

Edited by Mary Beckman, Joyce F. Long

Foreword by Timothy K. Eatman

"In an environment in which some governors insist a college's worth should be measured only by the number of graduates getting high-paying, high-demand jobs, this book reminds us that many students achieve a different kind of education: one that cultivates an ethos of investigative care about solving problems faced by the very communities in which they live and will work. That's the kind of education that really prepares graduates to be the workers our country needs: competent,

(Continues on preceding page)